Politics, Censorship
and the English Reformation

POLITICS, CENSORSHIP
AND
THE ENGLISH REFORMATION

by
DAVID LOADES

Pinter Publishers
London and New York

© David Loades, 1991

First published in Great Britain in 1991 by
Pinter Publishers, 25 Floral Street, London WC2E 9DS

British Library Cataloguing in Publication Data
A CIP catalogue record for this book is available from the
British Library

ISBN 0 86187 861 2

For enquiries in North America please contact PO Box 197,
Irvington, NY 10533

Library of Congress Cataloging-in-Publication Data

Loades, D. M.
    Politics, censorship, and the English Reformation / by David
Loades.
        p.   cm.
    Includes bibliographical references and index.
    ISBN 0-86187-861-2
    1. Great Britain – Politics and government – 1485–1603.
2. Censorship – Great Britain – History – 16th century.
3. Reformation – Great Britain.   I. Title.
DA310.L8   1991
320.941′09′031 – dc20   90-23111
                                                              CIP

Typeset by Florencetype Ltd, Kewstoke, Avon
Printed and bound in Great Britain by Biddles Ltd of Guildford and Kings Lynn

Contents

Preface

The essays in this collection have been written at intervals over about thirty years, and they represent my continuing interest in certain aspects of the English Reformation. Many of them are concerned with printing and publishing, which was always a front line in the constant skirmishing between Tudor governments and their critics. Whether the printed word ever exercised much influence over the political actions of Englishmen in the sixteenth century may be doubted, but since both the governments and their opponents believed that it did, and acted accordingly, the doubt is academic. The remainder could all be broadly described as dealing with ecclesiastical politics, and are for the most part by-products of two books, *The Oxford Martyrs* (Batsford, 1970), which investigated the impact of the royal supremacy upon church and society between 1530 and 1558, and *The Reign of Mary Tudor* (Benn, 1979) which covered all aspects of that five-year period. Inevitably, there is a degree of overlap, particularly where I have returned to a particular topic many years after writing the first essay; but each paper has something distinctive to say, and the coherence of argument would have been destroyed by selective editing. Consequently, most have been reproduced in their original form, with only such editorial attention as has been deemed necessary to draw attention to relevant later scholarship. Any cross-references, comments and updating have been added in square brackets. The exceptions to this generalisation are the introduction, which is new and endeavours to set the essays against the overall background of Reformation politics; Chapter 11 'Martin Luther and the Early Stages of the English Reformation', which was read at the German Historical Institute in 1982; and Chapter 10, 'Books and The English Reformation prior to 1558'. This last has appeared only in a French version, which was edited to fit the requirements of a collaborative volume; the version printed here is the original English text from which the French translation was taken. Chapter 6, 'Relations between the Anglican and Roman Catholic Churches in the Sixteenth Century' is a shortened version of the original, which also covered the seventeenth century.

Since this is a collection and not a monograph, there is no single interpretative theme, but I hope that I have made it clear that, in my opinion, the royal authority impinged upon religious developments in England at every level and throughout the sixteenth century. The popular faith which really mattered was faith in the Crown. This does not mean that those who lived or died for their vision of Christianity were self-deluded, merely that they were a creative minority whose impact upon the church was mediated through the responses of government. It could hardly be otherwise at a time when confessional unity was considered to be essential to political stability, but England was distinctive in the ease and completeness with which successive rulers switched their theological allegiance. I entirely accept what recent 'revisionist' historians have written about the prevalence of religious conservatism, and the relative health of the pre-Reformation church at the popular level. Nevertheless Protestant straws were needed to make the Anglican bricks, and some of these are also scattered in the pages that follow.

My main debts of gratitude on this occasion are to the original publishers for allowing the essays to be reproduced – specific acknowledgements are listed – and to Mrs June Hughes for retyping the whole text.

David Loades
University College of North Wales
July 1990

Acknowledgements

The chapters in this book include papers that originally appeared as follows:
1. *The Urban Classes, the Nobility and the Reformation* (German Historical Institute, 1979), 128–30.
2. *The Bulletin of the Institute of Historical Research*, XXV, 1962, 87–97.
3. *The Journal of Ecclesiastical History*, XVI, 1965, 54–66.
4. *Religion and National Identity* (Studies in Church History, XVIII, 1982), 297–307.
5. *Faith and Identity* (Studies in Church History, subsidia VI, 1989, 99–108).
6. *Rome and the Anglicans*, ed. W. Haase, 1982, 1–53.
7. *Transactions of the Cambridge Bibliographical Society*, III, 1960, 155–60.
8. *The Transactions of the Royal Historical Society*, 5 series, XXIV, 1974, 141–50.
9. *Too Mighty to be Free; censorship and the press in Britain and the Netherlands*, 1988, 9–27.
10. *La Réforme et le Livre*, ed. J.F. Gilmont, 1989.
12. *The Province of York* (Studies in Church History, IV, 1967), 65–75.
13. *The Last Principality*, ed. D. Marcombe, 1987, 101–117.
14. *Continental Reformers and the English Reformation* (Studies in Church History, subsidia II, 1980), 59–70.
15. *Miscellanea Historiae Ecclesiasticae*, VIII ed. B. Vogler, 1976, 343–355.
16. *Humanism and Reform in Britain and the Continent: essays presented to Professor J.K. Cameron* (Studies in Church History, subsidia, 1991).

Introduction: The Reformation and the English State

Whatever the English Reformation may have been, it was not a spontaneous religious revolution. Nor was it, even in broad outline, a straightforward confrontation between Protestants and Catholics. As Christopher Haigh has recently pointed out, it was extraordinarily difficult for contemporaries, even those in senior ecclesiastical or political positions, to understand what was going on around them – and impossible to forecast what would happen next.[1] This was partly, at least, because the medieval church was a collection of practices, habits and attitudes, rather than an intellectually coherent body of doctrine. Christian theology may have had an intelligible coherence to those who had spent many years in the schools mastering its subtleties, but even at that level there was no general agreement. Thomist disagreed with Augustinian, Dominican bickered with Franciscan. Even on central issues such as justification or transubstantiation there was room for disagreement. In theory doctrinal disputes were decided, and had been decided for many centuries, by the authority of the Pope or by General Councils, but papal and conciliar decrees formed a vast body of case law, which was not consistent, and in which the searcher was very likely to discover what he wanted. Consequently, for the vast majority of laymen, and for many ordinary clergy, the church was what the church did, rather than what it taught or believed. It was a visible and tangible world of devotion, centred upon the inaccessible mystery of the mass, and the comfortable rituals of confession and absolution; a world of images and intercessors, in which the supernatural was constantly invoked to cope with the physical and spiritual hazards of daily life. The image of the crucifix must be held in the sight of the dying, advised the author of the *Ars Moriendi*, published in 1491; stories of the saints should be read for their comfort, and holy water cast 'for avoiding of evil spirits'.[2] It was also a very social world. Pilgrimages and processions, feasting and atonement were corporate actions, embracing the whole community, and those who did not take part were regarded with suspicion or frank hostility. The parish church was a popular meeting place, and a symbol of the pride and identity of its people – hence the competitive building programmes and lavish ornamentation.

In the early years of the sixteenth century foreign observers commented upon the conspicuous piety of the English. Many Londoners, particularly the women, heard mass every day, wrote one, and those who could read frequently recited

the office of Our Lady in a low voice 'after the manner of churchmen'.[3]
Nevertheless this general picture, authentic as it undoubtedly is, should not be
allowed to occupy the entire canvas. Every society has its dissident minorities,
and late medieval England was no exception. Most of them tend to be lumped
together under the general name of Lollards, but as recent research has revealed,
the exact nature of Lollardy tends to become elusive under close examination.[4]
The dissidents, in fact, were no more intellectually coherent in their beliefs than
were the orthodox. They took the inevitable shortcomings of the clergy far more
seriously than their neighbours did, and objected to precisely those practices of
corporate devotion which featured so largely in popular piety. When images
were held in high regard, the Lollards sought to burn them; when the host was
an object of adoration, the Lollards declared that it was nothing but mouldy
bread. The priestly order as such was worthy of no respect and conferred no
authority; only the grace of God could make a man worthy to celebrate the
sacraments. It has been fairly said that Lollardy was not so much a sect as a state
of mind. Apart from an enthusiasm for vernacular scripture, Lollard protest was
largely negative, and usually private. Given the active hostility of the ecclesiastical authorities, such reticence is understandable, but it was also natural to the
type of spirituality that Lollardy represented. Protest against the wealth and
materialism of the church was endemic in Latin Christendom – the Waldensians
and the Fraticelli are other examples – and led to an emphasis upon the
inwardness of piety. Sometimes this was expressed in a total rejection of all the
outward forms of worship, but more often it was partial or selective. For this
reason, heresy was often in the eye of the beholder rather than in the intention
of the person accused. A Wycliffite treatise on images, written in the early
fifteenth century, expressed the viewpoint of a moderate dissident:

> Since Christ was made man, unlearned men are allowed to have a poor crucifix in
> order to have in mind the hard passion and bitter death that Christ suffered
> voluntarily for man's sin. And yet men err foully in this crucifix making, for they paint
> it with great cost, and hang much silver and gold and precious clothes and stones
> thereon and about it.[5]

Such attitudes, and other similar doubts about the validity of the majority
culture, were widespread and unquantifiable. Probably the apparent upsurge in
Lollard activity in the early sixteenth century had more to do with increased
vigilance by the authorities than it did with any evangelical campaign. Lollardy
was potentially subversive, but it lacked even the most rudimentary leadership
and organisation. Christopher Haigh has pointed out that Lollards were often
unpopular with their neighbours simply because they did dissent from prevailing
practices, and by weakening the consensus were seen to be undermining the
credibility of the community in the sight of God.[6] Nevertheless, to dismiss them
as insignificant, and to concentrate upon the plentiful evidence for the strength
of mainstream piety, is to make the Reformation in England unnecessarily
difficult to understand.

   The late medieval church operated at every level of intellectual sophistication
and the popular dissent represented by Lollardy was paralleled by similar doubts
and unease among the educated and influential. In Germany and the Low
Countries popular emphasis on cults, and on the more materialistic aspects of

works theology produced a reaction inclining to mysticism and contemplation, the so-called *Devotio Moderna*. This style of piety was particularly popular among the bourgeoisie and the more earnest clergy. It was not heretical in any doctrinal sense, but was regarded with suspicion by conservative prelates because it represented a loosening of the bonds of ecclesiastical discipline, which could be most easily enforced by a strict insistence upon outward forms. Christian humanism similarly distanced itself from popular piety, and during the late fifteenth century came to command the support of many of the best and most conscientious minds in the church. Erasmus and his English friends, such as John Colet, John Fisher and Thomas More, were keenly aware of the need for reform. Not only should the clergy set a better example in holiness of life (a plea which could be echoed from every period), but the laity should place less exclusive reliance upon rituals and tangible objects.[7] Better that pilgrimages, images and consecrated objects should disappear than that they should be seen as satisfying the whole of a man's spiritual needs. Sincere prayer, honest contrition, and a genuine awareness of Christ's sacrifice were needed to bring a man to salvation, and without them no amount of money spent on garnishing a shrine or building a new steeple on the parish church could possibly avail. It was because he already held such views that Erasmus was at first sympathetic to Luther's onslaught upon indulgences, and remained sceptical throughout his life on the value of images and monastic vows. Erasmus never challenged the authority of the church, or embraced Luther's view that the scriptures were the exclusive source of the faith, but he did place great emphasis on the need for an accurate and available Bible from which the people could be properly instructed. This 'new learning' did not have the radical implications of Lollardy, and it was far more articulate and unambiguous, but many of the spiritual anxieties which it expressed were similar. More importantly, it operated in England (as elsewhere) at the highest social and intellectual level, and was particularly strong at Henry VIII's court.[8]

Consequently it is not necessary to postulate any widespread dissatisfaction with the church, or a high level of popular anti-clericalism, in order to account for the progress of the English Reformation. Recent convincing demonstrations that the great majority of people seem to have been completely satisfied with the church as it was are therefore somewhat beside the point. At no time before the adoption of universal adult suffrage (and not always then) did it matter what the majority of ordinary people thought about issues of public policy. Only when resentment was sufficiently strong to persuade men to risk their lives, their livelihoods and their families by armed rebellion, did they impinge on the government of the state. The people whose opinions mattered in the sixteenth century were those who controlled resources, whether money, produce or manpower, and in England that meant the aristocracy, the gentry, and the corporations of the major cities, particularly London. It was precisely these people whose education and connections with the court and the universities made them most accessible to the 'new learning', and it was from that root, rather than from Lollardy or German Lutheranism, that the evangelical leadership of the 1530s arose. The Great Bible and the Bishops' Book, the reform of the calendar and the destruction of pilgrimage shrines came about because the king and his council so decided, not because there was any great demand for them. Luther in fact was a complication of only marginal relevance to these reforms. Because of the condemnation of his ideas in 1520 and 1521 he was of more use to the conservatives than he was to the evangelicals. They could happily brand any attack upon traditional practices as heretical if Luther had advocated it, irrespective of the fact that its prime movers in England owed nothing to Luther, and were even hostile to many of his ideas. In fact the German reformer had very few wholehearted disciples in England at any time, and a mere handful before 1540.[9] Historians of the Reformation have confused themselves quite unnecessarily by attempting to classify the early reformers in categories which became real only in the next generation. Was Robert Barnes, for example, a 'Lutheran'? He certainly had friendly contact with Wittenberg, and embraced the central Lutheran doctrine of justification by faith alone. But he remained orthodox on the important issue of the eucharistic presence. Was Cranmer a 'Lutheran' because he rejected the authority of the papacy and advocated the vernacular Bible? The very term 'Protestant' is anachronistic before 1530, and none of the principal architects of the English Reformation can be accurately so called before 1547. William Tyndale held theological views more radical than those of Luther, and closer to the Swiss reformer Ulrich Zwingli, but his important contribution was an English translation of the New Testament. *The Obedience of a Christian Man* may have appealed to the king, but its author was not allowed to hold any office in England.[10] So those who point out that Protestantism did not come to power during the reign of Edward VI as a result of any considerable pressure from below are absolutely right. But of course the same could be said of Sweden, or Denmark, or later of the Netherlands. Only in some of the imperial free ciites, such as Strasburg or Magdeburg in the early days of Lutheran euphoria did the established authorities change their religious stance to accommodate the wishes of their citizens.[11]

Before the death of Henry VIII in 1547 the English Reformation consisted of two related but distinct programmes. The first was a movement of evangelical reform, which owed a little to Lollardy, and a little to contemporary movements on the continent, but most to that form of enlightened piety which is known as Christian humanism. The second was the king's prolonged campaign to rid himself of his first wife, which culminated in the establishment of the royal supremacy. It is now generally recognised that the 'divorce' was not the only reason for Henry's one truly revolutionary move,[12] but it was the effectual cause, and the critical question, upon which the whole history of the English Reformation depends, is 'How did he get away with it?' What persuaded his peers and prelates, together with the gentry and citizens of the House of Commons, to endorse so extraordinary a course of action? It was certainly not an overwhelming hostility to the church as an institution, nor was it anti-clericalism in the ordinary sense. Part of the answer lies in the immense prestige of the Crown, and in the loyalty which the king could command as king. Partly also it was due to a long history of indifference to the papacy which, it was rightly felt, had done nothing to improve the spiritual condition of the English church – a failure very recently and very obviously manifested in the person of the Cardinal Legate, Thomas Wolsey. Moreover, it seems likely that very few took the king's claims to jurisdictional autonomy seriously. They were seen as moves in a political game, to be bargained away in return for the desired objective, and consequently not worthy of the appalling risks of overt opposition.[13] For every one like John Fisher and Thomas More, who was prepared to make a principled stand, there were hundreds who could see no valid reason for doing so. Henry was a Christian prince, who was likely to make every bit as good a job of running the church as the Pope had done – indeed he might well do it better as he was supporting a number of reforming initiatives. At the same time, obedience to a lawful sovereign absolved all sins. If the king was leading the realm on the wrong track, then he would answer for it, not those who were merely doing their duty as the scriptures urged them to. Moreover, Henry was an intimidating personality at the height of his powers, who had demonstrated his willingness to deal ruthlessly with those who crossed him. It was later claimed that he bullied the parliament into submission, but the truth seems to have been that there was no concerted will to resist him, and that many could see advantages, both for the church and for themselves, in the course he proposed to follow – if he really followed it.

Politically, the potential opposition was spreadeagled by Cromwell's tactics during the crucial years 1532–5, and when resistance did finally appear in the autumn of 1536 it was too late, and too confused in its motivation. The Pilgrimage of Grace was certainly a large-scale movement, but religious conservatism was only one element in its make-up, and it failed to make any explicit attack on the king's authority.[14] Stephen Gardiner, Bishop of Winchester and chief ideologist of the royal supremacy, never swerved in his loyalty to the central doctrines of traditional Catholicism. But for him the power of the Pope, and the existence of monasteries and pilgrimage shrines were *adiaphora* (things indifferent) which could (and should) be left to the determination of Christian princes.[15] The sacraments of the church remained, as Cardinal Pole later acknowledged, inviolate; so the English church in the latter part of Henry's reign was schismatic, not heretical. The political struggle between reformers and conservatives at court swung backwards and forwards, but within the parameters laid down by the royal supremacy. The king continued to burn heretics, and to execute papists as traitors, but the factional strife of the 1540s was not between Catholics and Protestants. Overtly Protestant literature continued to be banned, and much that was written in English was published abroad.[16] It is true that the boundary between Henrician reformers and Protestants was beginning to blur by 1547 – but no one could openly denounce the mass while Henry lived, unless it was from a safe distance. Nevertheless, without the royal supremacy the English Reformation – if it had ever come – would have been quite different; and with it the Catholic church could never be safe, in spite of the masses prescribed in Henry VIII's will.

The revolution that finally came in the years 1547–52 was almost entirely the work of that supremacy. The reforming faction, which had gained the ascendancy in the last months of Henry's life, emerged in less than two years as overtly Protestant, and used its control of the constitutional machinery to transform the worship and doctrine of the church. Edward VI was a minor throughout his reign, and the authority of the Crown impaired in practice, if not in theory.[17] Nevertheless there was no effective challenge to the religious policy that each of his chief ministers pursued in turn. This was not because the country at large was happy with a Protestant church. We know perfectly well that the destruction of

the traditional rites and practices was bitterly resented, and that supporters of
the 'new ways', even among the gentry and aristocracy, were few. However, the
main point which Henry VIII had wanted to make – that the faith of his
subjects was the king's business – had been well taken. Upon what ground
should the religious conservatives have stood during these years, given the
consensus support which the royal supremacy had achieved? Both Stephen
Gardiner and the Princess Mary faced this dilemma, and each endeavoured to
resolve it by maintaining the validity of Henry's settlement.[18] Protestants may
have been few, but there was hardly such a thing as a true Catholic in England
during Edward's reign. Gardiner and Mary appealed to the supremacy as Henry
had exercised it against the supremacy as Edward's council chose to exercise it –
an illogical and fruitless exercise which had only a nuisance value against those
in power. Both undoubtedly felt that the legislation of 1547 and 1550 violated
true Christian doctrine and imposed heresy, but neither as yet was prepared to
see the root of their difficulty where it truly lay – in the royal supremacy itself.
That supremacy had indeed changed its nature with Henry's death, because it
could no longer be represented as the personal authority of a divinely ordained
king. Instead it had become part of the public authority of the Crown, and the
church had become something like a department of state for ecclesiastical
affairs. On the whole the political nation accepted this, not because it believed
the new doctrine to be true, but because it had taken out a large investment in
the royal supremacy in the form of secularised monastic and chantry property.
At the same time, once Protestantism was in power, and had armed itself with a
liturgy and confession of faith, it naturally began to attract more adherents.
Considering that it was the work of an unpopular minority government, and
that it was associated in the popular imagination with Swiss and German
influences, the Protestant settlement made a surprisingly deep impact on
parochial life. Nevertheless, in spite of the efforts of the king's council, and of
evangelical preachers and writers, the conversion of England was almost entirely
a question of laws and edicts which, as Martin Bucer recognised, 'the majority
obey very reluctantly'.[19] As such, it was extremely superficial; but the important
thing was that it happened, and demonstrated that there was nothing in the
Ecclesia Anglicana which could stand up to political manipulation by the Crown.

The succession of Mary, and her subsequent reversal of religious policy merely
emphasised the same point. In spite of the continuing popularity of the
traditional practices, and widespread enthusiasm for the mass, their restoration
was the result of government action. As Robert Parkyn noted with indignation,
there were many clergy and congregations whose minds were 'wholly bent' on
restoration, but who could take no action until a 'public commandment' by
proclamation or statute gave them leave.[20] 'Religion as King Henry left it' was
the prevailing demand. Unlike either Protestantism or Catholicism, the
Henrician church had been distinctively English, and however controversial the
king's policies may have been in the 1530s, by the last years of his reign he had
his people solidly behind him, especially when they felt that either the emperor
or the French were likely to attempt the restoration of the Pope's authority by
force. However, Mary could not be satisfied with her father's settlement.
Whatever she may have said as princess, as queen she was determined to restore
the traditional Roman jurisdiction, and Stephen Gardiner, her first Lord

Chancellor, fully supported her. He had learned by bitter experience that the royal supremacy was not compatible with an immutable and universal faith, and when he was pushed to the point of choice, he abandoned his long advocacy of the supremacy. Other senior ecclesiastics, such as Edmund Bonner and Cuthbert Tunstall, shared his conversion, but the undoubted logic of their position made little impact on the laity. By exercising the full weight of her authority Mary did restore the papacy, but only after difficult and protracted negotiations. There was little enthusiasm for Rome, even among those who welcomed the conservative reaction most enthusiastically, and the complications introduced by the queen's marriage to Philip of Spain made matters worse. That marriage was unpopular for a variety of reasons, but it was accepted for the same reason that Henry's marriage to Anne Boleyn had been accepted – because it represented the clear will of a lawful sovereign. For reasons of his own, Philip took a leading part in the negotiations for reconciliation, so that it appeared (much to the chagrin of both Gardiner and Reginald Pole, the Cardinal Legate) that England had been restored to the church on a Habsburg initiative. And when, two years later, Philip was at war with Pope Paul IV, and excommunicated, the English church suffered in consequence.[21]

The association of the Roman church with Spain was largely unwarranted, but it was extremely unfortunate for the long-term future of Mary's religious programme. In fact the queen herself barely understood, and did not attempt to introduce, the Catholicism of the Counter-Reformation, of which Spain was already the champion. The spirituality of her church was insular, and looked back to the humanist reformers of the 1520s and 1530s – before the Protestants had destroyed their non-dogmatic and pietistic programme. She restored very few monasteries, and made no attempt to resurrect the great pilgrimage shrines. The writings of Bonner, Brookes and Watson were homiletic and exhortatory rather than polemic. So it was particularly ironic that what was, in effect, a very English style of Catholicism should have become splattered with so much of the mud that popular prejudice hurled against the Spaniards. The beneficiaries of this, and to some extent its instigators, were Mary's enemies, the Protestants. There were, for obvious reasons, more of them by 1553 than there had been in 1547, because not all the conversions of Edward's reign had been opportunistic. They were still not numerous as a proportion of the whole population, but they were disproportionately strong in London, and among the gentry of the Home Counties. Starting cautiously in the autumn of 1553, they waged an increasingly relentless propaganda war against the queen both from refuges abroad and from hiding places in England. Being largely a religion of and for the literate, Protestantism produced both more and better polemics than the established church, and consequently left a much bigger imprint on the history of the reign than either its support or its political power would have justified. The church struck back with a persecution which was principled rather than political – an attempt to extirpate heresy as a disease of the body politic, rather than to defeat a rival party. As a result the image of Protestantism began to change; instead of being a foreign intrusion, and the tool of unscrupulous power-seekers like the Duke of Northumberland, it became a cause that respected men would die for. It also began to appear English, partly thanks to its vernacular liturgy and Bible, and partly thanks to the Spanish image of the persecuting church.

When Mary died in November 1558, the Protestants were still a small minority, but their political position was strong. Thanks to Mary's childlessness, and Philip's other preoccupations, Elizabeth (who shared at least some of their convictions) was able to bring them back into her government. This could hardly have come about if Mary had not effectively killed the Henrician option that most Englishmen would still have preferred. With one exception, her bishops were good Catholics who would not contemplate a return to the royal supremacy, and the senior clergy assembled in convocation early in 1559 endorsed their stand.[22] Consequently the options facing the new queen were either a continuance of the status quo, or a return to the royal supremacy backed by a Protestant settlement. She chose the latter, and the fact that she could find enough able Protestant clergy to form a credible bench of bishops belies some of the more extreme claims for the Catholic loyalties of early Elizabethan England. However, it is broadly true that Protestantism returned to power in England on the shoulders of the royal supremacy, as it had first gained that power in 1547. There were good reasons why the political nation was prepared to accept that situation. One was that it needed Elizabeth, and the settlement was her choice, just as the papacy had been Mary's. Another was that it removed all lingering doubts (never entirely set at rest by the agreement of 1555) about the right of the laity to possess former ecclesiastical property. And a third was that, as long as it endured, it ensured the subservience of the church to secular jurisdiction. Professor Scarisbrick has recently argued that the laity actually played a larger part in the pre-Reformation church than they did subsequently, because there were so many lay guilds and religious fraternities, whereas the Anglican establishment was entirely clerical.[23] As far as it goes this argument is valid, but one has only to compare the bishops of Henry VIII with those of Elizabeth to see the decline of the church as a power within the state. England eventually became a Protestant country when conservatives were supporting the Prayer Book rather than the mass; or, as Professor Collinson has put it 'when the insomniac historian stops counting protestants and starts counting recusants'.[24] That situation was not reached until the second half of Elizabeth's reign, and it owed a lot to the queen's longevity and political success.

Whichever way you look at it, England as a Protestant state was the creation of the political power of the Crown. But that does not mean that the reformation was not a genuine spiritual force. The convictions of Hooper, or Ridley, or indeed of Matthew Parker, were not conjured up by political convenience. There would have been a Reformation in England, even without Henry VIII's 'Great Matter' and the establishment of the royal supremacy – but it would have been quite different. Perhaps the humanist reformers would have revitalised the church along their own lines, and remained within the Roman jurisdiction. Perhaps there would have been religious rebellion and civil war. However, history is about what happened, not about what might have happened, and the Reformation that actually occurred in England was not the result of popular evangelism, nor of anti-clerical fury, nor of widespread disillusionment with a corrupt and inadequate church. Rather, it was the result of a monarchy that wished to have a church amenable to its national and secular purposes, and used whatever religious lever appeared to be available. In fact Protestant theology was not particularly amenable to political control, even through the Godly Prince, but then the English have never taken theology very seriously.

Notes

1. C. Haigh, 'Introduction' to *The English Reformation Revised*, Cambridge, 1987.
2. *Here begynneth a lytyll treatyse . . . called ars moriendi* (1491); *A Short Title Catalogue of books printed in England, Scotland and Ireland, and of English books printed abroad, 1475–1640*, ed. A.W. Pollard and G.R. Redgrave; revised by W.A. Jackson, F.J. Ferguson and K.F. Pantzer, 2 vols. London, 1976, 1986 (STC), 786, sig. Ai^v; cited by Susan Brigden, *London and the Reformation*, Oxford, 1989, pp. 21–2.
3. *A Relation . . . of the Island of England*, ed. C.A. Sneyd, Camden Society, XXXVII, 1847, p. 23.
4. J.A.F. Thomson, *The Later Lollards, 1414–1520*, London, 1965; M. Aston, *England's Iconoclasts*, Oxford, 1988.
5. Aston, *England's Iconoclasts*, p. 127.
6. Haigh, *English Reformation*. Avoidance of the mass was the most common ground for suspicion; 'Thou art an heretic, for thou tookest not thy rights at Easter'. Brigden, *London*, p. 17.
7. Eamon Duffy 'The Spirituality of John Fisher', in *Humanism, Reform and the Reformation; the Career of Bishop John Fisher*, ed. B. Bradshaw and E. Duffy, Cambridge, 1989, pp. 205–31. Fisher more truly belonged to the ascetic tradition of the *Devotio Moderna*, but it was also this aspect of humanist piety which appealed to him.
8. Maria Dowling, 'The Gospel and the Court; Reformation under Henry VIII', in *Protestantism and the National Church in Sixteenth-century England*, ed. P. Lake and M. Dowling, London, 1987.
9. Erwin Doernberg, *Henry VIII and Luther*, London, 1961.
10. C.H. Williams, *William Tyndale*, Stanford, California, 1969, *passim*.
11. Steven E. Ozment, *The Reformation in the Cities; the Appeal of Protestantism to Sixteenth-century Germany and Switzerland*, New Haven and London, 1975, pp. 121–3.
12. J. Guy, *Tudor England*, Oxford, 1988, citing several specialist articles and monographs.
13. Haigh, *English Reformation*; D. Loades, *Politics and the Nation, 1450–1660*, London, 1986, pp. 161–5.
14. M.H. and R. Dodds, *The Pilgrimage of Grace, 1536–7; and the Exeter Conspiracy, 1538*, Cambridge, 1915; C.S.L. Davies, 'The Pilgrimage of Grace Reconsidered', *Past and Present*, XLI, 1968, 54–76; Davies, 'Popular Religion and the Pilgrimage of Grace', in *Order and Disorder in Early Modern England*, ed. A. Fletcher and J. Stevenson, Cambridge, 1985, pp. 58–91.
15. J.A. Muller, *Stephen Gardiner and the Tudor Reaction*, London, 1926, pp. 61–3; R.H. Pogson, 'God's Law and Man's: Stephen Gardiner and the Problem of Loyalty', in *Law and Government under the Tudors*, ed. C. Cross, D. Loades and J. Scarisbrick, Cambridge, 1988, pp. 67–90.
16. See Chapter 10, 'Books and the English Reformation prior to 1558'.
17. As Gardiner himself admitted 'A King's authority to govern his realm never wanteth, though he were in his cradle. His place is replenished by his Council . . .'. Nevertheless a minority government always lacked the full authority of a mature king. W.K. Jordan, *Edward VI; the Young King*, London, 1968, *passim*.
18. D. Loades, *Mary Tudor; a Life*, Oxford, 1989.

19. Bucer to Brentius, 15 May 1550; *Original Letters, Relative to the English Reformation*, ed. H. Robinson, Parker Society, 1847; II, p. 542.
20. A.G. Dickens, 'Robert Parkyn's Narrative of the Reformation', *English Historical Review*, LXII, 1947, 58–83.
21. D. Loades, *The Reign of Mary Tudor*, London, 1979, pp. 428–57.
22. Elizabeth made several attempts to persuade otherwise amenable bishops, such as Nicholas Heath, to accept a return of the supremacy, but without success. The only bishop who did accept was William Kitchen of Llandaff. The resolution of convocation demonstrated that there were no potential Henrician bishops among the deans and archdeacons who comprised the lower house. N.L. Jones, *Faith by Statute; Parliament and the Settlement of Religion, 1559*, London, 1982.
23. J. Scarisbrick, 'Layfolk and the Pre-reformation Church', in *The Reformation and the English People*, Oxford, 1984, pp. 1–18.
24. P. Collinson, *The Birthpangs of Protestant England: Religious and Cultural Changes in the Sixteenth and Seventeenth Centuries*, London, 1988, p. 10.

Part I: Politics

1 The Royal Supremacy: A Note in Discussion

We must never forget, in discussing the relationship between the English Reformation and that which occurred elsewhere, that England was in two respects distinctive. On the one hand there was an indigenous heretical tradition – the Lollard movement – going back a century and a half; and on the other hand the monarchy took a deliberate, and unique, initiative. The royal supremacy was not merely a pragmatic seizure of ecclesiastical property and jurisdiction, it was a theoretical claim, put forward with all the trappings of high principle and Divine law. As such, it had nothing whatsoever to do with doctrinal Protestantism, and indeed later Protestants endeavouring to adhere to the principle of *sola scriptura* sometimes found its doctrine an embarrassment. When princes or city magistrates in Germany decided to embrace the Reformation they normally did so either in response to pressure from below or out of a desire to exploit a political or economic opportunity. In either case they were making a positive reaction to a Lutheran (or possibly Swiss) reform movement which was already present and powerful. Such a situation did not exist in England. Before 1529 Lutheran and Swiss reforming ideas were known only to a handful of academics and merchants, and the Lollards had no influence at court or in the Council. Henry VIII was at first motivated by a purely political quarrel with the papacy over his marriage, but since this involved theological – or at least canonical – issues of a complex nature, he soon began to discover religious principle to sustain him.[1] Henry was a man of officious conscience, who needed to believe that God was on his side, and this quickly led him to the conviction that the Pope's authority was usurped, and had no foundation in Divine law. It was in this frame of mind that, between 1533 and 1535, he allowed Thomas Cromwell to draft and manage through parliament the Acts which carried the royal supremacy into effect. These Acts still owed very little to Protestantism, either in their conception or in their passage, but such Protestants as there were in England by 1535 naturally supported Henry's attack on the papacy. Since the king was in fact carrying out a jurisdictional revolution of the first importance he needed all the support he could get, and was even prepared to extend a cautious welcome to Tyndale's *Obedience of a Christian Man* or Simon Fish's *Supplication of Beggars*, in spite of the blatant heresy of their authors. By 1536 Henry's position had changed somewhat. In that year both Catherine of Aragon and Anne Boleyn died, thus leaving the king canonically free, but he rebuffed papal attempts to negotiate a settlement. However it may have started, by that time his rejection of Roman jurisdiction had come to rest on conviction. The theory of the royal supremacy owed far more to Marsilius of Padua[2] than it did to Luther or Zwingli, and its principal defender, Stephen Gardiner, was a lifelong enemy of Protestantism.[3] Nevertheless by 1536 Henry and Cromwell had set out to use the supremacy to implement a reforming programme in the English church which had many Protestant features.[4] For this reason, and because of the still delicate political situation, Protestant preachers and writers who were prepared to be reasonably discreet were given a good deal of official patronage and encouragement. Protestant ideas therefore spread, and the attempts of the conservative clergy to suppress and punish them were inhibited. The results of this can be most clearly seen in London, where furious quarrels broke out between conservatives and reformers who each had their centres of power and influence.[5] The episcopate was deeply divided, with conservatives such as Stokesley, Gardiner and Tunstall on the one hand trying to tread carefully to avoid suspicion of papist sympathies; and reformers such as Cranmer, Latimer and Shaxton on the other hand having to defend themselves against charges of heresy. The balance was not stable, and for a few years after 1540 the conservatives were in the ascendant, but Henry showed no sign of being willing to surrender the supremacy, and had his heir educated by Protestant tutors,[6] perhaps to prevent any backsliding in that direction. Thus in 1547 the supremacy passed into Protestant hands, and the Reformation received the full backing of the state, at least for a few years.

All this makes it very difficult to assess the 'popular Reformation' in England. Such a movement had scarcely begun before it was caught into political issues, so that by 1535 it was impossible either to embrace or to reject reforming ideas without the action appearing to have political significance. One cannot therefore compare London or Norwich in the 1530s with Strasburg or Bamberg in the 1520s, because the same opportunities for the spontaneous or independent evolution of religious parties did not exist. Of course there were in the English towns, as in those of Germany or Switzerland, political issues of a local nature which affected religious alignment, but they were dominated almost from the first appearance of continental reformed ideas by the overriding fact that the king had rejected the authority of the Pope, and had made similar rejection by his subjects an acid test of loyalty to the Crown.

Notes

1. J.J. Scarisbrick, *Henry VIII*, London, 1968, pp. 163–4; H.A. Kelly, *The Matrimonial Trials of Henry VIII*, Stanford, California, 1976, pp. 222–3. [The *Divorce Tracts of Henry VIII*, ed. E.J. Surtz and Virginia Murphy, Agers, 1988.]
2. *Defensor Pacis*, an edition of which was published in England in 1535.
3. S. Gardiner, *De Vera Obedientia Oratio*, London, 1535.
4. G.R. Elton, *Reform and Reformation*, London, 1977, pp. 157–8.
5. Much light has been shed recently upon the situation in London in the 1520s and 1530s by the work of Susan Brigden. *London and the Reformation*, Oxford University

Press, 1989.
6. More accurately, tutors who subsequently emerged as Protestants. The exact views [of Sir John Cheke and Richard Cox before 1547 can only be deduced.]

2 The Essex Inquisitions of 1556

As a well-known centre of Protestant strength, Essex suffered severely from the Marian persecution. Foxe recorded the activities of Bishop Bonner within the county in savage terms, and many Essex men and women featured in the edifying woodcuts which illustrated the early editions of the *Actes and Monuments*. Behind the spectacular self-sacrifice of the martyrs, however, lay a pattern of persecution and defiance on a less exalted plane, with which the martyrologist was less concerned, and whose records are scanty and fragmentary. Unable to face the consequences of resistance, and unwilling to conform, many people in the worst-affected areas fled. Some went overseas to join the well-known congregations in Emden, Frankfurt, or Geneva; others took to the woods and shared the fortunes of such outlawed gospellers as George Eagles, the notorious 'Trudgeover'. Some, and these are the least known of all, simply packed up and moved away to a quieter area until the troubles should be over.

These fugitives represented a serious leak in the government's coercive system, and a growing embarrassment. Some time early in 1556 the decision was taken to act against them in the only practicable way, by cutting off their means of sustenance. By the statute of 5 Richard II, st. I, c.2, the penalty for departing the realm without royal licence was the forfeiture of goods. The exaction of such a penalty, however, depended on a knowledge of who had gone, and what goods they possessed. In most cases the real wealth of the exiles was in land, and the confiscation of their movables would not do them sufficient harm to justify the expense and trouble of confiscation. Consequently the council introduced a Bill into parliament in the autumn of 1555 to extend the penalty for contemptuous departure to the lands of the offenders. In December, to the queen's bitter anger, the Commons rejected the Bill,[1] and the measure did not become law until the statute of 13 Elizabeth, c.5, which was directed against the Catholic exiles. In the absence of a statutory weapon the government was forced to employ other means. If the lands of the fugitives could not be confiscated they could still be sequestered to achieve the same immediate result.

The problem of those who had fled within the realm was less pressing because for the most part they were humble men who did not enjoy the same protection, or indulge in such open defiance. Legally they had committed no offence by simply leaving home, but in any case it was not necessary to confiscate their property. It could simply be taken into custody as a surety for their return. They were not fugitives in the technical sense of the word because they had been neither convicted nor indicted of felony, but no formal process was necessary for the Crown to take up vacated rights pending claim.

The obvious means of exploiting both these openings was that later to be prescribed by the Elizabethan statute, and anticipated at this time: the appointment of commissions to investigate potential distraints, and act upon their findings. The entries reproduced in the following pages record the existence, and some of the findings, of two such commissions which operated in Essex during the autumn of 1556. Similar commissions were appointed to investigate the resources of individual exiles, such as the Duchess of Suffolk, but as far as can be ascertained at present, these entries are unique. They are regional in their application, and cover both classes of fugitive. Both their matter and their form raise interesting problems. Although it might seem reasonable that such commissions should be appointed for Essex, and not for less disaffected counties, there is no logical reason why, out of the nineteen hundreds and half-hundreds, twelve should have been visited, and not the other seven. The northern and the central hundreds were covered, why not the southern? Bearing in mind that the second return is clearly incomplete, breaking off in the middle of a sentence, we may assume that the whole record is incomplete. This is supported by the fact that Foxe mentions an exactly parallel commission sitting at Beccles in Suffolk during the previous May,[2] for which no records appear to survive. Although the commissions themselves are specifically stated to be letters patent under the Great Seal, there is no trace of them on the patent roll. Apparently the survival of these two, or more accurately one and a half, returns upon the Memoranda Roll is arbitrary. The commissioners were instructed to make their returns into the exchequer, but either they were dilatory in doing so or the Remembrancer's clerk was equally negligent about recording them; the latter is more probable. The only case which was to arise out of the returns referred to the missing part of the Colchester entry. How many other commissions and similar administrative actions escaped the records through such carelessness or deliberate negligence, we are never likely to know.

To make any valid deductions from these documents, it is necessary to tread with the greatest care. Statistically their evidence is meaningless. Beyond confirming the natural assumption that only a minority of the fugitives went overseas, they can tell us nothing. Even the most cursory glance at other sources reveals that the presentations do not tell the whole truth, and it would be most unsafe to assume, for instance, that the hundreds of Clavering and Dunmowe were in fact innocent of offenders. It would appear, from the evidence given here, that Thomas Crawley was a yeoman of moderate wealth, whereas in reality he was the head of a substantial county family. Alone of those whose names appear here, he is noticed by Miss Garrett among the continental exiles.[3] He settled in Frankfurt, where in January 1557 his property was valued at 700 florins. On returning to England after Mary's death he probably sat in the first parliament of Elizabeth, as member for Aylesbury, Bucks. The £7 tenement in Elmden that the jury presented was only a small fraction of his property, which included the manor of Wendon Lofts and a good deal of chantry land purchased in the previous reign. Similar discrepancies can be discovered in other returns. William Asshley and John Rygges died in 1568 and 1563 respectively, and each left land and stock which show him to have been a yeoman of some means,[4] despite the fact that no property is mentioned in connection with his flight.

It is probably safe to assume that the jurors were unenthusiastic, and evaded their duty whenever possible, but the extent of their partiality cannot be accurately assessed. To judge from the wills of Harry Somersham and John Asser[5] it would seem that their property was fully presented, so it is not safe to discount all the returns as being far short of the truth. Probably the honesty of all the returns varied from hundred to hundred. According to Foxe the jury at Beccles was malicious and made a large number of presentations, but the tendency in Essex was the reverse. In this connection the attitude of the sheriff and commissioners was of vital importance. The sheriff empanelled the juries and could select such men as he thought most appropriate. The commissioners, if they were not satisfied with the way in which the jurors were performing their duties, could demand others of a more amenable mind. If the returns were defective for the government's purpose, all those associated with them must share the responsibility. Of course it is quite possible that a man like Crawley was presented by the juries of all the several hundreds where he owned property, and only this one has survived, but it is significant that no distraint is mentioned. In only four cases did the commissioners report that they had taken the land or goods of the accused into custody. In seven cases no property was mentioned at all, and in three cases the property was in the custody of other parties, as a result of transactions of which the juries claimed ignorance. The only complete return shows that, as a result of the commissioners' investigations, goods to the value of £9 18s.4d., and lands to the annual value of £2 8s.8d., belonging to three individuals were placed in the hands of official receivers. Although Lord Rich is castigated by Foxe as a persecutor, he was certainly not a zealot. Both he and Lord Darcy had narrowly escaped punishment for their association with Northumberland, and neither was likely to be enthusiastic over the sequestration of the property of a fellow gentleman such as Crawley.[6]

What happened to these small properties after sequestration is largely a matter for conjecture. The only exchequer case arising from such a distraint was that of John Mott of Great Wigborough, which was tried in the Easter term 1557.[7] Mott had been presented at Colchester (presumably on the missing part of the return), when his goods had been inventoried to the value of £16 9s.0d., and it was recorded that his farm and stock was in the possession of his father, John Mott senior. The latter had been distrained upon to answer the value of his son's stock, and now pleaded that the distraint was unjust as he had fairly purchased the stock from his son. Whether he had in fact done so, or the transfer was a mere technicality, the barons allowed his plea and the goods were returned to him. To judge by the wills that we have already noticed, most of the property must have been returned, although when, or how, cannot be said with certainty. Most probably it was quietly resumed upon the accession of Elizabeth.

All those fugitives of whose state there is any evidence, here or elsewhere, were substantial yeomen at least, and whatever precautions they may have taken to protect their interests it was surely a powerful stimulus that drove them from their homes. With the exception of Thomas Bowtell we have no evidence of what they did in their exile. Most eventually seem to have returned, and picked up the threads of their lives where they had dropped them, but the disruption must have been considerable. No doubt humbler people who had no property also fled. In their fate the government was not interested on this occasion because it could gain no hold over them.

Despite the necessity for caution in drawing conclusions from these records, it is clear that these commissions largely failed of their intended effect. Despite the sonorous phrases in which they were addressed, the commissioners seem to have been unenthusiastic; and the jurors were certainly partial. Potentially such a commission was a powerful administrative weapon, but in this case it failed to overcome the normal handicaps of Tudor administration. Whether, in this respect, it was typical of special commissions in general, it is impossible at the moment to say. The fact that such a method was used to supplement the normal machinery of administration is well known, but these documents emphasise that we know very little about the extent of its use, or the success it achieved.

Public Record Office, K.R.E., Memoranda roll, 1556–7 (E159/337, Recorda section, Michaelmas term, rr. 244, 267.

Anglia
Essex

[r.244] Memorandum quod Ricardus Ryche miles dominus Riche Iohannes Wentworth miles Robertus Mordaunt Willelmus Barners Ricardus Weston Iohannes Wyseman de Canfeld Thomas Myldmay & Willelmus Chyshyll armigeri venerunt coram baronibus huius Scaccarii viii die novembris hoc termino in propriis personis suis et exhibuerunt Curie huic litteras domini Regis et domine Regine sub magno Sigillo suo eis directas vacuandas quadam certificatione supra premissis capta quarum quidem litterarum patientium tenor sequitur in hec verba // Philip and Mary by the Grace of Godd King and queene of Englande Spayn ffrance both Ciciles Ierusalem & Ireland defendours of the fayth Archdukes of Austria Dukes of Burgoyne millayne and brabant Countes of hapsburg fflanders and Tyroll / To oure trusty and right well-beloved Iohn Wentworth knight and to oure wellbeloved Robert Maudante William Barnard Rychard Weston Iohn Wiseman of Canfeld Thomas Mildmay and William Cheshull Esquyers gretinge / fforasmuch as it ys given us to understande that dyverse and sondry of our subiects inhabiting and dwelling within the hundreds of chelmesforde Wytham halfe hundrethe Dunmowe uttesford & Freshwell Clavering halfe hundrethe and harlowe within our countye of Essex have of late withdrawen themselves and be fledd and departed out of this oure realme unto the partes of beyonde the Seas without oure especiall licens contrary to their dutyes of allegiance where they do still remayne in contempt of us & the lawes and statutes of this oure realme in that case made and provided / And we mynding to understande the truthe of the premisses to thentente we may be truly answeryd of the goodes and cattalls of them and of every of them as reason ys / And trustyng in youre fidelityes wysdoms and discretiones we have appointed and assigned you to be our commyssioners and by these present do geve unto you and three of you full powers & auchoritye by all the wayes and meanes ye can devise to examen serch trye and fynde out aswell by the othes of good and lawfull men inhabiting within the saide hundreds of any of them aswell within the liberties as without as allso by Inquisicions deposicions examenacons or otherwyse what tyme the same our subiects & eny of them fledd and departed out of our saide realme as aforesaid / And what goodes and cattalls they and every of them had or were possessed of at the tyme of theyre severall departures or at any tyme synce / And what goods and cattalls the same were and of what pryce and value and in whose handes and custody the same goods and cattalls & any parte thereof then were or do nowe remayne / And whether they or any of them had or helde any landes tenements & heredytaments by lease for term of life or yeares yet enduring or otherwise and for howe manye yeres / And in whose tenure holding or occupacyon the same landes tenementes or heredytaments then were or nowe be / And what persons have since the tyme of theyre severall departures had and received the revenues and profitts of suche landes tenementes and heredytaments and when howe and by what means and to whose handes the saide leases be come / And after such Inquiry othe and examinacyon so duly had and made our pleasure and Comandment is that all the goodes cattalls & leases & every of them which shall or may come to your knowledge ye shall cause to be seased and gathered together to our use / And the same or the iust valewe thereof to put and Comyt under safe custody so to remayne to oure use until we shall take furder order for the delivery of the same / And moreover we will and commande you for the better accomplishement of this our commyssion & for a playne declaration of your doings in that behalf to make or cause to be made substantial inventories and bookes in due playne and perfit forme declaryng & mencioning all & singular the particularityes & specialtyes of alle the goodes cattalls leases & offyces whiche they or any of them had or helde at the tyme of theyre severall departinges as aforesaid / And where also we understande that dyverse of our subiects despisinge the catholique faithe & religion by us restored & set forth within thys our Realme have in contempt thereof & of our lawes withdrawn themselves from their severall habytacions & dwellinges and remayne abrode in places secret and unknowen where they have neither iust occasion or commandment to abyde / Our pleasure & commandement is therefore & we gyve unto yo by these present full power & aucthoritie to make lyke inquisicion serche & examynacon within the saide hundredths & every of them of all & singular such persons as have withdrawen themselves & departed from ther saide severall habytacons & dwellings & the tyme of their departure / And what gooddes & cattals they & every of them had and were possessed of at theyre severall departures or at eny tyme sence / And what goodes & cattalls the same were & in whose handes & custody the same goodes & cattalles & eny plate thereof then were or do now remayne / And whether they or eny of them had or helde any landes tenements or heredytamentes by lease for term of yeres yet enduringe or otherwyse and for how many yeres / And in whose tenure holding or occupacyon the same landes tenements or heredytamentes then were or nowe be / And what persons have synce the tyme of theyre severall departures had and received the revenues & profittes of such landes tenements leases & heredytamentes / And when howe & by what meanes & to whose handes the same or eny parte thereof is come / And after such Inquery serche and examenacyon so duly had & and made Oure pleasure & commandment ys that all the goodes cattalls & leases of them and every of them wyche shallbe or may

come to your knowledge as aforesayde ye shall cause to be put under your sure &
safe custody / And to make substantyall bokes & Inventoryes of all the same &
every parte & parcell thereof in suche manner & forme as before is expressid
& declared / And finally we will & commande you or three of you to make
Inquisition of the premisses & to fulfill execute & accomplisshe all & every
other thinge & thinges whiche aswell by vertue of this our comysson as also by
the saide estatute are to be fulfylld & don / And also thereof & of alle youre
doinges in that behalfe to certify us into our Exchequer in writing under your
seales or the seales of three of you as aforesaid with diligence / And further we
woll & commande our Sheryf of oure saide county of Essex that he shall cause to
come before you or three of you at such dayes and places as ye shall appointe
such & as many honest menne of hys balywicke aswell within libertyes as
withoute by whome the truthe in the premisses may be better inquired of tryed
and knowen straightly charging and commanding all maiors sheryffes baylyffs
constables & all other our officers ministers & faithfull subiects that they &
every of them by ayding helping assisting & at your commandement in the due
execution hereof as they tender our pleasure & will avoyde the contrary at theyr
utmost perills / In witnes whereof we have caused these our letters to be made
patents / witnes ourselves at our manor of Eltham the thirde day of Auguste in
the thirde and fourthe yeares of oure reignes /

Et tenor certificationis predicti unde superius fit invencio sequitur in hec
verba /

The certificathe of Sir Richarde Ryche knight lorde Ryche Sir Iohn Wentworth
knight Robert Mordaunte William Berners Richard Weston Iohn Wiseman of
Canfield Thomas Myldmay & Willm Chyshull esquyers commissioners of our
sovraygn lorde & ladye phillipe & mary by the grace of Godde Kinges & Queene
. . . (etc) concerninge all & every suche person & persons lately inhabiting &
dwellinge within the hundreths of chelmsforde Wythem halfe hundrethe
Dunmowe uttesforde & Freswell Clavering halfe hundrethe & harlowe within
the county of Essex as of late have withdrawen themselves & be fledde &
departed out of this realme unto the partyes of beyond the seas without the
Kinges and Queenes maiesties speciall licens / And also of all & every
suche person & persons which for religion have departed from theyr severall
habytacions or dwellinges & remayne in other secret places within this realme
by vertu of the Kings and Queenes highnesses commyssion to them directed
dated the iii day of August in the thirde and fourthe yeares of their reignes /
othes & verdictes of sondry iuries in this behalf sworne & charged at muche
Dunmowe in the said countye the xv daye of September the third and fourthe
yeres aforesaid / Accordynge to dyverse articles underwritten as hereafter more at
large may appere /

The hundrethe of uttlesforde & Fressewell

The Iury there have presented that Thomas Crawley late of Elmeden ys fledd
beyonde the seas the first yeare of the queenes maiesties rayne / Whether yt was
for Religion or Whether he had lycens or not the iury knowe not / What goodes
and cattalls he had at the tyme of hys departure the iury knoweth not / in whose

possessyon they were at the tyme of hys departure or nowe bene they knowe not /
Certayne landes & tenements in Elmeden to hym and to hys heyres in fee simple
callid (blank) in the handes and occupacyon of Iohn ffremont of Elmeden
ffermor of the same beinge of the yerely value of vii li / The saide Thomas
Crawley hathe receyved thissues & proffits of the saide landes sithen hys
departure as ferre as the saide iury knoweth / The saide Iohn ffremont holdeth
the same landes & tenements by lease for the terme of certeyne yeares And one
Thomas mede now claymeth the same landes in fee symple by bargayne and sale
of the sayde Thomas Crawley /

The said iurye have presented that Thomas Bowtell of Newporte ponde is
fledde for religion into Wiltshire aboute a yere and a halfe laste paste but into
what parisshe the iurye knowe not / The same Thomas Bowtell dyd carry such
gooddes & cattalles as he had with hym into Wilteshere where he dwelleth The
saide gooddes & cattalls do remayne where he dwelleth in hys possession &
keeping / The same Thomas at the tyme of his departure had to ferme the
hospitall with thappurtenances in Newporte aforesayde for the terme of viii yeres
then to come and nowe is in the occupacion of one Willm Okeman fermor
thereof but what it is worthe yerely above the rente the iure knowe not /
Whether the said Thomas Bowtell receive any profette yerely of the saide Willm
Okeman for the saide ferme the saide iurye knowe not / Whether the saide
Willm Okeman have any lease from the sayde Thomas Bowtell of the saide
hospital the saide iury knowe not /

Memorandum that in the residewe of all the townes villages parisshes &
hamlettes within the said hundrethe there is no cause worthy of presentment
tooching the articles above rehersed as the saide iurye hath certyfyd /

The halfe hundreth of Wyttham

The iurye have presented that Thomas Boys & his wife of muche Braxted are
fledd for religion abowte vi weekes laste paste unto some secrete places within
this realme unknowen unto the iurye / The gooddes & cattalles of the saide
Thomas Boyce as doth appeare by an inventory hereof made do amounte unto
the some of xviis ivd / The saide goodes & cattalles are comytted by the Kinges
& Queenes maities commyssioners to the custody & safe keping of Richard
Savell /

The same iury have in likewise presented that Iohn Somersham & hys wife of
muche Braxted aforesaide are fledd for religion about xvi weekes last paste but
whether they be gone beyonde the seas or remayne in secret places within this
realme the iurye knowe not / The goodes & cattalls of the saide Iohn Somesham
as doth appeare by an inventorye thereof made doth amounte to the some of
xlviis viiid / The saide gooddes & cattalls are comyted by the Kinges & Queenes
maiesties commyssioners to the custody & safe keping of the saide Richard
Savell / The same Iohn Somersham hath to ferme one tenemente & certayne
landes in much Braxted till michaelmas come xii moneth of the yerely rente of
xxxvs ivd nowe in the occupacyon of the saide Richard Savell / And hys wife at
the tyme of hys deparure hadd the thirde of a tenemente there and hir parte
thereof was worthe yerely xiiis ivd / Thissues & profettes of the saide ferme

above the rent are valued nothing for that they are scantly worthe the saide rent / The saide ferme is comytted by the Kinges & Queens maiesties commyssioners to the occupacyon of the saide Ric. Savell and the rent of hit whiche shalbe due to michaelmas next coming is then to be answered to the Owner thereof /

The said iury have presented that harry Somersham & his wife of muche Braxted aforesaide are fledd for religion aboute xvii weekes laste paste but whether they be gone beyond the seas or remayning in secrete places within this realme the iurye know not / The gooddes & cattalles of the saide harry Somersham as doth appeare by an Inventory thereof made dothe amounte unto the some of vi li xxis vid / The saide goddess & cattalls are comytted by the Kings & Queenes maiesties commissioners to the custody & safe keping of the saide Richarde Savell / The same harry Somersham hath to ferme one tenemente & certayne landes in much Braxted till Witsontyde come xii moneth of the yearly rente of xxviiis / And an other tenements in the same parisshe till michaelmas come xii moneth of the yerely rent of xxxs nowe in the occupacon of the said Ric Savell / Thissues & profettes of the saide fermes above the rentes are valued nothing for that they are scantly worth the sayde rents / The saide tenementes are comytted by the Kings & Queenes maiesties commissionerss to thoccupacon of the saide Ric. Savell And the rente of them whiche shalbe due at michaelmas next coming is then to be answered to the owners of the same /

The saide iurye have presented that Thomas Cobbered of Keldon is fledd for religion aboute xvii wekes laste paste unto some secret places within the realme unknowen to the iury /

The same iury have presented that Iohn Alyn of Terlinge is fledd for religion into the partyes of beyonde the seas /

Memorandum that in the residewe of all the townes villages parisshes & hamlettes within the saide half hundreth there is no cause worthy of presentment touching the articles above rehersed as the saide iury have certefyd /

The halfe hundrethe of Clavering

Memorandum that in all the townes villages parisshes & hamlettes within the saide halfe hundreth there is no cause worthy of presentment touching the articles above rehersed as the iury there hath presented:

The hundreth of harlowe

The iury there hathe presented that William Garryce of harlowe taylor is fledd for religion aboute Easter was twelve moneth & remayneth in secret places within this realme unknowen to the sayde iury /

Memorandum that in the residewe of all the townes villages parisshes & hamlettes withyn the saide hundreth there is no cause worthy of presentment towching tharticles above rehersed as the saide iury have certified /

The hundreth of Chelmesford

The iurye there have presented that Iohn Asser of Stoke & Buttesbury ys fledd for religion & remayneth in secret places within this realme unknowen to the saide iurye / The goodes & cattalls of the saide Iohn Asser is in the price of v kyne prysed at xxvis viiid the coine amounting in the whole to the some of vi li xiiis ivd / Two of the saide kyne are comytted by the Kings & Queenes maiesties commissioeres to the custody & safe keping of harry stande & Rumbolde Tavener / And three kyne the residewe are distrayned by Iohn browne of Bylerika for lxs of rente / The same Iohn hath in fee symple parte of a marshe in Estylbury being worth by the yeare xxxiiiis nowe in the occupacon of one (blank) Rogers of Tylbury aforesaide / And the saide Iohn Asser shall have in reversion after the dethe of his mother yet living a tenemente with viii acres of free lande worthe by the yere xvis / The yerely rente & profittes of the saide marshe yerely as is aforesaid xxiiiis (sic) The saide Rogers taketh the profyt of the saide landes by what tytle or aucthority the saide iury knowe not /

The saide iury have presented that Iohn Hamper of the saide stoke & Buttesbury bacheler ys fledd for religion but whether or to what place the saide iury know not /

The said iury hath in lykwise presented that Iohn Rygges of the saide towne of Stoke & Buttesbury is fledd for religion but whicther or to what place the saide iurye knowe not /

The same iury hath in lykewise presented that William Assheley of Retinden single manne is fledd for religion but whicther or to what place the saide iury know not /

Memorandum that in the residewe of all the townes villages parisshes & hamlettes within the saide hundreth thereys no cause worthy of presentment touching the articles above rehersed as the saide iurye have certified /

The hundreth of Dunmowe

Memorandum that in all the townes villages parisshes & hamlettes within the saide hundreth there is no cause worthy of presentment touching the articles above rehersed as the saide iurye have certefyed /
Anglia
(r. 267) Memorandum quod Iohannes Comes Oxon. Thomas Darcy miles dominus Darcy de cheche Edwardus Waldegrave miles Willelmus Bendlowes serviens ad legem Iohannes Wyseman de ffelsted Georgius ffelton et Thomas Sicleden armigeri venerunt coram Baronibus . . . secundo die Decembris hoc termino in propriis personis suis et exhibuerunt Curie huic literas domini Regis & domine Regine sub magno sigillo suo eis directas . . .

(The Commission which follows is identical with the first
except that it refers to the hundreds of Hinckford, Tendring, Lexden,
Thurstable, Winstree and the town of Colchester)
Et tenor certificationis predicti unde superius fit invencio sequitur

in hec verba // Essex // Inquisitio capta pro hundredo de hynkeford apud villam Colchestr' in Comitatu predicto xxviii die septembris anno regni phillipi & marie dei gratia . . . (etc.) tercio & quarto Coram Thoma Darcy milite domino Darcy de cheche Willelmo Bendlowe serviente ad legem Georgio ffelton & Thoma Sylesden Armigeris commissionaribus predictis domini Regis et domine Regine virtute cuiusdem Commissionis sue eisdem commissionaribus directe & huic Inquisitioni annexae per sacramentum Iohannis Bower de Branktree Willelmi Baldwin de Bocking Thome Lawrence de eadem Iohannis Harrell de Systed Henrici Tompson de Halsted Anthonii Barber de eadem Roberti Mutton de ffelsted Thome Pannell de Stebbing Rogeri ffytche de Canfeld Iohannis Walklyn de Shalforde Iohannis Lamberde de Wethersfelde Thome Parker de eadem Thome Mascall de ffynchingfeld Iohannis Livermer de eadem Henrici Bygge de Redeswell Roberti Pannell de eadem Iohannis Chote de Stanborne Thome Anneys de Assheyne Willelmi ffynche de byrdbroke Willelmi Chapman de Sturmere Thome hande de Bumpstede ad Turrum Thome ffynche de eadem Ricardi Skotte de Gassefelde Walteri Bantoste de Hengham ad Castrum Roberti Bladen de eadem Iohannis Payne de Hengham Sible & Iohannis de Toppesfelde inhabitantium infra predictos Qui dicunt super sacramentum suum quod Robertus Wortham nuper de Branktree infra hundredum predictum fugiebat pro certis offensis heresie per ipsum commissis contra fidem catholicam a Branktree predicta ultimo die maii Anno regni domine Regine nunc primo usque ad locos & partes huius regni Anglie predictis Iuratoribus ignotos / Et quod idem Robertus Wortham eodem die quo fugam fecit habuit / possidebat hec bona & Cattalla hic sequentia que tempore captionis huius Inquisitionis remanebant apud Branktree predictam videlicet quandam dimissionem sine interesse pro termino certorum Annorum extunc venturo de et in uno campo vocato bromefelde quam Thomas Sadlyngton tenet pro termino quattuor Annorum solvendo eidem Roberto heredibus vel Assignis suis in fine predicti termini quatuor Annorum sex libras legalis monete Anglie prout per dimissionem predictam gerendam dat quinto die Aprilis anno regni predicto domine Regine primo supradicto plenius liquet / Et dicunt etiam Iuratores predicti quod Thomas Stetyll & (blank) uxor eius nuper de Bocking infra hundredum predictum fugiebant et seipsos subtraxerunt pro consimilibus offensis heresie a Bocking predicta tercio die Aprilis Anno regni dominorum Regis & Regine secundo & tercio die Aprilis Anno regni dominorum Regis & Regine secundo & tercio usqe ad alios locos et partes huius regni Anglie predictis Iuratoribus ignotos / Et quod idem Thomas dicto die quo fugam fecit habuit & possidebat hec bona & Catalla hic sequentia que tempore captionis huius Inquisitionis remanebant apud Syble Hengham infra hundredum predictum videlicet unum stratum vocatum a flock bedd unum luterium & unam supellectilem valoris vis viiid unam parem luteriorum ad valorem xvid tres patinas putras unum candelabrum & unum poculum vocatum a posnet precii xxiiid & unum kettell precii viiid que quidam bona & Cattalla in toto attingunt ad valorem Xs iiid [sic] Et dicunt etiam Iuratores predicti quod Iohannes Hullington &

(Here the record suddenly ends in the middle of r267v)

Notes

1. *Journals of the House of Commons*, 6 Dec. 1555. The opponents of the measure were led by Sir Anthony Kingston, who was imprisoned in the Tower as a result.
2. John Foxe, *Actes and Monuments*, 2 vols, London, 1610, II, p. 1894.
3. C.H. Garrett, *The Marian Exiles*, Cambridge, 1938, p. 137. John Alyn, although he is stated to have gone 'into the partyes of beyonde the seas', does not seem to have left any record of his presence there.
4. The wills of Asshley, Rygges, Asser, John Somersham and John Mott are all preserved in the Essex Record Office. Reference numbers D/ABW 1/159, D/AER 9, D/ABW 2/60, D/ACR 6, D/ACW 8/94. All naturally show a strongly Protestant formulation, and Asser refers to his executors as 'beloved frendes in the lorde'.
5. Somersham left a house and two tenements, with various small sums of money amounting to about £4. Asser left a house and tenement, about £30 in cash, and some stock.
6. It is interesting that although the cause of offence was religious, all the commissioners were laymen and local gentry. The government made extensive use of the ordinary channels of secular administration in the pursuit of its religious policy.
7. Public Record Office, Exchequer, King's Remembrancer, Memoranda Roll, Easter Term, 4 & 5 Philip and Mary (E159/338), Recorda section.

3 The Enforcement of Reaction, 1553–8

The religious settlement of 1553–4 rested no less upon the royal authority than its predecessor, or that which followed in 1559. Like the Elizabethan establish-ment it was the result of political compromise. To base a persecuting regime upon compromise was, as Elizabeth realised, both illogical and dangerous, but Mary's convictions did not allow her to acknowledge, or enable her to understand, the foundations upon which her church was built.

From a strict Roman Catholic point of view, all the ecclesiastical legislation of Henry VIII and Edward was invalid, and the correct course would have been for Mary, on behalf of her realm, to have submitted and sought absolution immediately upon her accession. Writing on 2 October, Cardinal Pole urged her to cast aside all considerations of worldly prudence:

> Nor has it even to be debated in Council whether obedience to the head of the church should be acknowledged or not, as that has already been determined by the council of God. But in the Royal Council the Queen has merely to make manifest her debt to God and His Church . . . .[1]

The cardinal's exile had left him very ill-qualified to pronounce upon the situation in England and, anxious as Mary was for a reconciliation, she had no hesitation in rejecting this extreme advice. In consultation with Gian Francesco Commendone, a papal chamberlain who had visited England secretly during August, she had besought a private absolution for herself and Gardiner so that she could undergo the ceremony of coronation with a clear conscience.[2] At the same time, however, she realised that any question of a general absolution would have to wait until parliament had signified its willingness by repealing the existing statutes. Commendone appreciated this point, and advised the Curia that it would be premature to send a legate until the situation had been clarified.[3]

The queen's natural zeal was curbed by the urgent advice of her cousin the emperor, proffered through his ambassador, Simon Renard. Renard's influence over Mary was considerable from the first, and he was consistently cautious and pessimistic: 'the thing most to be feared', he wrote in October 1553, 'is that the Queen may be moved by her religious ardour and zeal to attempt to right matters at one stroke, for this cannot be done in the case of a people that has drunk so deep of error.'[4]

He was constantly preoccupied with the danger of rebellion, an attitude which was intensified after the end of October by the rapid progress of his negotiations for a marriage alliance. The existence of such an explosive political issue made the emperor and his agents doubly concerned to prevent religious disturbances. Under this pressure Mary followed a political rather than an ideological approach to the problem of a settlement, although this was against her own instincts.

Looked at from this point of view, there was not one problem but several, and Renard consequently urged a 'step by step' policy which should divide her potential enemies and conquer them in detail.[5] A proportion of the Protestants were foreign refugees, and should be expelled forthwith; thereafter the revival of Roman Catholic worship and its enforcement by the use of the royal supremacy would be possible. Beyond this point the real difficulties would begin. The key to a 'Catholic establishment', as everyone realised except Pole, was the question of the ecclesiastical lands. This was not a religious issue, but it intimately concerned the nature of the church as an institution: 'it is my duty to inform your Majesty', wrote Renard to his master, 'that the catholics hold more church property than do the heretics . . .[6].' This enormous vested interest could be detached from the Protestant cause, as the emperor realised, but could only be reconciled to the papal authority by a political bargain which would leave the English church dependent upon the monarchy through lack of other resources. If such a compromise were reached, the church in England would remain fundamentally the church 'by law established', whether its doctrines were Protestant or Catholic.

The imperialists could afford to be complacent about this prospect, because they hoped thereby to purchase a dynastic victory which would ensure England a Catholic monarchy for several generations. The papacy, on the other hand, was not at first inclined to gamble with the future of the English church for the benefit of the Habsburgs. Only after a year's delay, when it had become apparent that without such a surrender there would be no 'Catholic establishment' in England, did Julius III reluctantly give way; all that time the English legate was detained in the Low Countries on the emperor's orders.[7]

This delay meant that there were two distinct stages in the Catholic reaction, one carried out in the queen's first parliament, the other in her third. The first stage consisted of two Acts, of which one, '. . . against offenders of Preachers and other ministers of the Church' was purely disciplinary, while the other repealed all the Protestant legislation of the previous reign, and enacted that

> all suche Divine Service and Administration of sacramentes as were most commonly used in the Realme of Englande in the last yere of the reigne of oure late Sovereine Lorde king Henrie theight, shall be from and after the xxth daye of December in this presente yere of our Lorde God (1553) used and frequented throughe the hole Realme of Engelande.[8]

It is significant that the first statute, although carefully reserving the rights of the church courts, effectively placed the whole responsibility for enforcement upon the justices of the peace. Some, including Renard, thought that 20 December would be the signal for widespread religious disturbances, but they were wrong.

A number of Bills announcing the change were torn down, and there was a certain amount of hooliganism but nothing that amounted to a rising.[9]

An attempt by the Lord Chancellor, Stephen Gardiner, to build upon these foundations in the second parliament of the reign was frustrated. Gardiner's influence in the council had been seriously impaired by his temporising attitude towards Wyatt's rising in January and February 1554, and his leading place had been taken by Lord Paget. In an effort to re-establish himself, Gardiner attempted to lay blame for the rising exclusively upon the Protestants, and advocated severe measures against them. These measures apparently included the establishment of a 'form of Inquisition', a proposal which was strenuously and successfully resisted by Paget,[10] partly out of antipathy to the chancellor, and partly because of his desire for a general pacification. A bill 'against heretics and seditious preaching', which seems to have embodied Gardiner's proposals, was sent up by the Commons to the Lords on 26 April, but was thrown out on 1 May, at the third reading.[11] Parliament was dissolved on 5 May, and the following day Renard reported that Paget was in disgrace at court over his part in this rejection. Renard was, if anything, more hostile to the chancellor's policy than Paget himself. His eye was firmly fixed upon the summer, when Philip ought to be coming to claim his bride. It was essential that by then the country should be in 'a good quiet', and he indignantly accused Gardiner of deliberately stirring up trouble in an attempt to prevent this consummation.[12] The lever that enabled Paget to overturn this bill was the fear of sequestration, a possibility which Gardiner had envisaged, but had been unable to provide against.[13] He had, indeed, introduced a measure entitled '. . . that (neither) the Bishop of Rome nor any other spiritual person shall Convent any person for Abbey lands'; but, although there is no record of the provisions of this Bill, it is difficult to see how it could have been effective. The chancellor may have been prepared to endorse the property-holders' title on behalf of the government, in exchange for severer measures against heresy, but he could not commit the papacy, nor affect the ultimate issue of reconciliation.

That issue could be successfully faced in the third parliament because two important developments had taken place during the summer. The royal marriage was completed in an atmosphere of remarkable calm after Philip's arrival in England at the end of July and, at the beginning of August, Pope Julius III bowed to the inevitable and authorised Cardinal Pole to negotiate the question of church lands. The only obstacle thereafter remaining was Pole's own reluctance to compromise the churches' title, and when this was overcome at the beginning of October, the negotiations began in earnest. The results of these negotiations were embodied in the statute 1 & 2 Philip and Mary c. 8, which repealed 'All Statutes Articles and Provisions made against the See Apostolick of Rome since the xx yere of King Henry theight', and stipulated the penalties of praemunire for '. . . disturbing (the lay possessioners of land) under Pretence of any spiritual jurisdiction'. This political bargain was accompanied, and partly concealed, by scenes of spectacular religious emotion. At the end of November the whole parliament assembled and with penitent tears besought the legate's absolution for twenty years of schism and heresy.[14] The *Te Deum* sounded in Rome, and Catholic Europe rejoiced, but it was an insubstantial victory, as the events of the next four years were to show. The immediate consequence was the victory of Gardiner's clerical party in the council and the implementation of that policy of persecution which they had been advocating for the previous twelve months. Defeated in an attempt to secure the exclusion of the praemunire clause from the Statute of Repeal, the chancellor was successful in securing the revival of three medieval statutes empowering royal commissioners to arrest heretics, confirming the death penalty for heresy, and decreeing the forfeiture of goods and lands by those convicted.[15] John Rogers was burned less than a month after the dissolution of parliament.

The persecution that followed, so mild by contemporary standards, caught the imagination of contemporaries and historians alike. From the first, Renard denounced it as a folly which would bring the whole alliance to ruin. Describing the scenes which had accompanied Rogers's death, he wrote:

> Some of the onlookers wept, others prayed God to give him strength . . . not to recant . . . others threatening the bishops . . . the haste with which the bishops have proceeded in this matter may well cause a revolt.[16]

In political terms, even in the terms of ecclesiastical policy, he was right; the English church was in no condition to be strengthened and edified by *autos-da-fé*. As he anticipated, the Spaniards came in for a large share of the blame, although their responsibility for inspiring such a policy does not seem to have been great.[17] Gardiner initiated the persecution, almost certainly because he believed that the genuine heretics were few, and their removal would leave the merely disaffected leaderless and compliant. Foxe described his attitude as follows:

> (he) . . . had got the laws and the secular arm on his side . . . so that the people, being terrified with the example of these great learned men condemned, never would nor durst once rout against their violent religion.[18]

After a few months, however, when severity was having the reverse of the desired effect, '. . . seeing his device disappointed, and that cruelty in this case would not serve to his expectations, (he) gave over the matter as utterly discouraged'.[19] Although he certainly believed in the dangers of heresy *per se*, he was mainly concerned with the order and security of the church. The queen's approach, on the other hand, was that of personal piety and religious duty. 'Touching the punishment of heretics', she wrote in February 1555:

> I believe it would be well to inflict punishment at this beginning, without much cruelty or passion, but without, however, omitting to do justice on those who chose, by their false doctrine, to deceive simple persons, that the people may clearly comprehend that they have not been condemned without just cause.[20]

Such an attitude was proof against arguments of policy. Mary, who so strenuously objected to the title of 'Supreme Head', in fact controlled the church in England no less than her sister was to do, and was largely responsible for the failure of the settlement by which she set so much store.

There was no shortage of individual religious enthusiasm in England in 1554, but the church as a Christian community was woefully deficient. The struggles and conflicts which had heightened the zeal of a small minority had reduced the rest to apathy and confusion. Not only had the lands of the church been confiscated, but plate, vestments, and sometimes the very lead from the roofs, had been plundered in the name of reformation. The situation that Cardinal Pole found when he visited the diocese of Lincoln in 1556 could be paralleled by many instances from other parts of the country. [21] Cures were vacant because the incumbents had fled or died, and had not been replaced; over 120 churches were in serious disrepair. The furniture and valuables removed by the Edwardian commissioners had not been returned, in spite of the queen's express command. Endowments were in the hands of the local gentry, who appropriated them to their own use. Beside this picture of decay, the half-dozen cases of heresy brought before the cardinal appear insignificant. Both Renard and Surian, the Venetian ambassador, agreed that the religious life of the country was deplorable and demoralised. The former made repeated references to empty churches and meagre congregations, writing on one occasion: 'Most of the churches here are in ruins, such is the peoples faithlessness.'[22] The latter, whose testimony is the more striking because of his habitual shrewdness and lack of exaggeration, reported in April 1557 that few Englishmen were really Catholics, although many conformed through fear.[23] This situation did not represent the triumph of militant Protestantism but of materialism and bewilderment.

Against such adversaries the weapons of repression and persecution were wielded in vain. The Protestants certainly resisted with zeal, and often with heroism, but many of those who suffered from the attentions of the Marian bishops were not followers or colleagues whom Cranmer, Latimer and Ridley would acknowledge.[24] A few of them were wild fanatics, whom no establishment would have tolerated, like 'father Browne, the broker of Bedlam' who was conducting conventicles in 'a typling house next the sign of the Mermayde' in London in 1555. Brown appears to have denounced 'my lord chancellors religion' and 'Cranmers, Latymers and Rydleys religion' with almost equal venom.[25] A few were criminal delinquents, whose contribution to the cause of the Reformation consisted of murder, assault and vandalism. The greatest number, however, were petty offenders who seem to have been simply ribald or careless. The Yorkshireman who called the censing of the altar 'a gay Yole layke',[26] or the Brompton man who suggested that his vicar, opening the church doors with his cross, was about to 'ronne at the quintine with God Almightie',[27] were representative of a widespread popular attitude. Gardiner's attempt to embrace such cases within the category of heresy, which was reflected in the queen's injunctions to the justices of the peace, issued in March 1555,[28] was a grave mistake. Such a lack of discrimination added greatly to the difficulty of the persecutors' task. Both the ecclesiastical and the secular administrations were overstrained to enforce peace and uniformity by such means. So great was the shortage of zealous and reliable clergy that the demands of the ecclesiastical courts led them to be concentrated in the cathedral cities. Very many ordinary parish priests made the merest pretence of conformity, but were unmolested because there was no one to replace them. Others were deprived, usually for taking wives, penanced, and re-inducted elsewhere.[29] It was not likely that such men would infuse into the restored Catholic faith that spiritual vitality which it so conspicuously lacked.

In spite of the ceaseless activity of the church courts, the nature of the 'Catholic establishment' was such that the chief burden of enforcing uniformity fell upon the council and the justices of the peace. Only by them could offenders be arrested, conventicles broken up, and punishments inflicted. On many days letters to local officials for such purposes occupied a substantial part of the council's recorded business.[30] The justices were even harder pressed, for only they had the knowledge and the power to police their neighbours, and staff the numerous local commissions which were set up to investigate religious delinquency. It was inevitable that Catholic orthodoxy should be used as a test of loyalty, and injunctions such as those which the queen sent to the magistrates of Norfolk in May 1554 invariably coupled the necessity to suppress sedition with the enforcement of religious conformity, and the 'Godly and catholic ensample' which should be set by the justices themselves.[31] Such instructions were even less enthusiastically carried out than most. Quite apart from the fact that some justices, especially in the south-east, had Protestant sympathies, preoccupation with their own affairs and with the ordinary maintenance of law and order led most to relegate the defence of the church to a very low priority. These secular-minded gentlemen had no desire to be the instruments of a persecuting clergy. Anti-clericalism was strong in all walks of life, from those who murmured in the taverns that 'the priests were (coming back) to take their revenge',[32] to the Lords of parliament who resisted the reintroduction of the heresy laws on the ground that they established clerical jurisdiction over the laity.[33] The members of parliament did not consider that their bargain with the church placed them under the orders of the hierarchy.

The persecution was also unpopular with the laity for other reasons. It seemed to be a device for subduing the country to foreign tyranny; and it was directed against an extremely vocal minority who exploited its propaganda value to the full. Most important of all, after a few months it was a patent failure, and sheriffs, justices of the peace and other officials grew more and more reluctant as the reign advanced. In June 1555 special letters had to be sent by the council to a number of Kentish gentlemen ordering them to assist at executions in Rochester, Dartford and Tonbridge.[34] Gaolers openly sympathised with Protestant neighbours committed to their charge, and occasionally allowed them to escape; the keepers of Colchester, Rayleigh and Ipswich prisons were at different times in trouble on this account, and in July 1556 one of the keepers of the King's Bench fled to avoid the consequences of a similar action.[35] By July 1557 council letters had to be sent to the sheriffs of Kent, Essex, Suffolk and Stafford, the Mayor of Rochester and the bailiffs of Colchester, demanding to know why sentences for heresy had not been carried out.[36] The following month the Sheriff of Essex, Sir John Butler, was fined £10 by the council for condoning the reprieve of a woman sentenced at Colchester.[37] By this time the extreme reluctance of officials in the south-east amounted to almost open defiance. So alarming had the situation become by July 1558 that Bonner was impelled to write to Pole suggesting that sentences for heresy should be carried out swiftly and secretly, to avoid the possibility of disturbances, and so the presence of numerous secular assistants.[38] By this time even the leading advocates of the persecution had lost all sense of its original purpose. They had forgotten what Gardiner had realised with perfect clarity – that every burning was a defeat.[39]

There is no necessity to dwell upon the strength that Protestantism derived from the blood of its martyrs, even if some of them were rather tainted sacrifices.

There is nothing more stimulating to a cause than inefficient persecution. How many genuine Protestants there were in England is a much more controversial issue. The records of the ecclesiastical courts and commissions are clearly no guide, for, although they provide the names of many who fled or were proceeded against, as Edward Underhill boasted, 'Some were preserved still in London that never bowed their knees unto Baal; for there was no such place to shift in, in this realm as London . . .'.[40]

If so prominent a reformer as Mathew Parker could remain in England unmolested, very many humbler people must have done the same.[41] Most of them probably made some gesture of conformity, but many seem to have taken no pains to hide their real opinions. Sir Henry Bedingfield discovered to his surprise in 1555 that the people of Woburn and Wickham Market were for the most part 'very protestauntes', seduced thereto as rumour had it, by Lord Russell, and 'certayn other gentlemen of his sect'.[42] In a quiet corner of Essex, in the same year, four parishes were still using the proscribed Edwardian services,[43] and conventicles were of very common occurrence, to judge from the number that were detected and broken up. Even in Yorkshire, which was notoriously conservative, and where there was no opposition to the restoration of Catholic worship, there was, nevertheless, an element of dissent, in places quite a strong one. Of the 330 recorded wills that were drawn up in the county during Mary's reign, 80 – almost a quarter – show traces of Protestant influence. In most cases this influence amounts to no more than the omission of the usual Catholic invocation of the virgin and saints, but 18 clearly express the Protestant belief in salvation by faith alone.[44] Since all the pressures of fashion and conformity would have been against such an expression, it is reasonable to assume that these were convinced reformers. No firm conclusion can be drawn from such limited evidence, but the indications are that the Protestants, although a small minority of the population as a whole, may actually have been more numerous than the Catholic zealots who persecuted them. Even in London and Essex, where they were strongest, they did not form a majority, but, as is so often the case with minority groups, their determination and polemical talents gave them an influence quite out of proportion to their numbers.

The extent of that influence can best be judged by the increasing resistance that the persecuting zeal of the queen and the council encountered. That increase did not signify evangelical success so much as a change in the Protestant image. The memory of their association with the unpopular regime of Northumberland faded as they became associated with opposition to Spain, and the preservation of English independence from Habsburg encroachments. It is ironical that Mary, who was so much concerned to restore the separate secular and ecclesiastical jurisdictions, should have suffered uniquely from the entanglement of her religious and political policies. This point is emphasised by the relative ease with which Catholic ceremonial was restored in the early part of the reign. In conservative Yorkshire, 'Preastes unmariede was veray glade to celebratt & saye masse in Lattin withe mattings & evin songe thereto, accordynge for veray ferventt zealle and luffe that thai had unto God & his lawes . . .'.[45]

Thus the ritual was in use all over the country by the beginning of September 1553. Active opposition to the change was confined to a few isolated incidents in London and the Home Counties. Passive opposition seems to have been more widespread, but certainly did not amount to a serious challenge to the royal authority. As Robert Parkyn wrote:

> In many places of the realme, preastes was commandyde by lordes and knyghttes catholique to say masse in Latin . . . as haithe been uside beforne tyme, butt suche as was of hereticall opinions myghtt nott away therwithe, but spayke evil theroff, for as then ther was no actt, statutte, proclamation or commandement sett furthe for the sayme; therefor many one durst nott be bold to celebratte in Latten, thowghe ther hertts was wholly enclynede that way . . .[46]

This attitude partly explains why there were so few disturbances when the Edwardian services became illegal on 20 December. Another explanation lies in the fact that the leaders of orthodox Protestantism, such as Cranmer, had always preached submission to the secular power, and remained substantially consistent when that power was turned against them.[47] Most of those who indulged in acts of sacrilege, or violence against priests, seem to have been 'sectaries' rather than adherents to the doctrines of the 1552 Prayer Book. Flight and evasion were very common among the latter, who frequently sought refuge in the indifference of their neighbours, but deliberately dissociated themselves from resistance to the queen as such.

When Gardiner sent for 'the Churchwardens and substancyllest of xxx parishes of London' in January 1554 to demand why they had not restored the Latin services, they replied evasively that '. . . they had don what lay in theym'.[48] Injunctions were ignored, rather than defied, in a manner which makes it hard to distinguish passive opposition from general carelessness and indifference. It took over a year to re-establish the ceremonial in St Paul's, and the mayor and aldermen only took their places in the revived processions when sharply ordered to do so by the council. Such a situation was no doubt very unsatisfactory, but it had its advantages. The reluctance of the majority of the Protestants to indulge in militant self-advertisement gave the authorities, both secular and ecclesiastical, an opportunity to build up the inner strength of the church before facing the problem of deliberate nonconformity. It also gave the government an opportunity to demonstrate the success of its concordat with Rome in driving a wedge between the Protestant interest and the landowning interest. These advantages were thrown away by the persecution which, by seeking out heresy, forced many to declare themselves who had no desire to do so. In the circumstances it was inevitable that religious dissent should be associated with opposition to the queen, but the reverse implication resulted only from the victory of the clerical party in the council. Gardiner's attempt to blame the Protestants for the rebellion of 1554 rebounded on his head, for, by associating resistance to the Spaniards with resistance to the church, he made the dissenters far more popular than the currency of their beliefs could have done.

Thus, when Michieli reported in April 1555 that the crowd which assembled to witness a burning in Essex had become so threatening that an attack on the officials was feared,[49] he was not necessarily describing the reactions of a Protestant mob. Similarly, the virtual curfew imposed during executions in London after January 1556,[50] was designed to curb disturbances for which religion provided the excuse, but the unpopularity of the government's secular policies the real motive. Popular opinion, in this respect as in so many others, was inconsistent and difficult to describe in general terms. The restoration of Catholic ceremonial had, on the whole, been well received, and crowds of Londoners had knelt by the wayside to receive the legate's blessing when Pole returned from exile.[51] Yet it was certainly not for humanitarian reasons that the burnings had made the government 'odious to many people', as Michieli reported in June 1555.[52] There seems, indeed, to have been a wide discrepancy between the meaning attached by the government to the restoration of the Roman Catholic Church, and the light in which that restoration was generally seen. The reactions, both of the members of parliament and of many ordinary people, indicate that when carried out, both at the parochial and national levels, it was assumed to mean simply a change of form. The intervention of inquisitorial bishops and their staffs, and the ceaseless attempts of the council to stir up the local administration on their behalf, caused both surprise and resentment. The queen demanded a very much more wholehearted devotion to her church than the nature of its erection justified, or the religious life of the country could provide. Almost the only significant acts of Catholic piety during the reign came from the queen herself. There are only two recorded examples in the Patent Rolls of guild or chantry establishments by private individuals.[53] More significantly, when Mary proposed in November 1555 to return to the church those secularised properties still in the hands of the Crown, parliament strenuously opposed her on the ground that she could not so deplete the revenues of her successors.[54] When at length an attempt was made, early in 1558, to instil a little positive zeal into the church by admitting Jesuit preachers,[55] it was already too late. By then any foreign intervention could only have resulted in a further worsening of the situation.

After the death of Gardiner, the disgrace of Paget and the withdrawal of Renard, there was no powerful influence to restrain the queen's enthusiasm. She relied increasingly upon the unworldly Pole, and upon such lay confidants as Waldegrave, Englefield, and Rochester, which partly explains why we find the council concerning itself with such purely ecclesiastical matters as the eating of meat in Lent, and even stirring up the zealous Bonner to further efforts.[56] Mary's loyalty to the papacy led her to throw away the many advantages of her father's position, repudiating his policies with horror. Henry's position had become strong by the end of his reign and had won a wide measure of acceptance, not least as the result of over a decade of successful anti-papal propaganda. The queen reaped nothing but trouble from her adherence to principle. In spite of the concordat, the suspicions of the property-holders were never completely stilled and the papacy continued to be regarded as a 'foreign jurisdiction'. Ironically enough, in view of the powerful feelings which were aroused, neither the Pope nor the King of Spain enjoyed any real power in England. This was demonstrated in 1555, when the election of Paul IV led to a rupture between the two. Mary, divided in loyalty, adhered to her husband and refused admission to the papal envoys bearing Pole's recall; nor would she recognise William Peto as his successor. In spite of the queen's devotion, England was as distant in its attitude to the Pope as any other Catholic power. The Marian bishops were only admitted to the temporalities of their sees after '. . . having publicly renounced all words contained in the . . . bull (of presentation) prejudicial to the crown, and made (their) fealty'.[57]

The restored Roman Catholic church never struck root. The political follies with which it was associated, and the shortness of its duration make this so obvious that we may be blinded to the fundamental reasons for its failure. England in 1553 was not a Catholic country, any more than it was a Protestant country, although it contained many enthusiastic practitioners of both creeds. It was a secular community still thinking, largely to its own confusion, in religious terms. Whatever the restoration may have meant to the queen, to the Lords and Commons of the parliament, and to their colleagues on the commissions of the peace, it was an arrangement whereby traditional practices might be revived without sacrifice or substantial inconvenience. When it offered not peace, but a sword, and not the spiritual stimulus of a true Counter-Reformation, but a burdensome and obtrusive persecution, it forfeited any chance of reconstructing the religious life of the country. The demand for such a reconstruction was genuine, but the church failed to take its opportunity, or to retain the respect it had once enjoyed. Rather was that respect being transferred to its opponents, who were eventually to bring a livelier spiritual life to the next secular and political compromise over England's ecclesiastical institutions – that of 1559.

Notes

1. *Calendar of State Papers, Venetian*, v, 422. [*Cal. Ven.*]
2. The request was made through Henry Penning, a confidant of Pole. Penning's report, 21 Oct. 1553: *Cal. Ven.*, v, 429.
3. Cardinal Pole to the Master of the Sacred Palace, 8 Sept.; same to Pope Julius III, 7 Sept.: *Ca. Ven.*, v, 408, 406.
4. Renard to the emperor, 19 Oct. 1553: *Calendar of State Papers, Spanish*, ed. Royall Tyler et al. (London 1862–1964), xi, 307. [*Cal. Span.*]
5. The ambassador was also insistent from the first that Elizabeth was a source of danger: *Cal. Span.*, xi, 194.
6. *Cal. Span.*, xiii, 46.
7. It was not until 4 August 1554 that the negotiations were eventually authorised. Marc Antonio Damula to the Doge and Senate: *Cal. Ven.*, v, 526.
8. 1 Mary 2, c.2.
9. Renard to the emperor, 20 Dec. 1553: *Cal. Span.*, xi, 443.
10. Renard to the emperor, 12 Apr. 1554: *Cal. Span.*, xii, 216.
11. This was in spite of the presence of 19 bishops in the House: *Journals of the House of Lords*, London 1846, I, pp. 459–60. There is no record of the details of these proposals. [For a recent discussion of these events see J. Loach, *Parliament and the Crown in the Reign of Mary Tudor*, Oxford 1986.]
12. Renard to the emperor, 14 Mar. 1554; *Cal. Span.*, xii, 152. The chancellor made an attempt to hold the parliament at Oxford, which caused great indignation in London.
13. Renard had reported as early as 22 March that Gardiner was proposing to introduce a measure to safeguard the holders of abbey lands: *Cal. Span.*, xii, 170. This measure was passed by the Commons only four days before the 'heretics bill' was rejected by the Lords. The exact development of this tangled episode is far from clear.
14. There were several full descriptions of this sitting, notably that sent by Don Pedro de

Cordova to the King of the Romans on 10 Dec. 1554: *Cal. Span.*, xiii, 118. [See also Carlo de Frede, *La Restaurazione Cattolica in Inghilterra sotto Maria Tudor*, Napoli 1971.]

15. 5 Richard II, 2, c. 5; 2 Henry IV c. 15; 2 Henry V c.7. There were several dissentient voices raised against these measures, which may be connected with the fact that about forty members of the Commons withdrew to their homes before the session was over: KB27/1176 Rex XVI (Placita Coram Rege in the Public Record Office [PRO]) [This tentative explanation has not been accepted by others who have investigated the incident; see Loach, *Parliament and the Crown*.]

16. Renard to Philip, 5 Feb. 1555: *Cal. Span.*, xiii, 138.

17. Philip's mind was divided between his own zeal and deference to his father's wishes. The influence of his followers is uncertain; many of them were undoubtedly horrified by the prevalence of heresy in England (see e.g., *Cal. Span.*, xiii, 61), but the persecution was originated by the English clerical party, which was anti-Spanish. The presence of such strong persecutors at the English court as Alfonso à Castro (whose *Adversus Haereses* was republished in Antwerp in 1556 with an exhortatory dedication to Philip) suggests a secret influence over the queen's mind which may have fortified her determination, but cannot be blamed for the inception of the policy.

18. John Foxe, *Actes and Monuments*, ed. S.R. Cattley and G. Townsend, London 1837–41, VI, p. 703.

19. Ibid.

20. Memorandum by the queen: *Cal. Ven.*, vi pt. iii; Appendix 1647.

21. Pole's Visitation Articles and returns are printed in Strype, *Ecclesiastical Memorials*, Oxford, 1822, III. pt ii, 389–413 [*Eccl. Mem.*]. A similar visitation, with similar results, was conducted in the diocese of Canterbury by Archdeacon Harpesfield in 1557: *Catholic Record Society*, XLV, XLVI, 1950–1, ed. L.E. Whatmore and W. Sharp.

22. Renard to the emperor, 6 May 1554: *Cal. Span.*, xii, 243.

23. Surian to the Doge and Senate, 3 and 21 Apr. 1557: *Cal. Ven.*, vi, pt. ii, 1004, 1018.

24. The Protestant leaders were quick to denounce mere vandalism, but the confusion persisted, both at the time and since. The Marian authorities tended to treat all vandalism as heresy, and there has recently been a tendency among historians to regard all their victims as hooligans or sectaries. The evidence supports neither of these extreme viewpoints. Foxe, while occasionally guilty of concealing undesirable aspects of his subjects, provides a substantially accurate guide to the genuine Protestants.

25. Miles Huggarde, *The Displaying of the Protestantes*, London, 1556, (STC 13557), 121.

26. I.e. a sport, or game. A.G. Dickens, *Lollards and Protestants in the Diocese of York, 1509–1558*, Oxford, 1959, p. 232.

27. Strype, *Eccl. Mem.*, III, pt ii, 392.

28. British Museum (BM) Cottonian MS Tiberius B. II, fol. 99.

29. W.H. Frere, *The Marian Reaction in its Relation to the English Clergy*, Church Historical Society, XVIII, 1896, p. 78.

30. For example, 28 July 1557: *Acts of the Privy Council*, ed. J.R. Dasent, London, 1890–1929, VI, 135.

31. BM Cottonian MS Titus B. II, fol. 104.

32. Ambassadors to the emperor, 8 Aug. 1554; *Cal. Span.*, xiii, 23.

33. Renard to the emperor, 21 Dec. 1554: *Cal. Span.*, xiii, 125.

34. *Acts of the Privy Council*, v, 154: 30 June 1555.

35. Ibid., 316.

36. Ibid. vi, 135.
37. Ibid., 144. Butler was held responsible for the action of his deputy.
38. Bonner to Pole, July 1558: Petyt MS 538, vol. xlvii, fol. 3. Reported in the *Second Report of H.M.C.*, Appendix, 152.
39. Hence the apparently senseless outbursts of rage with which the commissioners frequently seem to have reacted to obstinacy.
40. 'The narrative of Edward Underhill' in E. Arber, *An English Garner*, (London, 1879–83), VI, 81. [It has recently been pointed out that some of the foreign Protestants also remained, keeping a low profile. A. Pettegree, *Foreign Protestant Congregations in Sixteenth-Century London*, Oxford, 1986].
41. In spite of the fact that Parker was a notorious Protestant and an associate of Northumberland, no attempt ever seems to have been made to apprehend him. A story related in the *Dictionary of National Biography*, that he fell from his horse while escaping from the government's wrath, is quite unsupported.
42. Extract from the Bedingfield Papers, printed in the *Transactions of the Norfolk Archaeological Society*, IV, 1855, 150.
43. *Acts of the Privy Council*, v, 150: 23 June 1555.
44. Dickens, *Lollards and Protestants*, p. 220.
45. Dickens, 'Robert Parkyn's Narrative of the Reformation', *English Historical Review*, LXII, 1947, 80.
46. Ibid., 79.
47. See especially, Cranmer's letter to Peter Martyr, written from prison in 1555, printed in *Original Letters Relative to the English Reformation, 1537–1558*, ed. H. Robinson, Parker Society, 1846–7, I, 30.
48. *Chronicle of Queen Jane*, ed. J. Nichols, Camden Society, XLVIII, 1849, 34.
49. *Cal. Ven.*, vi, 45.
50. *Acts of the Privy Council*, v, 224: 14 Jan. 1556.
51. Don Pedro de Cordova to the King of Romans, 10 Dec. 1554: *Cal. Span.*, xiii, 118. Similar scenes had greeted Bonner on his release from the Tower.
52. *Cal. Ven.*, vi, pt. I, 94. It is fairly clear that, quite apart from Protestant sympathisers, by 1555 heresy was no longer regarded by most people in the south-east as being in itself a justification for death. No such sympathy was shown with the victims of equally barbarous punishments at Tyburn.
53. On 11 February 1555 a licence 'notwithstanding the statute of Mortmain', was granted to William Roper Esq. of Eltham to found a chantry in the church of St Dunstan-without-Westgate, Canterbury (*Calendar of the Patent Rolls, Philip and Mary*, London, 1936–9, II, 225). On 25 July 1556 the Guild of Jesus in the chapel of St Faith at St Paul's cathedral was re-erected: ibid., III, 274. There were certainly some other foundations but they were not numerous. [See D. Loades, *The Reign of Mary Tudor*, London, 1979, p. 352.]
54. Michieli to the Doge and Senate, 18 Nov. and 3 Dec. 1555: *Cal. Ven.* vi, 251, 270. The Bill was eventually passed by the exercise of the full weight of the Crown's authority, by 183 votes to 120.
55. Count Feria to Fr Ribadeneyra, S.J., 22 Mar. 1558: *Cal. Span.*, xiii, 370. The failure to introduce an effective Counter-Reformation in England was partly due to the rupture of relations with the papacy after the election of Paul IV in 1555, and partly to the dearth of trained and competent preachers capable of speaking the English language. No serious attempt was made to tackle this problem until the development of the seminary system: J.H. Crehan, 'St. Ignatius and Cardinal Pole', *Archivum Historicum Societatis Jesu*, XXV, 1956, 72–98.
56. *Acts of the Privy Council*, vi, 18, 216, 276. [See also G. Alexander, 'Bonner and the Marian Persecutions', *History*, LX, 1975, 374–92.]
57. *Calendar of the Patent Rolls*, Philip and Mary, III, 158.

4 The Origins of English Protestant Nationalism

In 1580, in his *Answer to a Seditious Pamphlet*, William Charke wrote

> He that smiteth our religion woundeth our commonwealth; because our blessed estate of policie standeth in defence of religion, and our most blessed religion laboureth in maintenance of the commonwealth. Religion and policie are, through God's singular blessings, preserved together in life as with one spirit; he that doth take away the life of the one doth procure the death of the other.[1]

This was, of course, a partisan point of view. However, the extent to which it had won general acceptance among Englishmen of all social classes can be demonstrated by reference to the Armada crisis of eight years later. Not only did pamphleteers like Thomas Deloney appeal for patriotic effort:

> That . . . all with one accord
> On Sion hill may sing the praise
>   of our most mighty Lord.[2]

but recusant apologetic makes it clear that the Catholics were fully aware of the prevailing opinion that papists could not be good Englishmen.

Such a situation had not been created overnight by the war with Spain, nor was it simply the product of a well orchestrated propaganda campaign by William Cecil and his friends since 1559. Papal policy had been, and still was, a major contributory factor. *Regnans in Excelsis*, military adventures in Ireland, and ill-concealed support for assassination attempts against Elizabeth, played directly into the hands of those who wished to regard the papacy as the foreign enemy *par excellence*. 'That wicked and illfated conspiracy', wrote the Jesuit Robert Southwell of the Babington plot, '. . . did to the catholic cause so great mischief that even our enemies, had they the choice, could never have chosen ought more mischievous to us . . .'.[3] But even Pius V and his successors did not create the situation that Southwell and the later appellants were to find so distressing; they had merely deepened and confirmed prejudices which were already powerful when Elizabeth came to the throne.

The English had a long-standing reputation for xenophobia. 'They have an antipathy to foreigners', an anonymous Italian had written about 1500, 'and imagine that they never come into their island, but to make themselves masters of it, and to usurp their goods . . .'.[4] The Flemings and the French had borne the brunt of this unlovable characteristic since the fourteenth century, but the Italians themselves had not escaped, and the papacy was a sitting target in 1533. However litle justification there may have been for such an attitude, charges that the Pope was removing great quantities of money from England featured prominently in the early parliamentary attacks on his jurisdiction.[5] Moreover, one of the reasons why the king succeeded in pressing these attacks to a conclusion was that remarkably few Englishmen seem to have regarded the papal authority as important to their religious faith. Consequently the anti-Roman polemic which accompanied and followed the work of the Reformation parliament was much less directly helpful to the early Protestants than is sometimes supposed. The emphasis was all upon the usurpation of royal authority which had resulted from the unscrupulous use of spiritual sanctions, rather than upon any perversion of the doctrine or practices of the English church. Indeed, most defenders of the royal supremacy were more concerned to mobilise religious allegiance in support of the king than they were to urge the duties of reform upon him:

> howe muche more aught all Christians to obey their princes absolutlie when thei the kinges themselves are nott only members of the self bodie of Christ, but also ministers of the Christian justice . . .[6]

or, as Stephen Gardiner put it, 'The king our master hath a special case bicause he is an Emperor in himself and hath no superior.' Naturally, Protestants such as Tyndale or Barnes welcomed the royal supremacy, but their alliance was unwelcome to, and unacknowledged by, Gardiner and the conservative nobles. Indeed the Bishop of Winchester consistently argued that the royal supremacy would be seriously weakened by association with heresy.[7] After Henry VIII's death, in the course of his rearguard action against the publication of Cranmer's *Homilies*, he described himself as 'a good Englishman', and observed 'It is incredible that a king shuld set forth a boke tending to the subversion of hys owne estate . . .'.[8] In taking this attitude, Gardiner probably spoke for the bulk of English opinion, gentle and simple. Popular reactions to the introduction of the Prayer Book in 1549 suggest no great enthusiasm for either Protestantism or the Pope. Even in Devon and Cornwall, where hostility contributed to a major insurrection, there was no demand for a settlement with Rome. *De vera obedientia* had done its work too well for its author's peace of mind. By 1547 to be 'a good Englishman' meant to support the 'king's proceedings', and that loyalty had made the country more willing to accept a legislated Reformation than Gardiner had anticipated, or was prepared to acknowledge.

Without the royal supremacy the advance of Protestantism, first to a position of influence under Cromwell's protection, and then to power under Somerset and Northumberland, would have been impossible. Nevertheless it must be remembered that to many supporters of the supremacy, heresy was not only anathema in itself, but subversive of the whole political and social order:

> Libertie lept over this lande
>   Lusty at its owne will
> Letchery to breake wedlockes bande
>   Likewise doth luste fulfyll . . .[9]

Such views were reinforced by the fact that there appeared to be nothing particularly English about Protestant doctrine, which was more associated in the popular mind with Germany, or with the foreign congregations which sprang up in London under the protection of Edward VI and his council. By 1553 any advantage Protestantism may have gained from the Edwardian supremacy had been largely neutralised by Northumberland's unpopularity, by his apparent subservience to the French, and by the influx of Swiss and south German reformers after 1549. The warning of Ridley that Mary might well marry a foreigner, and subject the realm to an alien king, as well as to the 'Anti-Christ of Rome' went unheeded even by committed Protestants.[10]

The new queen's conservative and Catholic supporters did their best to capitalise on this situation, and were given useful ammunition by the restiveness of some of the more extreme Protestants in London. 'O develyshe libertye', wrote Miles Huggarde, 'I wolde to God that Germany had kept thee still'. Nevertheless, Mary's determination to marry Philip of Spain considerably marred her image as 'a good Englishwoman', and initiated a protracted propaganda campaign against her as 'A Spanyarde at heart', and one who despised and distrusted her native-born subjects.[11] This campaign was not, initially at any rate, the work of Protestants, most of whom professed their loyalty to the queen. Probably the French ambassador, Antoine de Noailles, who had instructions to inhibit the marriage to the best of his ability, was behind a lot of it.[12] However, there also seems to have been a spontaneous popular dislike of Spaniards, particularly in London, which antedated Noailles efforts and was a source of anxiety to Simon Renard from the beginning of the negotiation. Charles V had recognised that Englishmen hated 'all foreigners' when he had first instructed Renard to proceed,[13] but the ambassador was soon reporting that a Spanish connection presented particular difficulties. Rather surprisingly, in view of past history, the English were professing their willingness to get along with Flemings or Brabanters, but declaring that they could not live with Spaniards.[14] It is possible that Renard (who was a Franc-Comptois) was simply hearing what he wanted to hear, but equally likely that the unpopularity that Philip and his entourage had earned for themselves in the Low Countries between 1549 and 1551 had communicated itself across the narrow sea. The Spaniards had certainly begun to acquire an evil reputation for themselves in Italy and Germany before 1553, and it was not to be long before 'the horrible practices of the Kyng of Spayne in the Kyngedome of Naples and the miseries whereunto that noble realme is brought . . .' were being exploited for propaganda purposes in England.[15] Whatever their 'real' motivation, Wyatt and his followers professed to be acting 'for the avoidance of strangers', and were fully conscious of the dangers of trying to utilise French support.[16] Although the rebellion failed, the xenophobic fires which it had fanned to life smouldered on, and Renard was soon uneasily reporting that the Londoners had crowded to dip their handkerchiefs in Wyatt's blood, and were muttering that noble blood ought not to be shed for the sake of foreigners.

The government's reaction to these events, and indeed to the anti-Spanish agitation as a whole, was to blame them on the Protestants, pouring scorn upon the latters' professions of loyalty.

And to thinent that they may move men more easily to such a mischevouse enterprise, they cloke the matter with a goodly pretence, and tell them that they entend nothynge elles but to deliver the poore commons from oppression . . . They tell them besyde that everye man is bounde to love his contrye, and to seke for the preservation thereof . . . As for theyr prince (they saye) they wyll dye and lyve with him . . .[17]

The gist of the official view was that there was no widespread opposition to the marriage, but that the Protestants were seeking to create it as a patriotic smokescreen for their nefarious activities. This position also seems to have been partly shared by some Englishmen who did oppose the match. John Bradford, in *The copye of a letter*, written against Philip's coronation in 1556, justified a fresh outburst of invective on the grounds that previous attacks had been produced 'by the develishe device of certayne heretickes . . . thinking thereby to grounds in the hartes of all people . . . many abominable heresies'.[18] He then went on to profess his own allegiance to the Catholic faith, 'which the Queenes Majestie moste graciously setteth oute at thys present . . .'. By the time this tract was written the animosity between the two nationalities was manifest, and had been demonstrated in violence, bloodshed and mutual recrimination. This hatred knew no religious boundaries, and was in the murky tradition of Jack Straw and the Evil May Day, but two circumstances conspired to ensure that some of the mud which was hurled at the Spaniards also bespattered the Catholic church. One was the undoubted importance of Philip's personal initiative in bringing about the reconciliation of the realm to the church at the end of 1554.[19] The other was the unfortunate coincidence (if such it was) that a religious persecution of unprecedented severity was launched while the foreign king and his militantly orthodox entourage were in residence.[20] Robert Parkyn, Henry Machyn, and other humble religious conservatives who had welcomed the restoration of the mass with paeans of joy, showed no such enthusiasm for either the Pope or the persecution, to say nothing of the Spaniards. When these circumstances are added to the assiduous (if somewhat sparse) efforts of the government's own propaganda, it is not difficult to see how the Protestants were given the opportunity to sail for the first time under patriotic colours.

By 1555 some of them, at least, were willing to grasp this opportunity. A strand of patriotic enthusiasm had been woven into English Protestantism many years earlier. Rejoicing over the birth of Prince Edward in October 1537, Hugh Latimer had written to Cromwell, '. . . verily (God) hath shewed himself God of England or rather an English God, if we consider, and ponder well all his proceedings with us from time to time . . .'[21]

Bale's *History of King John*, drawing on earlier reformers such as Tyndale and Barnes, and showing an adroit mixture of Protestantism and anti-papal nationalism, was published in 1538. Bale is, of course, a key figure in the development of this strand of thought. As early as 1536 in his unpublished history of the English Carmelites, *Anglorum Heliades*, he had devoted the preface to a lavish display of patriotic sentiment.[22] This was partly in homage to the antiquarian John Leland, for whom he had a great admiration in spite of the latter's determined religious conservatism, but partly also because his *patria* seems to have taken over much of the loyalty which before his conversion he had devoted to the Carmelite order. For whatever reason, by the time he came to write the *Image of both churches* in 1545, Bale had come to identify the opening of the sixth seal with the release of the gospel by John Wycliffe: 'The second sabbath here, or lyberte of God's truthe, hath had his shewe in England already, yf ye marke it wel . . .'.[23] At the same time, in his *Chronycle concernynge . . . syr John Oldcastell*, he characterised the fifteenth-century Lollard as a patriot and an English saint. By 1555 Bale and his friend John Foxe had made considerable progress in constructing a distinctively English historiography of the Reformation, in which the persecution then raging featured as a trial of God's Elect, and the English Protestants in general as a 'godly remnant' of the true church. However, it would be a mistake to suppose that either Bale or Foxe postulated a unique dispensation of providence for England. In arguing that God had vouchsafed a particular providence to their fellow countrymen, they were not denying the equally authentic vision of their German or Swiss friends. In 1560 Bale was to write that he had 'alwaies bene of thys opinion, that St Jhons Apocalips hath as well his fulfilling in the particular nacion as in the universal church';[24] but he did not say, and clearly did not believe, that such a 'fulfilling' could be in one nation alone. Pendleton's *Homily* 'of the nature of the church', published in 1555, observed the same phenomenon from a hostile point of view:

> in this tyme . . . some (were) saying in Germany, here is Christ, here is the churche; some in Helvetia; here is Christ, here is the churche; other in Boheme; here is Christ, here is the churche; and we in England . . .[25]

As long as the Protestant vision of England retained its eschatological priorities, that is well into the seventeenth century, it is proper to speak of *an* Elect Nation, but not of *the* Elect Nation.

However, in the context of the persecution, and of the problems presented by Mary's 'ungodly proceedings', that distinction was not of first-rate importance. What was needed was a means of mobilising English national feeling for the defence of the gospel, and it was in this connection that anti-papal and anti-Spanish prejudices were of the greatest value. 'O lord', prayed one pamphleteer in 1554, 'defend thy elect peple of Inglond from the handes and force of thy enemyes the Papists.'[26] As the reign progressed the inhibitions which had hindered the earlier generation of Protestant leaders from direct attacks on the queen were gradually abandoned. In place of prayers that the queen's heart would be turned from idolatory we find savage invective, like the *Admonition to the Town of Callais*, denouncing

> . . . Another Athalia, that is an utter distroier of hir owen kindred, kyngdome & countrie, a hater of her own subjects, a lover of strangers & an unnatural stepdame both unto the & to thy mother England . . .[27]

Mary, it was alleged, was not only a papist and an idolator, but had reduced the realm to a state of abject defencelessness, 'so debilitated and weakened as well in worthy capitaines and valiante soldiers as in money, municions & victual, that she is scant able to defend & releve hir selfe . . .'. At the same time the Protestants were at pains to display their own patriotic credentials: '. . . next after God', wrote John Ponet in 1556, 'men be borne to love, honour and maintene their country'.[28] To Christopher Goodman two years later, the removal of Mary was both a patriotic and a religious duty, and he lamented the folly of Wyatt and his friends in not having called more explicitly upon the Lord. After 1555 events also conspired to strengthen the arguments of Goodman and those who thought like him. The child which Mary passionately desired, and which she believed herself to be carrying from October 1554, failed to appear. Despite her continued and rather pathetic hopes, the prospect of a Catholic succession, and the continental possessions that would have gone with it, steadily withered after July 1555. Harvest failure in that and the following year were followed by famine and the sweating sickness, leading to heavy mortality. Then in June 1557 came war, and after a hopeful start the disastrous and deeply felt loss of Calais.[29] In 1554 John Christopherson, in celebrating Mary's victories over Northumberland and Wyatt, had drawn the conventional conclusion that such triumphs were evidence of divine favour. By 1558 the corollary was obvious, and it did not require a committed Protestant like Goodman or Traheron to see it.

In fact the military weakness of England in the latter part of Mary's reign was more myth than reality, but it was a myth to which the English council subscribed for reasons of its own.[30] The Catholic Miles Huggarde accepted it no less than the author of the *Admonition*, making valiant, if not very convincing attempts to blame it on the heretics rather than the queen. Since England had fallen from the unity of the church, he claimed,

> it hath fallen from the grace of God into all kyndes of wickedness, skarcitie falshode deceyt and other abhominable vices, and from the accustomed valiaunce in feates of arms into effeminate myndes . . .[31]

In fact Mary's accumulated misfortunes drove the Catholics on to the defensive at a time when they might legitimately have expected to exploit a position of strength. As a result we find pamphleteers endeavouring to defend the church on quasi-patriotic grounds, and testifying in the process to the success that the protestants were having with the 'morning star of the reformation'. As George Marshall wrote:

> All the olde heresies that heretofore
> Were put in use by John Wykleffe here
> Were confuted by William Wylford
> He was a famous clerke and an Englishman borne.[32]

Mary's death in November 1558, at the relatively early age of 42, was of course the crowning mercy from the Protestant point of view. Not only did it end the persecution by making way for the sympathetic Elizabeth, it also appeared to justify those prophetic voices which had forecast a brief though fiery purgation for the Elect. John Bale had written in 1553:

> we shall finde mercie in time convenient and though he scourge us with these uncircumcised soldiers of Satan for a time yet (as David saithe) When he is angrie he will remember mercie; and restore his blessed gospel to us again with habundance of blessinge/in case we will (like obedient children) take his chastisings in good parte.[33]

Athalia had come, if not to a sticky end at least to a speedy one. And it is not surprising that many saw in this the intervention of an offended Deity. During the troubled period from June 1557 to November 1558, when the newly reconciled England was deeply at odds with the papacy of Paul IV, and when both the realm and its ailing queen were consistently neglected by their alien lord, the deeply rooted xenophobia of the English people took a further, and critically important step towards association with doctrinal Protestantism.

However, none of this would have been decisive if Elizabeth had not been a Protestant herself. Cautious and enigmatic she may have been, but Mary had not trusted her conformity, and she had been right. The settlement of 1559 could not depend for success upon the support of the Protestants alone. Despite their euphoria they were too few, and had too little support among the aristocracy. Consequently it was of the greatest importance that they, and the queen, could call upon the powerful and growing sentiment of patriotism to rally the country behind a church which few really liked but which had the immense advantage of being 'mere English'.

> My swete realme be obedience to gods holy commandment and my
> proceedings embrace,
> And for that that is abused shalbe better used, and that within
> shorte space

says 'Bessy', in William Birch's famous ballad of 1559.[34] As the more determined Catholics departed reluctantly into exile, John Aylmer was able to rally his fellow countrymen with the conviction that Elizabeth represented decisive proof of God's particular favour:

> Think not that God will suffer you to be spoiled at their hands, for your fall is his
> dishonour; if you lose the victory, he must lose the glory.[35]

How well the still precarious triumph that Aylmer celebrated would have stood up to the kind of misfortunes that overtook Mary, we cannot know. In the event England was to enjoy a long period of peace and relative prosperity, and nothing succeeds like success. By the time of the Armada it was possible to assume (although not with complete accuracy) that Protestantism and patriotism were the same thing – but that had required in the mean time a lot of work, and the benign face of fortune – or providence.

Notes

1. *STC* 5005; sig C 1 r & v.
2. Thomas Deloney, 'Three Ballads on the Armada Fight', *Tudor Tracts*, ed. A.F. Pollard, London, 1903, p. 491.
3. J.H. Pollen, *English Martyrs, 1584–1603*, Catholic Record Society, V, 1908, 314.
4. *A Relation of the Island of England*, ed. C.A. Sneyd, Camden Society, 1847; repr. in C.H. Williams, *English Historical Documents*, V 196.
5. For example 'Forasmuch as it is well perceived by long approved experience that great and inestimable sums of money be daily conveyed out of this realm to the impoverishment of the same, and specially such sums of money as the Pope's Holiness, his predecessors, and the Court of Rome by long time have

heretofore taken . . .' (23 Henry VIII, c. 20).

6. William Thomas, 'Pelegrine'. BL Add. MS 33383 fol. 19.

7. This was the burden of a number of letters written to Somerset during the latter part of 1547. J.A. Muller, *The Letters of Stephen Gardiner*, Cambridge, 1933, pp. 378–438; D.M. Loades, *Oxford Martyrs*, London, 1970, pp. 52–6.

8. Muller, *Letters*, p. 416.

9. STC 13559.5. A *newe ABC paraphrasticallye applied* by Miles Huggarde, London, March 1557.

10. J. Ridley, *Nicholas Ridley*, London, 1957, pp. 303–4.

11. In spite of her Spanish blood, Mary had never previously been accused of being a foreigner; however, commitment to her mother's cause gave some substance to the charges which began to be voiced after her accession. H.F.M. Prescot, *Mary Tudor*, London, 1952; D.M. Loades, *Two Tudor Conspiracies*, Cambridge, 1965.

12. E.H. Harbison, *Rival Ambassadors at the Court of Queen Mary*, Princeton, 1940, pp. 57–88.

13. Emperor to his ambassadors in England, 23 June 1553. *Calendar of State Papers, Spanish*, ed. Royall Tyler et al., London 1862–1964, xi, 60–65. [*Cal. Span.*]

14. Simon Renard to the bishop of Arras, 9 Sept. 1553. *Cal. Span.* xi, 227–8.

15. For example STC 10024.

16. Loades, *Two Tudor Conspiracies*; M.R. Thorp, 'Religion and the Wyatt Rebellion', *Church History*, XLVII (iv), 1978, 363–80.

17. John Christopherson, *An exhortaton to all menne to take hede and beware of rebellion*, London, 1554 (STC 5207), sig. B iv.

18. *The copye of a letter sent by John Bradforth to the right honorable lordes the erles of Arundel, Darbie, Shrewsbury and Pembroke*, London, ? 1556 (STC 3480) preface.

19. D.M. Loades, *The Reign of Mary Tudor*, London, 1979, pp. 219–21.

20. Philip's possible share in the responsibility for the persecution has been extensively, but inconclusively, discussed. Nevertheless the senior ecclesiastic in his household, Alfonso à Castro, the Bishop of Cuenca, was a well-known and energetic advocate of persecution.

21. *Sermons and Remains of Bishop Latimer* PS, 1845, 385. [See also J.W. McKenna, 'How God Became an Englishman', in *Tudor Rule and Revolution*, ed. D.J. Guth and J.W. McKenna, Cambridge, 1982, pp. 25–43.]

22. BL Harleian MS 3838; J.P. Fairfield, *John Bale*, West Lafayette, Indiana, 1976, pp. 50–1.

23. *Image of both churches*, II, sig. K vii.

24. *The first two partes of the Actes or unchast examples of the Englyshe votaryes*, London, 1560, sig. xvii. Fairfield, *John Bale*, p. 87.

25. Homily 'of the nature of the churche', *A profitable and necessarye doctryne with certayne homelies . . .*, London, 1555 (STC 3281.5) p. 33.

26. *A praier to be sayd of all trewe christians against the pope and all the enemies of Christ and his gospell*, London, May 1554, Society of Antiquaries broadsheet 36A.

27. Robert Pownall, April 1557 (STC 19078).

28. John Ponet, *A Shorte Treatise of politike power*, Strasburg, 1556 (STC 20178) sig. E vi.

29. The council made strenuous efforts to blame the Protestants for the fall of Calais, and the Lord Deputy, Thomas Wentworth, was arraigned for high treason. These charges, however, seem to have done nothing effective to divert responsibility. C.S.L. Davies, 'England and the French War, 1557–9', in *The Mid-Tudor Polity, 1540–1560* ed. J. Loach and R. Tittler, London 1980, pp. 159–85.

30. Loades, *Mary Tudor*, pp. 378–80. The council was anxious to save money by refraining from aggressive policies on the grounds of military incapacity.

31. Miles Huggarde, *The Displaying of the Protestants*, London, June 1556, (STC 13557) p. 922.
32. *A compendious treatise in metre*, London, 1554 (STC 17469).
33. *De vera obedientia*, Rouen, 1553 (STC 11585); preface by Bale, sig. A iii.
34. *A songe betwene the Queens majestie and Englande*, London, 1559, Society of Antiquaries broadsheet 47 (STC 3079).
35. J. Aylmer, *An Harborowe for Faithfull and Trewe Subiectes* . . ., Strasburg, 1559 (STC 1005), 35.

5 The Sense of National Identity among the Marian Exiles

> Dr Cox and others with him came to Frankfort out of England, who began to break that order that was agreed upon; first in answering aloud after the minister, contrary to the church's determination; and being admonished thereof by the Seniors of the congregation, he, with the rest that came with him made answer, That they would do as they had done in England; and that they would have the face of an English church . . .[1]

Thanks to the *Brieff Discours*, a partisan account published for polemical purposes almost twenty years later, the 'Troubles' which began with this gesture form one of the best known aspects of the Marian exile.[2] However, because of the context within which the compilers of that work were operating, it is usually seen simply as a liturgical conflict between the protagonists of the 1552 Prayer Book, and those of the Geneva rite, which had been printed in English as far back as 1550.[3] In fact the issues it raised were far wider, embracing the whole conduct of ecclesiastical affairs, and the nature of the English church. Replying to Calvin's strictures on 20 September 1555, David Whitehead wrote

> These, your friends, however, are altogether a disgrace to their country; for whatever has been bestowed from above upon our country in this respect, with exceeding arrogance, not to say impudence, they are treading under foot.[4]

Recent historians of the English Reformation, from Norskov Olsen to Richard Bauckham, have demonstrated that there was among English Protestants of the 1550s no concept of 'elect nationhood' in the sense postulated by William Haller.[5] If that came at all, it did not come until the 1590s. There was, however, a strong awareness of 'special providence' – that God had a particularly significant part for them to play in the preparations for His second comng. The roots of that tradition went back well before the Reformation, and probably originated in the similar convictions displayed by the French during the Hundred Years War. Both the kingdom of England, and the kingly office, enjoyed a special place in divine favour.

> 'Regnum Anglorum regnum Dei est'
> As the Aungell to seynt Edward dede wytenesse

a Yorkist propagandist had written in 1460, as a part of his attempt to demonstrate that the Lancastrian usurpation had been a particular affront to the

Deity.[6] The later tendency of English reformers to celebrate John Wycliffe as the 'morning star of the reformation' and to praise the 'Godly proceedings' of Henry VIII stemmed from the same root, and was regarded with incomprehension by their continental friends.

There was, consequently, something special about the way in which the English church had been reformed, and particularly about the person of King Edward VI – the young Josias who had been destined to restore the worship of the true God to Israel, but who had been removed because his people had shown themselves unworthy.[7] In so far as that special ingredient had been the royal supremacy itself, it was, of course, no longer available to the godly after 1553, and all the churches of the diaspora realised that they would have to find some other method, both of governing themselves and of preserving their identity. There were, however, other ingredients which could still be made use of. One of these was the continuity of the clerical office and authority, traced back to the pure days of the primitive church; another was the Articles of Faith, authorised by parliament in 1553; and the third was the English liturgy, similarly authorised in the previous year. It was to these distinctive ingredients of the *Ecclesia Anglicana* that Whitehead alluded in the letter already quoted when he wrote

> You must know that we do not entertain any regard for our country which is not agreeable to God's holy word. Neither in the meanwhile are we so ungrateful to our country . . . as rashly to despise the benefits which God has bestowed upon it.

The fact that the church in England was 'under the cross' by 1555 added point and poignancy to this defence. If suffering was a mark of the true church, then the persecuted remnant of the Edwardian hierarchy was more worthy of credence in adversity than it had been in power. If the doctrine and worship of the English church had been truly reformed in the latter days of King Edward, then whatever the failures of implementation that worship and doctrine was worthy to be maintained in exile and adversity, and should be so maintained:

> Nor have we such a mean opinion of the judgements of our countrymen who resisted ungodliness even unto blood, as that by reason of the clamours of individuals, possessing no weight whatever, we should brand them with the foulest marks of papistical impiety . . .[8]

Such arguments did not impress Whitehead's opponents, and indeed they contain distinct echoes of Charles V's judgment against Luther, or the general Catholic position on the traditions of the church. At the height of the struggle in Frankfurt John Knox preached a sermon, declaring roundly that it was precisely because of the abuses contained in the Prayer Book that God had turned his back upon the English church and withdrawn his 'Godly Imp'.[9] Calvin, although using more cautious language, clearly believed that the Prayer Book party in Frankfurt was more concerned with the validity of the English reformed tradition than it was with the Word of God. Cox and Whitehead responded vigorously. What they were doing was perfectly consistent with the Word of God. The 'English ceremonies' were things indifferent, and some, such as kneeling to receive communion and the use of the surplice, had been abandoned out of deference to the consciences of Calvin's friends, 'which might at that time have been piously adopted'.[10] The remainder were retained, not out of wilful obstinacy, but as a 'concession to the love of our country'. They were, they protested, not 'so entirely wedded to our country as not to be able to endure any customs differing from our own . . .', but since these customs did not contain the substance of their faith, merely a part of its form, they felt entitled to retain them within the constraints imposed by the circumstances of their exile. The magistrates of Frankfurt had given them permission to use 'the rites of our native country' and had been fully satisfied with the Forty-Two Articles as a summary of their doctrine. To some extent these justifications were disingenuous. The Prayer Book party were the aggressors in the 'Troubles', disrupting the previous understanding which had been reached with the senate of the city, and overthrowing the Genevan order and discipline which had previously been in use. The senate accepted this coup, simply because it appeared to be a decision made by the congregation itself, and did not transgress the limits of what they were prepared to tolerate. The main concern of the magistrates was that the English should not make a nuisance of themselves.

This, it soon transpired, was a forlorn hope because the removal of the Genevan discipline had left gaps and uncertainties in the structure of authority. The English tradition was that of an establishment, where no such uncertainties existed, and the role of the congregation itself was negligible. However, it was one thing to transpose a modified Prayer Book into the context of exile, and quite another to decide how to run a church which suddenly consisted of a number of isolated groups. There were bishops among the exiles, notably John Ponet, but episcopal oversight would not have been practicable even if it could have been agreed upon, and was scarcely suggested. The remaining alternatives were either appointment by the civil authority of the place in which the church was situated, or election by the congregation. The latter was universally adopted, for obvious reasons. However, the fact of election did not in itself fully define the relationship between the congregation and its officers, and it was that issue which was tried out during the next round of the Frankfurt 'Troubles', which began early in 1557. The origin of this dispute lay in an attempt by Robert Horne the pastor and Richard Chambers the deacon, to discipline one Thomas Ashley for critical remarks which he had made about their ministry.[11] Ashley understandably complained that Horne and Chambers were proposing to be judges in their own cause, and appealed to the congregation at large. Horne did not deny that he was proposing to act in the manner alleged, and according to one of his opponents took the view

> that, by his judgement, there is no ordinary way to meddle against the Pastors and Seniors, except they call themselves to be hearers of their own cause, and their own judges themselves. For other 'ordinary way' . . . neither he nor any other shall be able to show.[12]

In other words, the fact of election did not make the pastor, or any other officer, answerable to the congregation for the discharge of his duties. Also, since there was no provision for re-election or review, such officers held what was effectively a freehold of their posts until they should choose to lay them down. The majority of the congregation held this position to be intolerable, but tacitly admitted that Horne was right in his interpretation of the existing constitution. They therefore set out to draw up a 'New Discipline' which should remedy that situation, providing for two ministers in place of the original pastor, and for the annual re-election of officers. Horne and his friends objected to the first, on the grounds that it was contrary to custom and would breed confusion, but raised only a minor quibble about the second, presumably because the ministers (whose authority was really in question) were to be exempted. The main battle was joined over article 44 of the new order, which ran:

> Item, that the Ministers and Seniors, thus elected, have now authority as the principal members of the Congregation, to govern the said Congregation according to God's word and the Discipline of the church as is aforesaid: and also to call together and assemble the said Congregation for causes, and at times, as shall to them seem expedient.
>
> Provided always, That if any dissension shall happen between the Ministers and the Seniors, or the more part of them, and the Body of the Congregation, or the more part of them, and that the said Ministers and Seniors, in such controversy, being desired thereoto, will not assemble the Congregation: that then the Congregation may, of itself, come together and consult and determine as concerning the said controversy or controversies: and the said Assembly to be a lawful Congregation . . .[13]

To this Horne objected that it 'wiped away' the authority of the ministers and seniors, making them answerable to any temporary majority which might happen to arise, and was contrary to the terms upon which the church held its franchise from the city,

> That if there arise any dissentions or contentions among the Strangers, concerning religion or their discipline, they be set at one with all diligence by the Ministers and Seniors . . . And in case the matter cannot be appeased before the Ministers and Elders; let them know that the Senate of this City will take order therein . . .[14]

To which the supporters of the New Discipline responded:

> Except the matter be used as we have provided . . . both the authority and liberty of the Congregation is wiped away, and a mere tyranny established.

Although Horne admitted that there was no sensible alternative to the election of a minister in the circumstances of exile, in every other respect he was prepared to regard the senate of the city as a Godly Magistracy, with authority over the worship and doctrine of the church analogous to that of the Supreme Head to which they were accustomed.

The city fathers were not anxious to become involved, but they were anxious to see peace restored, and by intervening twice for that purpose embraced, unwittingly perhaps, the role that Horne wished to assign to them. But they had many other more important matters to attend to, and in spite of the failure of the arbitration which they set up in April 1557 were prepared to let the matter rest once it was clear that the majority view was going to prevail. They had no interest in defending Horne, either to establish the principle of their own authority or to safeguard a concept of the ministerial function more appropriate to an established incumbency than to a church in exile. Although the controversy rumbled on after Horne and Chambers had left Frankfurt, for all practical purposes the autonomy of the English congregation, and its ultimate authority over its own pastors, was accepted by all parties.

Whether similar controversies were fought out elsewhere is not clear. The congregation which was originally established at Wesel seems to have been rejected by the authorities there for refusing to subscribe to the Augsburg Confession, but settled finally at Aarau, where it apparently used the Genevan order both of worship and discipline without interference. The other two congregations established early in the exile, at Zurich and Strasburg, used a modified version of the 1552 Order, as is clear from correspondence between them and Frankfurt in October and November 1554. The original group in the latter city, led by William Whittingham and well pleased with their reception, had taken the ill-advised step in August 1554 of writing to the other congregations inviting their adherence. Zurich and Strasburg – the 'Learned men' as Whittingham somewhat disparagingly referred to them – responded cautiously, insisting upon adherence to the Prayer Book as a condition of any possible move.[15] When it became clear that Frankfurt had adopted the Genevan order, the others not only backed off, but probably began to plot that incursion into Frankfurt which resulted in the establishment of the English order in 1555, as we have seen. Neither in Zurich nor in Strasburg did disputes arise which threatened to involve the civil magistrates in the affairs of the congregations, and if there were quarrels over the nature of the ministerial authority, they have escaped the record. Strasburg did refuse burgher rights to some Englishmen who were suspected of purely political conspiracy, just as the magistrates of Frankfurt expelled John Knox for his intemperate attacks on Philip and the Emperor Charles V. The attitude of all the 'cities of refuge' seems to have been substantially the same. They were all within the Reformed (as opposed to the Evangelical) tradition; they were perfectly satisfied with the doctrine professed by their English visitors, whether explicitly through the Forty-Two Articles or not; and they were happy to leave them to run their own affairs, provided that they behaved themselves.

Nevertheless, considering that Zurich and Geneva had been in full communion since 1549, the differences between Bullinger and Calvin over the English order were significant. Calvin objected to it in the strongest terms, supported its opponents wherever they appeared, and welcomed them to Geneva with enthusiasm. There could have been no Prayer Book congregation in Geneva, whatever its professed doctrine, while Calvin's influence prevailed with the council. Bullinger on the other hand, while denying that he would wish to use it himself, was perfectly happy for his guests to insist upon it in their own congregation, as something appertaining to their own tradition, the faults of which were matters indifferent. This was entirely consistent with the advice he gave during the two Vestiarian controversies in England, in 1551 and 1563,[16] and indicates that his view of the discretion allowed to the Godly Magistrate was a good deal wider than Calvin's – perhaps reflecting the different circumstances in Zurich and Geneva. Calvin's only concession to national tradition in his dealings with the English was in the use of the vernacular, and that was not a concession, because it was a principle he held as strongly as they did. Consequently, wherever the Genevan Rite and Discipline were adopted by the exiles – at Aarau, Basle and Geneva itself – the only thing that distinguished the English congregations from their French or Swiss neighbours was the use of the English language. This complete, if temporary, absorption into the continental Reformed tradition made a profound and lasting impression on those who experienced it, detaching them not only from the liturgical tradition established by Cranmer and Ridley, but also from that broad interpretation of the role of the Godly Magistrate which had been necessary in England before 1553, and was going to be equally necessary after 1558. That this detachment was not carried out without some qualms, even on the part of its most earnest advocates, is indicated by Whittingham's claim in the early stages of the Frankfurt dispute that Cranmer had been about to produce a further revised order 'a hundred times more perfect' than that of 1552, had he not been prevented by the king's death.[17] As far as I am aware, no evidence of any such intention has ever come to light.

To what extent either side was motivated during the exile by intentions, or even plans, of returning to England is uncertain. Although the restoration of the gospel to England was a consummation devoutly to be wished, in practical terms it was only likely to come about through the death of Mary and her replacement with the more amenable Elizabeth. Given their distaste for the Prayer Book (which still represented Protestantism to most of the persecuted brethren who had remained behind) and their extremely limited view of the role of the Godly Magistrate, it is not surprising that the Genevans regarded the prospect with mixed feelings. Less than a month after the new queen's accession Christopher Goodman and his congregation in Geneva wrote to Frankfurt, rejoicing in the advent of the 'virtuous and gracious Queen Elizabeth' and proposing a common front among the returning exiles:

> that we may together reach and practice the true knowledge of Gods Word; which we have learned in this our banishment, and by God's merciful Providence seen in the best Reformed churches, That (considering our negligence in time past; and God's punishment of the same) we may with zeal and diligence, endeavour to recompense it . . .[18]

Significantly, by the time this letter was received, most of the Prayer Book congregation in Frankfurt had already left for England, and those who remained were under no illusions about the drift of their correspondents' intentions:

> 'For ceremonies to contend', they replied '(where it shall lie neither in your hands nor ours to appoint what they shall be; but in such mens wisdoms as shall be appointed to the devising of the same, and which shall be received by common consent of the parliament), it shall be to small purpose. But we trust that both true Religion shall be restored; and that we shall not be burdened with unprofitabe Ceremonies. And therefore, as we purpose to submit ourselves to such Orders as shall be established by Authority, being not of themselves wicked; so we would wish you willingly to do the same.'[19]

Although personal relations between many of the Prayer Book exiles and their co-religionists in Geneva and Aarau remained good, so that Horne and Chambers were able to pay an amicable call on Calvin during the summer of 1558, their visions of the English church remained a long way apart.

It is now generally recognised that Christina Garrett overstated the case when she argued (almost fifty years ago) that the whole Marian exile was a calculated 'withdrawal and return'. Few Englishmen imitated Edmund Grindal in making a serious attempt to learn the German language, but their hopes for the restoration of true religion in England were vague and apocalyptic, at least until the onset of Mary's last illness. That the servants of AntiChrist would be punished, none doubted. But with the end of the world so imminent, it was uncertain whether such punishment would antedate the Second Coming, or be part of it. Not suprisingly, it was Prayer Book men, such as Becon and Bale, who inclined to take the view that the gospel would be restored in England before the end: 'If we return unto the Lord our God', the former wrote, 'let us not doubt but that he will shortly turn unto us, mercifully behold us, and once again bless us with the benefit of his blessed word'.[20]

'We shall find mercie in time convenient', Bale had declared at the very outset of Mary's reign, and the popular scriptural parallel of the exile in Babylon pointed hopefully in the same direction. However, to draw comfort from that, it was necessary to accept England as a manifestation of Israel, which brings us back to the concept of the special providence. In the last analysis, the difference between the Prayer Book exiles and their opponents can be reduced to the strength or weakness of their sense of such providence. To those whose model of the Reformation was the Consistory of Geneva, the church in England had never been anything other than a second-best approximation – true Reformation 'seen through a glass darkly'. To those who desired 'the face of an English church' in their exile, on the other hand, the Edwardian church liturgy, Godly Prince and all, had been an authentic expression of the Will of God. They did not defend it as perfect, but they did accept that the royal supremacy represented the Divine purpose, and like Bullinger, were prepared to allow a fairly generous latitude in their definition of godliness. To a young queen who was keenly aware of the importance of being English, the availability of skilled and experienced clergy with such convenient principles must have carried a lot of weight in making the critical decisions of 1559.

Notes

1. A Brieff Discours of the troubles begonne at Franckfort, 1575; repr. and ed. Edward Arber, 1908, p. 54 [Discours].
2. A.F. Scott Pearson, Cartwright and Elizabethan Puritanism, Cambridge, 1925, pp. 144–6; M.A. Simpson, John Knox and the Troubles begun at Frankfurt, London, 1975. Patrick Collinson has identified the main editor of this work as Thomas Wood; 'The authorship of A brieff discours of the troubles begonne at Franckfort', Journal of Ecclesiastical History, LIX, 1958, 188–208.
3. The forme of common praiers used in the churches of Geneva; made by J. Calvyne, trans. W. Huycke, London, 1550.
4. Discours, p. 88.
5. W. Haller, John Foxe's Book of Martyrs and the Elect Nation, London, 1963; V.N. Olsen, John Foxe and the Elizabethan Church, Los Angeles, 1973; R. Bauckham, Tudor Apocalypse, 1978.
6. J.W. McKenna, 'How God became an Englishman', in Tudor Role and Revolution; Essays for G.R. Elton from his American Friends, ed. J.W. McKenna and D.J. Guth, Cambridge, 1982, pp. 25–43; quoting T. Wright (ed.) A Collection of Political Poems and Songs (Rolls Series, 14), 1861, II, 130.

7. 'Our king has been removed from us by reason of our sins, to the very great peril of our church', J. Hooper to John A. Lasco, 3 Sept. 1553, *Original Letters Relative to the English Reformation*, Parker Society, 1846, I, p. 100.
8. *Discours*, p. 88.
9. On 19 Mar. 1555: *Discours*, p. 55.
10. *Discours*, p. 8.
11. Ibid., pp. 99–100.
12. Ibid., p. 115.
13. Ibid., pp. 187–8.
14. Ibid., p. 188.
15. Ibid., pp. 31–7.
16. For a full discussion of this advice, see J.H. Primus, *The Vestments Controversy*, Leiden, 1960, *passim*.
17. *Discours*, p. 75.
18. Ibid., p. 225.
19. Ibid., pp. 225–6.
20. Thomas Becon, *Works*, ed. J. Ayre, Parker Society, 1843–4, III, p. 220.

6 Relations between the Anglican and Roman Catholic Churches in the Sixteenth Century

Introduction

In this chapter I do not intend to discuss doctrinal controversies, nor the work of Protestant evangelists or Catholic missionaries at the parochial level. My intention is to examine the political and diplomatic relationship between the two churches as represented by their respective heads – successive popes and English monarchs. Unlike the social history of puritanism and Catholic recusancy, this has not been a popular subject for research in recent years. The most considerable monograph specifically devoted to Anglo-papal relations, W.E. Wilkie's *The Cardinal Protectors of England* (1974), deals only with the period 1492–1534, and the substantial output of recusant historians has included only one work on the later period since 1955, a reprint in 1968 of C.G. Bayne's *Anglo Roman Relations 1558–1565*, first published in 1913. At the same time many books have appeared dealing with English Catholicism in general, or with particular aspects of it, which have discussed Anglo-papal relations incidentally or as a matter of context.

The most directly relevant are by G. de C. Parmiter, M.A. Kelly [G. Bedouelle and Virginia Murphy] on Henry VIII's divorce, C. de Frede [and G.R. Redworth] on the Catholic restoration under Mary, and P. McGrath on the political problems of the Elizabethan Catholics.[1] A number of scholars have written learned articles in the field, notably Leo Hicks, J.P. Crehan and R.H. Pogson; and some theses which have remained unpublished, notably those of T.P. Bostock [J.P. Marmion and V. Murphy].[2] English attitudes towards the papacy, both official and popular, have received rather more attention; from Elton, Scarisbrick, McConica [and Brigden] on the reign of Henry VIII;[3] from myself [and Jennifer Loach] on the reign of Mary;[4] and from Bossy, Cross, Trimble [and Haigh] on the later sixteenth century.[5] The most important recent book on post-Reformation English Catholicism, J.A. Bossy's *The English Catholic Community 1570–1850*, while not ignoring the continuous significance of the Roman authority, is primarily concerned with the internal evolution of the church, and there has been no analysis of papal policy towards England over a long period since Philip Hughes' *Rome and the Counter-Reformation in England.*[6] The Curia was seldom well informed about English affairs. The country was distant, and during the years of schism information was received mainly through exiles and third parties who were frequently biased, and often themselves ignorant. Also, virtually from the beginning of the schism the papacy showed an inveterate tendency to pursue two conflicting policies simultaneously. Until the end of the sixteenth century successive popes strove to foster and support the English Catholics by propaganda and missionary activity of a purely spiritual nature, while at the same time entertaining with scanty concealment schemes for the forcible reconversion of the country by a mixture of political assassination and foreign invasion. It is not surprising that Englishmen of the seventeenth century associated the propagation of the Catholic faith with violence and deception long after the papacy had abandoned such schemes as unworthy and unreal. Later popes continued to be plagued by a double policy, although of a less obviously contradictory nature. The shadow of political conversion lingered, although it was now embodied in hopes for the personal conversion of the monarch. In fact this way to reunion was as much the result of unreal political calculations as that of a victorious Catholic uprising, and almost equally damaging to the welfare and interests of the English Catholics.

The situation at the beginning of the sixteenth century

In the opening years of the sixteenth century relations between Rome and England were calm and amicable. Those relics of ancient warfare, the statutes of provisors and praemunire remained unrepealed, but no attempt was made to invoke them as long as Henry VII lived.[7] Henry was conventionally pious, and the three popes with whom he had to deal, Innocent VIII (1484–92), Alexander VI (1492–1503) and Julius II (1503–13), were all anxious to secure his political support. Consequently he was able to invoke the sanction of excommunication against his enemies in Ireland, to restrict benefit of clergy, to reduce the immunities of sanctuary, and to nominate to the episcopal bench at his own discretion. In return Henry gave a certain amount of diplomatic support, persecuted heretics, and supported the jubilee indulgence of 1501. The situation was one of unwritten concordat; apparently stable, but in fact at the mercy of changing circumstances and personalities. The development of the office of Cardinal Protector between 1492 and 1514, although appearing to provide a guarantee of continuity and good communications, was itself at the mercy of personal ambitions and animosities, as was demonstrated by the fortunes of Christopher Bainbridge and Adriano Castellesi.[8]

Anti-clericalism had been strong in England for many years, and fierce intellectual criticism of the church (already common in other parts of Europe) began to appear soon after 1500.[9] The church was an extremely useful institution from the king's point of view. It gave sanctity to his office and weight to his laws. It provided him with a career structure for his civil servants, and with tangible evidence of that divine favour which was so important in preserving the loyalty of his subjects. But the church also needed the king. Its wealth and complex landed endowments presented a standing temptation to lay harassment, and without royal backing the jurisdiction of its courts lacked substance. Both lay anti-clericalism and clerical humanism presented the monarchy with weapons of sharp correction against the church within its dominions should that church draw back from the political and administrative alliance to which it seemed committed before 1509. The church was thus in the classic position of a man serving two masters, and the closer the agreement between those masters the more tenuous did its autonomy become. Consequently one of the chief results of the goodwill which prevailed between England and Rome from 1485 to 1509 was that the English church became virtually a hostage for papal acquiescence in the policies of the English Crown. This was not in itself unprecedented, but continuous warfare in Italy and the addition of the powerful Lutheran challenge to existing criticism also contributed to the weakening of papal authority in England. These factors combined to make the English church uniquely vulnerable to royal pressure when Henry VIII's matrimonial crisis developed in the late 1520s.

Henry VIII: the matrimonial crisis

The circumstances of that crisis are too well known to need recounting, but it is worth remembering that to Clement VII it came as a bolt from a clear sky. The diligence and cordiality of English communications with Rome had waned after the old king's death, and both Leo X and Adrian VI had complained occasionally of unfilial negligence, but there had certainly been no breakdown of relations.[10] Some years ago Professor A.F. Pollard represented English policy between 1514 and 1525 as being harnessed to papal aims by the ambitions of Thomas Wolsey.[11] This view has now been effectively challenged,[12] but Wolsey's double position as chancellor and papal legate must have seemed to provide a guarantee against fundamental divergence, and King Henry had taken the trouble to enter the theological lists against Luther with his *Assertio Septem Sacramentorum*, a work which had contained, among other things, an unequivocal assertion of papal authority. At the same time, because of the way in which Wolsey had monopolised English business, Clement was unaware of the strength of the anti-clericalism that the cardinal was stirring up in England, and uninformed of Henry's state of mind. More important, England's established contacts in the Curia proved inadequate to manipulate its more intimate politics. This fact was to be of critical importance in the tense and dramatic conditions created by the sack of Rome, Clement's imprisonment in the Castel Sant'Angelo, and his escape to Orvieto in December 1527. For a time the Curia was shattered, the Pope unnerved and thoroughly alienated from the emperor. When the first English envoy, William Knight, made contact with Clement a few days before his escape, he found him almost pathetically anxious to win friends; but by the time that Knight had followed him to Orvieto, he was already less amenable. A man more familiar with Clement's character, or better provided with confidential information, might still have gained his point had he been prepared to offer prompt and generous relief of the poverty which was the Pope's most pressing anxiety. This Knight was unable to do, and his mission was already well on the way to failure when he was replaced by Gregory Casale with new instructions from Wolsey in January 1528.

Casale was a more skilful diplomat than Knight, and had the advantage of being an Italian, but he was never given adequate powers, and acted mainly as resident host to successive special missions which followed him in rapid succession over the next four years.[13] English importunity was the least of Clement's worries in the early months of 1528. He was quite willing to do the emperor any injury within his power, but understandably nervous of the possible consequences; and neither he nor his advisers, such as Cardinal Pucci, could understand why Wolsey was making such a fuss. In their eyes the sensible course would have been for the English cardinal to have judged the matter himself, and only brought the case to Rome should the validity of the king's second marriage be challenged.[14] To Wolsey such a course was a mere waste of time, since opposition to the Boleyn marriage was so strong that a challenge was inevitable. He was quite willing to judge the case, but only by virtue of a Decretal Commission which would have made his decision final, and not subject to appeal. This Clement adamantly refused to grant, although he was prepared to issue a general commission, and to make an informal undertaking to confirm the commissioners' decision. This unsatisfactory compromise, reached in April 1528, was the nearest that any of the English missions came to diplomatic success. By the summer of that year the imperial forces had withdrawn from the papal states, and by October the Curia was back in Rome. Clement's animosity towards the Emperor was waning, and with it any remaining chance that he would take resolute action in defiance of Charles' wishes.

Meanwhile Wolsey and his agents in Rome, principally Stephen Gardiner, kept up a feverish activity.[15] Cardinal Campeggio was to be joined with Wolsey in commission to hear the King of England's case, and part of this activity was directed towards overcoming his gout and his reluctance. The rest was fruitlessly expended upon renewed attempts to secure a Decretal Commission. Campeggio eventually reached England at the end of September, secretly instructed by Clement to use every possible pretext for delay, to find Wolsey and Henry consumed with impatience. By November, in an agony of exasperation the English cardinal was repeating over and over again that if Clement did not gratify his master swiftly it would be the end of papal authority in England.[16] Campeggio was unmoved by such extravagance. He was in an extremely difficult position, and saw only one real hope of satisfying the conflicting demands being made upon him – to persuade Catherine into a graceful withdrawal. While the legate pursued his hopeless quest, a series of developments further weakened Henry's position. A papal brief confirming the dispensation for his original marriage turned up in Spain, undermining the little that his diplomacy had achieved. In February and March of 1529 rumours of Clement's death, and his actual illness, caused further confusion and delay, while at the end of April the emperor's agents in Rome made a formal protest against the King of England's suit, and petitioned the Pope to revoke the case to the Curia. In these circumstances Henry's agents in Rome could accomplish nothing in the direction of amplifying the commission which had already been granted, and the king's only hope lay in getting a favourable verdict from Campeggio and Wosley as quickly as possible. The legates began work at length on 18 June, but it is clear that Campeggio never had any intention of giving judgment. Following Clement's instructions, and no doubt his own inclinations, he found a technical pretext to adjourn the court on 31 July, and soon after the case was revoked to Rome.[17]

Henry had been totally defeated by a mixture of his own incompetence and imperial pressure. Furious and humiliated, he now needed a scapegoat and a new policy. The former was easier to find than the latter, and predictably the weight of his displeasure fell upon Wolsey. The story of the chancellor's fall is too well known to need repetition, but it is important to realise that more was involved than the disgrace of a once trusted minister. Wolsey was a prince of the church, and the manner in which he was handled was of the gravest significance for the papacy which he theoretically represented. On 21 September, after several weeks of tension and uncertainty, he was deprived of the Great Seal; and on 9 October he was charged with offences against the statutes of praemunire, and speedily convicted. Objectively, the charges were absurd, since they involved the exercise of papal jurisdiction without the king's consent; but Wolsey put up no serious resistance, and no protest was forthcoming from Rome. Shortly after, Henry pardoned his old servant's praemunire, and by keeping him for some months in a demoralising limbo between hope and fear was able to take from him the temporalities of several of his benefices, and sundry ecclesiastical properties which were not Wolsey's to give.[18] Encouraged by intermittent gestures of renewed favour, in April 1530 the cardinal withdrew towards his province of York, and apparently began to entertain hopes of recovering his position with papal assistance. If these intrigues were real at all they can hardly have been substantial; but they provided sufficient pretext for the king to order his arrest on a charge of treason at the beginning of November. Wolsey died without coming to trial, but not before his fate had demonstrated that, to a man in his position, the panoply of legatine authority was at best a worthless protection and at worst a disastrous liability. Wolsey fell, not because he was a symbol of papal jurisdiction but because he had failed the king. Nevertheless, by the time he died his disgrace had become an integral part of that policy of ecclesiastical blackmail which marked the second stage of Henry's search for a solution to his 'great matter'.

The king's principal ally in this policy was the parliament which met in November 1529 – particularly the House of Commons.[19] In acting as they did the Commons were doing no more than picking up the threads of an ancient controversy, a controversy which had blazed up fiercely as recently as 1514. On that occasion true to the existing spirit of concordat, Henry had damped down the fires of anti-clericalism;[20] now he fanned them. There is no space here to discuss the proceedings of the so-called Reformation Parliament, but it is quite clear that by 1530 the king was strongly sympathetic to demands for ecclesiastical reform. He was also beginning to express new and disquieting opinions about the extent of his own role in that reform. Professor Scarisbrick has recently argued that the appearance of these ideas was not simply the result of Henry's desire to coerce the Pope, and his views carry weight.[21] Nevertheless, by the summer of 1530, when the English king had spent much time, effort and money endeavouring to strengthen his case at Rome, the bishops of his own realm were thoroughly alarmed by the pressure building up against them in parliament.

Bitterly as he disliked the idea, up to this point Henry had accepted the prospect of having to plead his cause at Rome, and had concentrated his attention on obtaining a favourable verdict. This phase culminated in early June with the dispatch to Clement of a petition bearing the seals of nearly a hundred English dignitaries, begging him to find for Henry, and dropping ominous (but vague) hints about alternative solutions. There was no chance of a favourable response. Emperor and Pope were by this time the closest of friends, and Charles' agents were committed to frustrating English efforts at every turn. In the face of this, by August 1530, Henry's attitude had undergone a critical change. Loud importunity had been replaced by a cool denial that the Pope had any jurisdiction to pronounce upon the King of England's marriage. The ancient privileges and customs of the realm, he declared, exempted Englishmen from being cited before foreign courts; the Pope's authority in England extended only to matters of heresy. Consequently there was no reason why the marriage question should not be committed to the Archbishop of Canterbury, in spite of the fact that Clement had inhibited all further discussion pending the outcome of Catherine's appeal. The Pope was in any case both a bastard and a simoniac, Henry alleged, and if the manifest justice of his claim was not admitted, he was fully prepared to appeal in his turn – to a General Council.[22]

Henry VIII; the royal supremacy

By the end of 1530 the king's thinking was more radical than that of any of his known advisers, and a source of acute embarrassment to his envoys in Rome.[23] When challenged by an indignant Pope to substantiate the claims that Henry insisted that they should make on his behalf, they could find nothing. Neither England's jurisdictional immunity, nor the king's vaguer claim to 'imperial' dignity could be supported by evidence from the Vatican archives. For the next fifteen months these envoys (principally William Benet and Edward Carne) strove by a variety of arguments, inducements and threats to get the king's case heard in England. They were unsuccessful, and Henry's own position lacked both logic and consistency. In spite of his belligerent claims, he was not yet fully committed to the doctrine of English autonomy, as the continued efforts of his envoys testified. At the same time a sweeping attack on the English clergy, culminating in charges of praemunire against both convocations, was allowed to peter out in a royal pardon and an equivocal submission.[24] Henry was certainly feeling his way towards a fully fledged concept of royal supremacy – all the elements of which were present in his mind – but both emotionally and intellectually he was irresolute. It was still possible as late as the beginning of 1532 that a change of heart on Clement's part could simply have restored the status quo; but Clement, understandably, took Henry's threats and blandishments with a large pinch of salt. He saw no reason, either political or canonical, to change his mind. The king thereupon moved from threats to action. How far the dramatic events of 1532 and 1533 were brought about by this stalemate over the 'great matter', and how far they were the result of long brooding about ecclesiastical jurisdiction, is hard to tell. The traditional thesis of a complete causal relationship between the 'divorce' and the break with Rome is no longer adequate. Henry held some views of a Caesaro-papist kind in the early 1520s, and it is quite probable that England would have come to a position similar to extreme Gallicanism even if there had been no matrimonial issue. On the other hand it would be unreal to maintain that the royal ultimatum based upon the Commons 'Supplication against the Ordinaries', or the Act in Restraint of Annates,[25] was not part of a campaign to force the Pope's hand. Henry was reaching the end of his resources. His attempts to secure a favourable nomination to the College of Cardinals had failed, and his ostentatious *entente* with Francis I, reached in late October 1532, provided no real guarantee of adequate political backing in the Curia. In the three years since the failure of the Blackfriars court he had battered the English church into a submission which would, in itself, have seriously disrupted Anglo-papal relations, but he had made not the slightest progress towards obtaining a favourable judgement on his case. All he had to show for his efforts was the fact that no definitive sentence had been pronounced against him.

This impasse was finally broken at the beginning of 1533, ostensibly by Henry's discovery of the fact that Anne Boleyn was pregnant. In reality that pregnancy was a symptom rather than the cause of the crucial decision. The death of Archbishop Warham on 22 August 1532, and the emergence of Thomas Cromwell as Henry's leading adviser in the last months of the year, are more likely to have been the decisive factors. The way was now open for the king to act upon the ideas which he had been voicing for some time, by appointing an amenable archbishop to settle his 'great matter' in England without further reference to Pope or Curia. Professor Elton has argued convincingly that Cromwell was the man who finally steeled the king's resolution,[26] and it was certainly he who organised the subsequent campaign which translated Henry's aspirations into legal and political realities. The progress of that campaign is familiar to all students of the period, and only certain features call for comment here. Clement was warned that new and dangerous moves were afoot in England, but Henry had been crying 'wolf' for years, and the Pope was not wholly without sympathy for his problems. Consequently he made no difficulty about confirming Thomas Cranmer's appointment as Archbishop of Canterbury, which, as things were to turn out, was to be the last effective act of papal authority relating to England for more than twenty years. At the same time, Henry refrained from burning his boats immediately. His excusators continued to plead in the Curia, even after Anne Boleyn had been crowned as his queen, and it was not to be until 1534 that papal jurisdiction was unequivocally excluded from England by parliament and Convocation. By that time, of course, the initiative did not lie entirely with the king. Clement responded to the English defiance with some moderation, but he could not ignore it. In Consistory on 11 July Henry's marriage to Anne was solemnly condemned, and he was ordered to take back Catherine, who was still his lawful wife pending the outcome of her appeal. He was given until September to do so, under pain of excommunication.

The king responded to the challenge by cancelling the commissions of his agents in Rome, and by sending Gardiner and Edmund Bonner to defy the Pope to his face by appealing to a General Council. By the end of 1533 Henry stood excommunicate (although the sentence had not been formally promulgated), and all direct communication between England and the Curia had ceased. For the remainder of his pontificate (until September 1534), Clement's attitude was remarkably supine. He gave no lead or encouragement to those Englishmen who wished to resist the royal supremacy, and played into the hands of that important and persuasive group who were arguing that only the king could cleanse the Augean stables of the English church.[27] Apart from Cromwell, John Fisher and Sir Thomas More, it seems that very few people either in England or in Rome understood the true significance of what was happening. Popes and English kings had quarrelled before; sooner or later, many must have thought, a negotiated settlement would be reached and all the high-principled language of the royal supremacy would be quietly forgotten. The new Pope, Paul III, was anxious for an accommodation, and spoke of reopening the king's matrimonial case.[28] Both Francis and Charles V were sympathetic towards an agreement which would have relieved them of the embarrassment of having to do business with a colleague who was under the ban of the church. Henry, however, would accept nothing less than a complete surrender to his claims; and the executions of Fisher and More in the summer of 1535 put an abrupt, if temporary, end to all talk of reconciliation. A second excommunication was pronounced against him, and bulls prepared absolving his subjects of their allegiance and declaring him deposed from his throne. By the summer of 1536, however, the pendulum had swung back again. Both Catherine and Anne were dead, and the Pope was willing to make sweeping concessions. The emperor was openly enthusiastic, and the shrewdest observers in Rome believed that a settlement would come in a matter of weeks.[29] Had the royal supremacy been nothing more than a device to secure the annulment of the king's first marriage, these expectations would have been justified. By this time, however, Henry was deeply convinced that all papal jurisdiction was wrongful and usurped; and his only interest in negotiation was to forestall the possibility that either the emperor or the King of France might be prevailed upon to execute the papal sentence against him.

This never seemed a very likely eventuality, but could not be altogether discounted, and Henry remained acutely suspicious of papal intentions. His suspicions were confirmed by Paul's reaction to the news of rebellion in England towards the end of 1536. The king's remote kinsman and arch-enemy, Reginald Pole,[30] was created a cardinal and dispatched northwards for the purpose of activating the bull of excommunication. Hopefully, this was to be done by the strength of the rebels themselves; but should that fail Pole was empowered to do his utmost to invoke the aid of other Christian princes. Pole arrived in the Low Countries only after the rebellion was over, and it is extremely uncertain that he would have been able to enlist any substantial support had he arrived earlier. Henry was furious over what he regarded as the treason of one of his own subjects, and Pole was fortunate to escape either abduction or assassination. Within a few years those members of his family who remained in England were to pay the price of his zeal in the papal cause.[31] For the time being the Pope's animosity had been frustrated, but there was no more talk of an amicable settlement. For at least as long as Henry lived the English schism would continue, unless it could be broken by armed invasion. Thus by the end of 1537 he was competing directly with the Pope for friendship and alliance, and a second polarity had been added to the existing Franco-Habsburg rivalry.

Consequently, English security depended upon the preservation of this pattern, and English diplomacy was consistently directed against any sign of a *rapprochement* between Francis and Charles, as well as against the ever-present threat of a General Council of the church. Towards the end of 1538 Henry appeared to be facing defeat on both fronts, and Pope Paul, now fully determined on his overthrow, prepared again to promulgate the bull of deposition against him. Just before the New Year Pole set out on another crusading mission, and in January 1539 the emperor and the King of France concluded a formal treaty at Toledo. England was seized by an invasion panic which probably placed the king in a stronger position than he had occupied at any time during the previous ten years, but the threat came to nothing. Disillusioned, Pole returned to Rome, and as the European balance returned to equilibrium, Henry drew back from his flirtations with the German Lutherans.[32] Within England his own peculiar brand of orthodoxy was reasserted and Protestant reformers passed under a cloud with the fall of their patron, Thomas Cromwell. An uncompromising Erastianism, which seemed to need no doctrinal support, was the unprecedented outcome of a decade of crisis at home and abroad.

The end of conservative Erastianism

By 1545, England again stood in peril of a Franco-Habsburg alliance, but in that situation the Pope had played no significant part. In December of that same year the long-awaited General Council began its work at Trent, but that assembly did not bring the danger that had been anticipated. On the contrary it resulted in a final, and somewhat mysterious, gesture of reconciliation from Rome. Paul was apparently so anxious to secure some English representation at Trent that in August 1546 he sent a secret emissary to Henry – one Guron Bertano – offering almost total endorsement of all that had been done in return for a formal submission. Nothing came of this overture, and very little is known about its reception. When the king died five months later, the political and religious situation which he left in England was uniquely unfavourable to reconciliation. Whether by his own intention or not, the tutors and councillors of his young successor were predominantly men sympathetic to doctrinal Protestantism;[33] from the papacy's point of view heretics as well as schismatics. For the next six years the religious history of England was to be one of legislated reformation, and the issues of controversy were between the Protestants and the conservative Henricians. During this period the authority of the Pope was principally a propaganda weapon, which each side used against the other as occasion served. Stephen Gardiner, whose *De vera obedientia oratio* was the principal intellectual defence of the royal supremacy, was also throughout the leader of the conservative group. Arguing against the introduction of religious innovations at the beginning of the new reign, he claimed that such changes played into the Pope's hands, since he '. . . wanteth not wit to beat into other princes' ears that where his authority is abolished, there at every change of governors shall be change of religion'. This was a substantial point, but of course Gardiner's opponents were quick to reply that the surest way to exclude papal authority was to remove popish doctrine and ceremonies. If papal jurisdiction had been grounded upon human custom rather than divine law, the same was true of the sacrifice of the mass. To the reformers there did not seem to be any logical reason to reject one Catholic tradition and retain others which were equally unscriptural in origin.

After striving for about four years to preserve his vision of a conservative royal supremacy, Gardiner eventually succumbed to the logic of this argument, and concluded that Catholic doctrine and papal authority were inseparable. Without unity of jurisdiction there could be no unity of faith.[34] The majority of his friends and followers, such as Cuthbert Tunstall and Edmund Bonner, came to the same conclusion, although they made no public announcement of their conversion and thus avoided facing charges of treason or praemunire. Their change of heart was to become fully apparent only in the following reign. Meanwhile it had become clear that many years of anti-papal propaganda, coming on top of a long tradition of anti-clericalism, had left the Pope with few friends among the English people. Even those who disliked Protestantism sufficiently to rebel against the introduction of the Prayer Book in 1549 had nothing to say in his defence – although they did ask for the rehabilitation of Reginald Pole.[35] In so far as the papacy entered into the political calculations of Edward VI and his mentors, it was purely as an external threat. Neither Paul III nor Julius III who succeeded him in 1550 made any further move against England; partly because they had other things to think about and partly, perhaps, because of the king's minority. On the other hand, neither would have objected had the emperor or King Henry II of France used the crusading pretext to make war on England for their own purposes. Henry VIII's excommunication had died with him, but his realm was now subjected to both schism and heresy – a position increasingly difficult to distinguish from that of the kingdoms of Scandinavia or the Lutheran principalities of Germany. In the event religion was not made an excuse for war, because as usual neither of the major powers wished to drive England into the arms of the other. Charles V maintained persistent diplomatic pressure to protect Princess Mary from the council's attempts to deprive her of the mass,[36] but otherwise religion played a negligible part in England's relations with her neighbours during this period – and the papacy none at all.

This situation was dramatically transformed by the death of King Edward, still under age, at the beginning of July 1553. John Dudley, Duke of Northumberland, the president of the council, who had embraced Protestantism in order to obtain the maximum advantage from the young king's personal convictions, was left to face the prospect of a Catholic successor. Unfortunately for his attempt to alter the succession, the papalist convictions of the lawful heir were not generally appreciated. In the dark days after her mother's death Mary had yielded to her father's pressure and accepted the royal supremacy.[37] Only a few of her intimates realised what anguish this surrender had subsequently caused, or how strong was her determination to repudiate it. In the crisis of 1553 Dudley and his friends conspicuously failed to mobilise anti-papal emotions against Mary; and since most of the Protestants were unwilling to support him on the grounds that he was a time-server and an exploiter of the gospel, his position quickly collapsed. Mary was almost universally acclaimed, on the mistaken assumption that she would restore her father's conservative Erastianism; 'religion as King Henry left it'. The queen and some of her less discreet supporters jumped to the opposite conclusion, and assumed that her easy victory was intended to be a mandate for a policy of full reaction. 'A miracle wrought by God for none other purpose . . .', as Reginald Pole was soon to express it.[38] Mary had spent her adult life far from the centre of power, and had been subjected to much humiliation and unhappiness. In this situation her two consolations had been her religion, and the friendship of her cousin Charles V. Now, in her time of triumph, conscience and loyalty spoke with different voices. The emperor was firmly convinced that the best interests of the Catholic church in England would be served by caution in ecclesiastical matters, and by a marriage between Mary and his own son, Philip, which would hopefully guarantee a Catholic succession and bring England permanently within the orbit of Habsburg orthodoxy. Such a marriage would also have the advantage of strengthening Philip's position in the Netherlands, and giving him the main credit for any reconciliation that might subsequently be negotiated between England and Rome.[39] He was therefore strongly opposed to any declaration of religious policy which might arouse powerful opposition in England until such time as the marriage alliance had been completed and Philip placed in a sufficiently strong position to ensure that such a policy could be successfully carried through.[40] At the same time Mary was desperately eager to restore England to the Catholic fold, and was urged in the same direction by letters from Reginald Pole, which not only represented this as the clear path of duty, but alleged that the whole legitimacy of her regime depended upon it.[41] Caution, ably represented by the emperor's ambassador Simon Renard, at first presented the more persuasive arguments, and Mary wisely refrained from making any public pronouncement on the subject of the royal supremacy.

Pope Julius III was well aware that the conservatism of the new English queen embraced the Roman jurisdiction as well as the mass. He was also aware of Reginald Pole's extreme enthusiasm for the reconciliation of his native land. On 5 August 1553 bulls were issued giving Pole the necessary powers to negotiate, and the messengers bearing them to Viterbo were met on the road by Pole's own messengers, hastening to Rome to request the mission. Such expedition was almost unprecedented and, as it turned out, mistaken. Julius knew better than to suppose that the reconciliation of England was simply a matter of despatching a cardinal legate. There was other work for Pole to do in the north, which happily coincided with a possible mission to England; the perpetual problem of peace negotiations between the emperor and the French.[42] Pole's commission embraced both tasks, thus bringing England back into the centre of papal diplomacy; but such a dual policy turned out to be a grave disadvantage to the English mission. Certainly Pole was, from the Pope's point of view, profitably employed in the months during which he was forced to wait for admission to England; but he became increasingly distracted and disillusioned. Even when he was safely installed, his energies were to be constantly diverted to international diplomacy, and many of the intractable problems of the English church received less attention that was necessary. In the short term Pole's hopes were raised too quickly, and his passionate advocacy of immediate submission went unheeded. Mary's surrender to 'worldly prudence' drove him to a despair which is only comprehensible in terms of his own experience and convictions. The nature of his original quarrel with Henry VIII, and even more his intellectual and spiritual struggles over the doctrine of justification, had left him convinced of the absolute centrality of the Roman obedience to the Catholic faith.[43] For the English conservatives the papacy might be a necessary prop and safeguard; for Pole it was very much more. Without Rome there could be no salvation, no law and no morality.

'I say', he wrote to Mary on 27 August, 'that the establishment of this obedience is a greater establishment of your right to the Crown than any confederacy whatever which might be formed with any foreign Prince, or than the goodwill of your people at home, both which things are unstable and . . . may fail'.[44] In this frame of mind, Pole could not be expected to appreciate the strategic considerations which dominated the emperor and influenced the queen, but the Pope was more sympathetic. His personal envoy, Gian Francesco Commendone, visited England secretly in August 1553, and talked to Mary at some length. To him she confessed the warmth of her affection for the Holy See, and her desire to make open submission on behalf of the realm, but she also explained the difficulties in her path.[45] Commendone was so far convinced as to recommend his master to be guided by the wishes of the queen, and to do everything in his power to smooth her chosen path. Consequently, Julius did not share his legate's indignant frustration, but patiently reassured Pole with his confidence of ultimate success.

Queen Mary and the legatine mission of Cardinal Pole

Within six months of her succession Mary had successfully dismantled the Protestant establisment of her brother's reign, negotiated a marriage alliance with Philip of Spain, and defeated all organised opposition. She had not, however, rid herself of the title of Supreme Head of the Church; and it had become abundantly clear that she would not be able to do so until the question of the secularised ecclesiastical lands had been settled. These were the lands of the dissolved religious foundations, taken by the Crown and subsequently sold. By 1553 they were widely distributed in the possession of gentlemen and noblemen who had bought them at fair market prices, and were determined to resist any attempt at resumption, either by force or by spiritual blackmail. Apart from the queen herself, and those senior clergy who had been recently 'reconverted', there was in any case little enthusiasm for the papacy in England – and much deeply engrained distrust. In order to overcome this distrust and make reconciliation a political possibility, more was needed than the restoration of the mass and traditional ceremonies. The Pope would have to be prepared to 'write off' the monastic and other lands, and to hope that in due course the piety of subsequent generations would re-endow the church to its former level. Naturally Julius found the prospect of bargaining with recalcitrant schismatics extremely distasteful, but by the summer of 1554 he was convinced that there was no other way, and on 28 June he wrote to Pole authorising him to make concessions. At the same time he instructed the legate to give the English reconciliation priority over all his other commitments.[46]

This was the first significant step forward since the bull of the previous

August, but Pole did not welcome it unreservedly. On an issue of this kind compromise was not in his nature; nor was he convinced that concessions were necessary. Despite its lack of outward success, his mission had not been altogether fruitless. Julius had authorised him to exercise his legatine authority from outside England, and he had in fact absolved a number of individual penitents, confirmed several episcopal appointments, and issued a steady trickle of dispensations – all in defiance of English law.[47] This evidence of goodwill, both on the part of the queen and of the private individuals concerned, Pole had taken to indicate that the extreme caution of Mary's policies was unjustified, and that Englishmen were much less averse to the Pope than was commonly represented. He was therefore extremely reluctant to give any undertaking on the question of church lands, and the negotiations hung fire – despite the abrupt withdrawal of all imperial opposition to his mission following upon the final celebration of Mary's marriage to Philip in July 1554. Philip was a warm supporter of reconciliation. Like his father, he believed that the church lands would have to be guaranteed and was prepared to take the initiative in such a negotiation himself. Between August and October pressure from all sides wore down Pole's resistance, and at length he agreed to accept a new brief which would give him explicit instructions to make the required surrender. The way was then sufficiently clear for him to be admitted to England as legate. The new brief, dispatched from Rome on 7 November, reached Pole on the eve of his meeting with parliament; it was judged sufficient by all parties, and an impressive ceremony of reconciliation followed. The emotions generated by that occasion moved both Mary and Pole deeply, but politically rocks still lay beneath the calm surface. Within a few weeks sharp disagreements had arisen over the exact nature of the guarantees which had been given to the 'possessioners', as they were significantly called. In the Pope's name Pole had waived all ecclesiastical censures, and agreed that the church would make no attempt to disturb the status quo. He had not acknowledged that the statutes dissolving the religious houses had given to the Crown a legal title which could be transmitted to the purchasers. The security of the latter thus depended on the papal dispensation itself, and no Pope could irrevocably commit his successors.[48] In the event the bargain was not disrupted; parliament duly repealed the royal supremacy, and the Bull of Plenary Indulgence followed in January 1555. Nevertheless suspicions lingered, and were soon to be sharpened into fear by the twists and turns of papal policy.

Julius III died on 23 March 1555, and his death had a most unsettling effect both upon Pole and upon the English situation in general. At first it was widely expected that Pole would himself be elected, and although he professed complete indifference, he knew perfectly well that such an advancement would put an end to his work in England almost as soon as it had begun. On the other hand, if he was not elected the new Pope might take a quite different view of the English mission, and the harmony between Pope and legate which was essential for success would disappear. The news of Cardinal Cervini's election as Marcellus II was consequently greeted with relief in England. Cervini was an old friend of Pole's, and immediately confirmed the legate's powers. However, within three weeks he too died, and uncertainty once more prevailed. This time the outcome was less fortunate. Cardinal Caraffa, who became Pope Paul IV, was not only a man of invincible obstinacy, but a lifelong enemy of the Habsburgs and a long-standing opponent of that school of liberal Catholic theology which Pole had led in the 1540s.[49] In spite of his high standing, the orthodoxy of the English cardinal has always been suspect in certain parts of the Curia, and Pole had never been completely free from the fear that his position was steadily being undermined during his long absence in the north. This fear was greatly intensified by Caraffa's election, and problems soon began to multiply. Like Marcellus, the new Pope confirmed Pole's commission, but he also issued a bull condemning the alienation of ecclesiastical property which seemed to threaten the whole foundation of the English settlement. After a great effort, Pole managed to persuade him to exempt England, and to confirm Julius' dispensation, but by the summer of 1555 the omens for future co-operation were not good. At this juncture the main difficulty was that Paul was not interested in the English situation as such, but only as an aspect of the general European crisis. He saw Pole primarily as a resident ambassador in England, and agent at large in north-western Europe.[50] In other words he reverted to Julius' original conception of the mission, before its priorities had been reorganised in June 1554. Pole, who was inclined to be daunted by the problems he faced in England and to seek escape by contemplating the pleasures of Italy, could ill afford this massive additional distraction. He was only too ready to agree with the broad interpretation of the crisis, and to divert his own energies, and those of his subordinates, away from the English church. Both he and Gardiner spent considerable time at the peace negotiations at La Marque during 1555; and in August of the same year Thomas Goldwell, one of the most zealous and effective agents of Catholicism in England, was sent on a prolonged mission to Rome in connection with the same negotiations.

The Catholic restoration in England had turned out to be a more difficult business than either Mary or Pole had anticipated. Neither had taken seriously the possibility of deeply convinced Protestant opposition, or had made plans for a campaign of orthodox evangelisation. Consequently they relied very heavily upon jurisdictional weapons. Pole, as we have seen, placed the Roman obedience at the centre of his faith, and believed that his main task was the reimposition of discipline. This priority was clearly reflected in the decrees of the legatine synod which he called during the winter of 1555–6,[51] and in the inflexible policy of persecution which was to bequeath such a disastrous legacy to subsequent generations of English Catholics. At least one recent scholar has argued that the Cardinal's reasoning was sound; and that for the vast majority of Englishmen the restoration of orthodox customs and habits was the most effective way to restore sound doctrine. Failure was not so much the result of a misconceived policy as of Mary's untimely death and Elizabeth's refusal to continue in the Catholic church.[52] There is some evidence to support such an hypothesis, but more to indicate that the self-conscious papalism of these years was a mistake. Conservative writers who rejoiced at the return of the mass studiously avoided reference to the Pope, and the development of Paul IV's own policies made him a disastrous liability to a church so orientated. Had the English mission concentrated on evangelisation, and had the restored Catholic church adopted a more Gallican attitude, it would certainly have been in a better position to survive the crisis that Paul brought upon it in 1557. If Pole calculated that explicit ultramontanism would preserve the English church from too close an association with England's political subordination to Spain, then he was disappointed. Ironically enough, the Roman obedience was becoming firmly linked with Spain in the minds of many Englishmen at precisely that time when the breakdown of relations between Paul and Philip threatened to bring the whole English mission to a grinding halt.

Sir Edward Carne, Mary's ambassador in Rome, had many occasions to complain of the Pope's neglect of his sovereign's affairs. In June 1556 he reported in despair that he had repeatedly failed to persuade Paul to deal with the episcopal vacancies at Winchester and Chester, both of which had been unfilled since the previous year.[53] Chichester, Lincoln, Peterborough and Carlisle all stood vacant for more than twelve months between 1556 and 1557; while Salisbury and Oxford, vacated in the latter year, were still unfilled at the end of the reign. The fault may not have lain entirely with Paul, but his lack of concern is manifest, and did no good to the English church. Finally, in April 1557, Carne wrote to say that the long-threatened blow had fallen. The Pope had decided to break off diplomatic relations with Philip for political reasons, and had 'revoked all his ministers and legates within the realms and dominions of . . . the king'. Worse was to follow. On 31 May 1557 Cardinal Morone was arrested on charges of heresy. Morone was Pole's closest friend within the Curia, and had been entrusted by Julius III with the special oversight of English affairs. Since the beginning of the mission he had acted as advocate and protector, encouraging Pole, keeping him supplied with news of Italian affairs, and making good some of his deficiencies as a politician. The arrest of Morone not only cut an exceedingly valuable line of communication between England and Rome, but gave an additional and sinister significance to the termination of Pole's commission. This was made more apparent by the Pope's reaction to Mary's indignant protests and expostulations. He was prepared to recognise the special needs of the English church, but no amount of intercession would persuade him to continue Pole in office. Instead, the cardinal was to return to Rome to answer 'certain religious suspicions', being replaced in England by an octogenarian Friar, William Peto, whose only qualification for the post was that he had once been a confessor to Catherine of Aragon! Mary was appalled and insulted. On 14 June Pole's recall was published in Rome, and a few days later he laid down his office, but the queen would not admit to England the nuncio who bore the actual letters of revocation. Nor would she accept Peto in his place.[54] If there were charges of heresy to be laid against Pole, she declared in an astonishing echo of her father's spirit, '. . . she would, in observance of the laws and privileges of her realm, refer them to the cognisance and decision of her own ecclesiastical courts'.

For the English cardinal these were months of acute misery. In spite of the obvious danger to himself and the threat to his work in England, his conscience prompted him to obey the Pope's wishes; but Philip and Mary were determined that he should not leave the country. As Archbishop of Canterbury (a position he had held since Cranmer's execution in 1556), he still had sufficient authority to sustain the English mission. The king and queen insisted that they had confidence in him, and in no one else, for this work. Pole replied unhappily that he must perforce obey their wishes, but that he could have no direct dealings with princes who were at war with the Pope. He withdrew from the court and retired to Canterbury. By the autumn the worst was over. Peace was patched up between Paul and Philip, and formal diplomatic relations were resumed. But the deadlock over the English mission was never broken. The Pope persisted in his desire to send Peto, but Mary was unrelenting in her refusal, and Peto himself declined to accept the office on the grounds of his age and unsuitability. Sir Edward Carne gave up the fruitless negotiation, and Pole continued to run the English church as *legatus natus* until his death in November 1558. In doing so, however, he compromised one of his deepest principles; and although in fact Paul accepted defeat with a bad grace and took no further action either against Pole or England, during the last year of his life Pole was a sick and despondent man. Instead of relieving the political gloom of 1558 with the courage of faith, he rather contributed to it. Military defeat abroad, and hunger and disease at home contributed to a vague but powerful feeling that God had testified against the Catholic queen and the church in which she so intensely believed.[55]

Elizabeth I: the sheltered years

Ironically, the simultaneous deaths of Pole and Mary were greeted with almost equal relief in England and in Rome. In spite of her doubtful birth, Paul seems at first to have regarded Elizabeth as an improvement on her obstinate half-sister.[56] She was not tied to Spanish policy, and she was free from the insidious influence of the half-heretical cardinal. Rumours quickly spread that the French were moving heaven and earth to persuade Paul to declare her a bastard, and to pronounce in favour of the title of Mary of Scotland. He may have considered doing so, but in fact Henry II made no formal move in that direction; and when Paul did begin to change his mind about the English queen it was not on account of French prompting. There is neither need nor space here to describe the development of Elizabeth's religious policy, which has been the subject of frequent scholarly reappraisals.[57]

During the first few weeks of her reign she gave no more than a series of ambiguous hints, which worried the English Catholics but passed unnoticed in Rome. But early in February 1559 the situation began to clarify. Sir Edward Carne was recalled, thus effectively breaking off diplomatic relations with the Holy See,[58] and a Bill for the resurrection of the royal supremacy was introduced into parliament. Elizabeth's intention at this stage is uncertain, but it seems likely that she contemplated a Protestant settlement from the first, and was initially frustrated by Catholic opposition in the Lords. Despite this hitch in her plans, Paul was substantially correct when, in March 1559, he described Elizabeth as 'being revolted from his obedience and this see'. Considering his choleric temperament, the Pope's reaction to these developments seems to have been surprisingly mild – almost indifferent. He may have been imperfectly informed, and his mind was certainly on other things, but the expected storm never came.

Between February and May Elizabeth was driven further into the arms of the English Protestants by the absolute refusal of the Catholic clergy, high and low, to have anything to do with the royal supremacy. She was caught between the recalcitrance of the convocations,[59] and the great weight of lay opinion, which demanded a return to national policies and a national church. The result was a settlement which was effectively a bargain between the queen and those Protestants who still upheld the Erastian principles of Cranmer and the other Edwardian leaders. However much Elizabeth might endeavour to cloud the issue in conversation with Catholic diplomats, she had effectively reverted to the situation of 1552. She was able to do this because, like her father and brother, she was protected by the European balance of power. Philip, mindful of his exposed position in the Netherlands, needed English support, or at least neutrality. He was haunted by the fear that the French, who were already strongly entrenched in Scotland, might seize any opportunity created by a papal initiative against Elizabeth to invade England in the cause of Mary Stuart. Consequently he swallowed his mounting dislike of Elizabeth's religious policy, and set out to prevent any open rupture between England and Rome. In a series of letters to his agents in Rome during May 1559, Philip urged them to inform the Pope that the position of the heretical party in England was by no means as strong as it appeared; the great majority of the population were good Catholics; and hopes were entertained of the queen's own conversion.[60] These latter hopes, of course, were based on her marriage to a Catholic prince – hopes which Elizabeth assiduously kept alive, to the intense alarm and annoyance of her Protestant councillors. These urgent representations seem to have had the desired effect. Paul was much less hostile to Philip than he had been two years previously, and was consequently inclined to allow him to apply his own remedies to the English situation. By July the Pope was strongly incensed against Elizabeth, describing her as a heretic and a bastard, but he took no formal action against her. Instead, he urged Philip to call upon the aid of the English Catholics, and to launch his own invasion from the Netherlands. Such a drastic course formed no part of Philip's plans, but his agents in Rome could hardly say so openly, and neither party took any further steps before Paul died on 18 August.

The new Pope, Pius IV, was not elected until the end of December, and being a statesman rather than a zealot, was not inclined to resort to sanctions until all the resources of diplomacy had been exhausted. Philip was therefore spared the need to make any difficult decisions about his relations with England for a long time. He could continue to make indignant noises about Elizabeth's heresy without having to withdraw his ambassador, and gradually came to terms with the fact that she was not going to marry a Catholic prince. But Pius, although cautious, was not neglectful of his responsibilities, and decided early in 1560 to send a mission to England in the hope of reopening direct communications. In one sense the moment was opportune, since Elizabeth was becoming increasingly involved in the revolt of the Scottish Lords of the Congregation, and her relations with France were correspondingly strained. She heard the news of the proposed mission with ill-concealed alarm, and the English council stepped up its activities against religious nonconformists. Although ostensibly conceived in a friendly and conciliatory spirit, the Pope's action was a calculated threat, and this was emphasised by the choice of Parpaglia, titular Abbot of San Saluto, to lead the mission. As an ex-member of Pole's household, Parpaglia was obnoxious to Elizabeth, and as a French sympathiser unacceptable to Philip. It was largely for this latter reason that the mission came to nothing. Philip's diplomacy first managed to get Parpaglia stopped, and then recalled, without Elizabeth having been forced to refuse him admission. English successes in Scotland culminating in the Treaty of Edinburgh in July 1560, and the steady weakening of French influence under the pressure of mounting domestic tension also contributed to this outcome.

These early years were critical for the stability of Elizabeth's new religious settlement. It was extremely important to her that the fragile alliance between Protestant nationalists like Cecil and Knollys, and conservative Erastians such as Arundel and Shrewsbury should hold together. This harmony was threatened alike by zealous puritans and by conscientious papalists. At first the former seemed to her to present the greater threat, since their enthusiasm for the destruction of traditional worship endangered that general acquiescence upon which the regime depended. Hence the apparent paradox of a Protestant queen curbing the puritans, while turning a blind eye to the continuance of Catholic practices.[61] Clandestine masses were neither here nor there, unless they became linked to a revival of papalism – in which case the queen's tolerance abruptly disappeared. From Elizabeth's point of view one of the principal dangers of missions such as that of Parpaglia was that they might provide just that element of leadership and inspiration which Catholic opposition in England had so far conspicuously lacked. Consequently the Pope's decision, towards the end of 1560, to reconvene the Council of Trent spelled a new threat to the fragile English church. Although Philip again attempted to dissuade him, Pius was determined to try a second time to get a nuncio into England, and an invitation to send emissaries to the council provided an ideal pretext. This time the man chosen was the unexceptionable protonotary, Martinengo. Martinengo arrived in the Low Countries in April 1561, bearing letters of friendly greeting to the English queen, in which the schism and heresy of her realm were blandly ignored. Pius' hope, clearly derived from misinformation about the English situation, seems to have been to detach the queen from her heretical advisers, and to persuade her by offers of friendship and support to revert to the policies and personnel of her sister's reign. Although he was thoroughly sceptical about this approach, Philip reluctantly supported it through his ambassador in London, De Quadra. Support of a kind also came from an unexpected quarter. Lord Robert Dudley, the queen's favourite, seeing his hopes of matrimony diminishing, was prepared to add his voice to De Quadra's in return for the latter's support of his pretensions to the Crown matrimonial.[62]

This unlikely diplomatic combination turned out to be no match for Cecil and his allies. About the middle of April De Quadra was hopeful of securing the necessary safe conduct for Martinengo, but by the end of the month his expectations had been completely dashed by a series of apparently fortuitous events.[63] A priest by the name of Coxe was arrested at Gravesend, and an investigation of his baggage produced evidence of very widespread evasion and defiance of the Acts of Supremacy and Uniformity; the trail led to several survivors of Mary's Privy Council, and several ex-bishops. Rumours of the appearance of a miraculous cross in Glamorganshire sparked off another investigation, and fresh evidence of extensive Catholic sympathies. A Jesuit named David Wolf turned up most opportunely in Ireland, in the middle of

Shane O'Neill's rebellious preparations. Full publicity was given to all these discoveries, and Protestant opinion became thoroughly alarmed. The queen herself took fright at such appearances of Catholic conspiracy, and on 1 May the Privy Council unanimously agreed to refuse Martinengo admittance. If there had ever been any possibility that Elizabeth would voluntarily reverse her religious policy, it vanished with this decision, and the Pope was left to digest the rebuff as best he could.

Pius made no further attempt at direct communication with England, and although hope of the queen's conversion still lingered in some quarters, it ceased to be a major political factor. For the remainder of his pontificate, until 1565, he sought ways and means to apply effective sanctions against Elizabeth and to ameliorate the position of the English Catholics. Pius was wise enough to realise that a sentence of excommunication and deposition would be futile without the willing support of the Catholic powers, and might serve only to stimulate the English government to the kind of fierce persecution from which it had hitherto refrained. Twice did the Pope contemplate such action, in 1561 and 1563, and both times drew back in the face of Spanish opposition and French weakness. Nor did his efforts on behalf of the English Catholics enjoy much more success. A petition from them, forwarded by De Quadra in 1562, sought guidance on the question of occasional conformity. To have permitted such a practice would have been to encourage that drift into Anglicanism which was already very marked, and which was a prime object of Elizabeth's gentle policy. On the other hand to prohibit it entirely would have meant forcing all substantial Catholics to make a specific choice between their religion and their worldly prospects. Pius dealt with the petition obliquely by referring it to the Inquisition as a hypothetical case. The Inquisition, as might be expected, issued a flat prohibition, which was subsequently transmitted to De Quadra, but not as a papal sentence. At the same time De Quadra himself was authorised to make good the lack of Apostolic authority in England by delegating to suitable priests those powers of absolution normally reserved to the hierarchy. These devices satisfied nobody, increasing the burden on Catholic consciences without providing any real leadership or pastoral care. However, in 1563 the first of a long series of patched-up religious compromises in France seemed to offer a hopeful precedent for England, and a new approach to Elizabeth was decided upon. This was to come, not from the Pope but from the emperor and Philip in the form of a suggestion that English Catholics might be accorded a recognised minority status similar to that accorded to the French Protestants. In the event it was Ferdinand alone who wrote, in September 1563, and his request was categorically rejected. Pius did not entirely give up at this point, but subsequent efforts were no more than hopeful intrigues of little significance. Coercion was politically impossible, so persuasion only remained, unless the papacy was to neglect its duty and abandon the English church altogether. The vitality of English Catholicism was at a low ebb by 1565, in spite of the prevailing preference for traditional religious practices. In addition to the 300 or so Marian priests who had refused the oath of supremacy and been deprived, numerous clergy continued to celebrate the old rites when opportunities presented themselves, but this kind of 'survivalism' hardly offered a dynamic alternative to the established church.[64] On the other hand a small number of dedicated academic exiles had settled in the Low

Countries and turned themselves into effective and voluminous propagandists.[65] It was these men who first became convinced that the Catholic church in England was simply dying of inanition, and that the natural instinct to avoid persecution lay at the root of the trouble. They were ready to urge militant action of all kinds, and some were also ready to take part in such action at the risk of their lives. In the new Pope, Pius V, elected in January 1566, they found a man willing to listen, and respond, to their urgings. Consequently the period of his pontificate, from 1566 to 1572, transformed relations between England and the papacy for the remainder of the century. Pius V was a zealot with nothing of the politician in his make-up, and Elizabeth found herself faced for the first time by a Pope who had already decided that her conservative sympathies were humbug, and that her removal by any available means was essential to the spiritual welfare of her subjects.

'Regnans in Excelsis', the years of total conflict

Even Pius was not so optimistic as to suppose, however, that God would act in England without substantial human agents. Should Elizabeth be either killed or deposed, Mary Stuart would almost inevitably succeed her, and at first the Pope was by no means convinced that this would be an improvement. Mary had scandalised the Curia by her behaviour in Scotland, and in 1566 would not have been acceptable to either Pius or Philip as Queen of England. Two years later this situation was dramatically changed by her flight to England, and imprisonment there. The loss of her Scottish throne, and effectively of her Scottish husband, made her a much more promising instrument for Spanish policy, at a time when Anglo-Spanish relations had been strained almost to breaking point by Elizabeth's confiscation of a large supply of bullion on its way to pay the Spanish forces in the Netherlands.[66] Also, by the beginning of 1569 Mary had made her peace with the papacy, and was already beginning to acquire something of the aura of a Catholic martyr. More important still, there was strong feeling among the conservative aristocracy in England against Cecil and his allies on the council, who were thought to be endangering the country by reckless Protestant policies. Consequently two separate but overlapping conspiracies developed during 1568 and 1569. The greater was designed to overthrow Cecil, to secure Mary's recognition as Elizabeth's heir, and to marry her to the Duke of Norfolk. The lesser (in terms of support) intended to depose Elizabeth and to place Mary on her throne, hopefully with Spanish and papal backing. The religious aspect of the former was conservative, but probably looked no further than a modification of the 1559 settlement; the latter was explicitly Catholic and ultramontane. It is difficult for the historian to distinguish between these two movements of opposition, and many contemporaries found it impossible, but the distinction was nevertheless of critical importance.[67] The great majority of those who were sympathetic to the first conspiracy were loyal to Elizabeth and would not have contemplated armed resistance under any circumstances. Those who were sympathetic to the second were quite prepared to fight, but were few and ill-equipped.

Thus it happened that the rebellion which actually occurred in 1569 was more the result of muddle and panic than of deliberate intention. The Earls of Northumberland and Westmorland were discontented conservatives who allowed themselves to be manoeuvred into open treason by followers and kinsmen who were more resolute and clear-sighted. Having set out to make a massive conservative demonstration on the lines of the Pilgrimage of Grace, they ended up controlling a small part of north-east England, and appealing to the Pope and the Duke of Alva for immediate aid.[68] When this appeal reached Rome, Pius was understandably convinced that the long-expected moment of truth had come. An agent of his own, one Nicholas Morton, had reported willingness to respond to a suitable papal initiative. Nicholas Sander, one of the most energetic of the English exiles, had also convinced him that many Englishmen would rise against Elizabeth if they could be reassured that they were not committing mortal sin in doing so. Consequently he replied almost immediately to the rebels' plea, assuring them of his moral and financial support. A few days later he signed the bull 'Regnans in Excelsis', excommunicating Elizabeth, and releasing her subjects from their allegiance. In spite of the exemplary speed of his reaction, Pius was too late. The earls' letter had taken from 7 November to 16 February to reach him; Alva had done nothing, and by the time the bull of deposition was issued, the rebellion had long since collapsed. Philip, although much less sympathetic to Elizabeth than he had been ten years before, was indignant at what he considered to be the Pope's precipitate and irresponsible action; and the English Catholics were impaled on the horns of a cruel dilemma.

'Regnans in Excelsis' was a declaration of war. For the first time men and women were required to choose between their religion and their allegiance, and the mass became a symbol of treason. There was no longer any room for Henrician doctrine. Had the papacy taken this unequivocal stand in 1559, Elizabeth might well have been forced to submit, but in ten years she had established herself securely, and Catholic loyalties had become confused and eroded. Nevertheless, the bull was not without positive results. It reaffirmed the Pope's leadership of the English Catholics, and helped to stop the slide into conformity. In other words it laid the foundations for that tough and resilient recusancy which was to be English Catholicism for the next 250 years. But the result would not have been achieved had it not been for the less dramatic but more constructive work of the English exiles, particularly the foundation of the English college at Douai by William Allen in 1568. Douai was specifically designed to train young Englishmen for the priesthood in order that they should return as missionaries to their native land. The training was long and rigorous, so that it was not until 1573 that the first students were ordained, and 1574 when the first missionary priests returned to England. By that time their task was a great deal more dangerous than Allen had originally intended. They were treated not merely as religious dissidents but as the spies and emissaries of a hostile foreign power. Labouring under the greatest difficulties, they achieved considerable success; not so much in the conversion of Protestants as in the strengthening of those who had never given up their loyalty to the old faith. Under the twin pressure of persecution and missionary evangelism the religious conservatives split. The majority conformed to the established church, while the remainder became increasingly resolute and identifiable recusants. Aided by the Douai priests, and later by Jesuit missionaries, Pius had succeeded in preserving a remnant of the English church in full communion with Rome; but in both human and political terms the price was extremly high.[69]

That price was paid mainly by the missionary priests themselves, many of whom suffered torture and death after the execution of the first seminarian, Cuthbert Mayne, in 1576.[70] To a lesser extent it was paid by the English Catholic laity, who suffered fines, imprisonment, civil disabilities, and imputations of treason which most of them were desperately anxious to refute. It was also paid in a different way by the papacy, which became to Protestant Englishmen not merely a symbol of cruelty and oppression (which it had been before), but of diabolical pride and hypocrisy. Pius V and the Popes who followed him, Gregory XIII (1572–85) and Sixtus V (1585–90) considered it their manifest duty to regain England for the Catholic church, and saw no contradiction in the simultaneous use of spiritual and political weapons. Gregory, for instance, founded the English college in Rome, launched the Jesuit mission, and in 1580 issued an 'explanation' of 'Regnans in Excelsis' which mitigated some of its starkness.[71] But at the same time he was repeatedly and deliberately involved in plots against Elizabeth's life, and in attempts to stimulate invasion, or rebellion in Ireland. In 1579 James FitzGerald was sent with his blessing to stir up his kinsfolk in Munster, and in the following year was joined by a force of 1500 Spanish troops under the papal banner. Under these circumstances it is not surprising that the English government treated priests as fifth columnists; yet their disavowals of political intentions were undoubtedly sincere. 'My charge', declared Edmund Campion in 1580, 'is . . . to preach the Gospel . . . (and) to cry alarm spiritual against proud vice and foul ignorance . . . I never had mind, and am strictly forbidden by our fathers that sent me, to deal in any respect with matters of state or policy of the realm, as things which appertain not to my calling.'[72] The tragedy of the English mission is contained in this contradiction. To the modern mind it must seem that both sides were as confused in their values as they were vehement in their protestations. When Sir William Cecil claimed, in his *Execution of Justice*,[73] that papists were not being punished for their religion but for treason, William Allen was quite correct to point out that since Catholicism was being treated as treason *per se*, this statement was meaningless.[74] At the same time Allen's own avowals of pure religious motivation accorded ill with his known advocacy of military attack on England, and with the letters which he wrote to Philip of Spain urging such a course upon him. As long as Catholics believed that the Pope had the power to depose an heretical sovereign, then their acceptance of papal authority made them potential traitors. It was to demonstrate this point rather than to provide evidence of actual treason that the so called 'Bloody questions' were put to captured priests, and the propaganda value of the answers was considerable. In fact only a handful of Catholics within England, either clergy or laity, were involved in political intrigues, but many of the exiles were deeply committed, and the English government was fully justified in taking the threat which they represented seriously.

The climax of these dangers came in the 1580s. In December 1580 the Cardinal Secretary of State privately but unequivocally sanctioned Elizabeth's murder: 'whoever removes her from this life', he wrote, 'with the due end of

God's service, not only would not sin, but would even be doing a meritorious deed . . .'.[75] The assassination of William of Orange in 1584 proved how immediate this peril was, and in 1586 the discovery of Babington's plot fulfilled Englishmen's worst suspicions. A number of young men from Catholic gentry families were involved, and the conspiracy not only cost Mary Stuart her life, but struck a very heavy blow against Catholic evangelism in England. 'That wicked and ill-fated conspiracy', wrote the Jesuit Robert Southwell in December 1586, '. . . did to the catholic cause so great mischief that even our enemies, had they the choice, could never have chosen ought more mischievous to us . . .'.[76] By the time this happened England was openly at war with Spain, Philip's deep reluctance having been gradually overcome by a mixture of English provocation and religious conviction. The old association between the papacy and Spain in English minds, forged in the reign of Mary, had been refurbished and was by this time stronger than ever.[77] For the first time since Henry VIII's excommunication over fifty years earlier, a Catholic power was ready and willing to impose the sanctions of the church upon an English monarch. William Allen and his fellow exiles were delighted: 'I think there can be very few indeed', Allen wrote to Philip in 1587, 'who love their country and religion who do not from their hearts desire to be once more subject to your most clement rule.'[78] If this letter was sincere, it was a measure of the immense distance which separated the militant exiles from their co-religionists in England, most of whom regarded the prospect of a Spanish invasion with almost as much fear and horror as did their Protestant fellow countrymen. The new Pope, Sixtus V, although not as enthusiastic as might have been expected and suspicious of Philip's motives, could hardly fail to lend public support to the enterprise. He made William Allen a cardinal and agreed to contribute a million ducats to the cost of the campaign. He did not, however, pronounce any additional sentence against Elizabeth and the 'Declaration' which appeared renewing her excommunication and explaining the pious intentions of the King of Spain bore Allen's name alone.[79]

Clement VIII: diplomatic stalemate and Catholic divisions

The complete failure of Philip's Armada left Allen in a very exposed position, and paved the way for those deep and bitter divisions which were to afflict the English Catholics over the next decade. It was not clear for several years that the Spanish danger had really been averted, and there was little improvement in the lot of the recusants. Nevertheless a sharp and explicit reaction took place against the views that Allen had expressed, both in his 'Declaration' and in his unpublished 'Admonition to the Nobility and People of England'. A number of Catholic works appeared, including Robert Southwell's *Humble Supplication to Her Majesty*, which expressed the warmest loyalty to Elizabeth in temporal matters, and rejected all association with Spain. It was, perhaps, fortunate that the English cardinal, who was the official ruler as well as the natural leader of the English mission, died in 1594. Thereafter the leadership of what might be called 'political' Catholicism devolved upon the Jesuit Robert Parsons, who was a less authoritative and prestigious figure. This, combined with the fact that the

English province was without any canonically appointed head for four years, enabled a little progress to be made towards a *modus vivendi* between the Catholics and the government. At the same time both the papacy and the English Crown began to move cautiously away from the entrenched positions which had been taken up over twenty years before. In 1589 Sir Christopher Hatton had made a passionate attack on the Pope in parliament, and as late as 1593 the council was still sponsoring strong anti-Catholic legislation; but by 1601 the government was quietly facilitating negotiations between English Catholics and the Curia. Similarly Clement VIII (1592–1605) was not a crusader in the mould of Pius V or Gregory XIII. He was prepared to consider reopening relations with the heretical queen, and saw no reason why he should be intractable for the sake of implementing Spanish policy.

The thirteen years of his pontificate saw a number of important changes in the situation of the English Catholics. Until Allen's elevation to the cardinalate the Catholic church in England had had neither structure nor discipline: '. . . no man subject to his fellows, no way to call disorders to accompt, no common conference, no sovereignty nor subjection; but every one lying severally and secretly by himself . . .', as Allen himself had written.[80] During the seven years between his elevation and his death, the cardinal had not been able to do much to remedy this situation, and the 'Cardinal Protectors of England' remained shadowy figures whose main function was to see that judicial proceedings involving Englishmen were brought to the attention of the correct officials in Rome. Consequently disciplinary problems were endemic, and were aggravated both by political activism and by the fact that the Jesuit missionaries were subject to no authority save that of their own superiors. The story of the 'Wisbech stirs' is too familiar to need repetition, but it was to be particularly unfortunate that the quarrel between the Jesuits and the secular priests should have become linked to political disagreements through the activities of Parsons. In 1595 the latter was instrumental in producing *A Conference about the next succession to the Crown of England*, which proposed a religious 'test' and argued strongly in favour of the claim of the Spanish Infanta. This document was in every sense provocative, and the storm which it aroused did more than anything else to bring the divisions among the Catholics to the attention of the rest of the country. Even this scandal, which seriously weakened the church in the face of continued pressure from the English government, failed to arouse the Pope to action. Both Parsons and his secular enemies put forward plans for a new ecclesiastical organisation in 1597, but neither was adopted. Finally, in March 1598 the Cardinal Protector issued a brief setting up an Archpriest with limited authority over secular priests working in England and Scotland, but no jurisdiction over either the laity or the Jesuits.[81] This scheme itself was both clumsy and insufficient, since it made no provision for episcopal functions, and the appointment of George Blackwell as the first Archpriest ensured disaster. Blackwell, although a secular, was strongly sympathetic to the Jesuits: 'All catholics must hereafter depend upon Blackwell', wrote one of the anti-Jesuit faction, 'and he upon Garnet (the Jesuit superior), and Garnet upon Parsons, and Parsons upon the Devil who is the author of all rebellions, treasons, murders, disobedience and all such designments as this wicked Jesuit hath hitherto designed against her majesty, her crown, her safety and her life.'[82] The

Archpriest's abrasive personality quickly stimulated his opponents to action, and before the end of 1598 two representative secular priests had been dispatched to Rome to petition the Pope for a canonically elected bishop to rule the English province. They also sought to obtain an inhibition against the political propaganda of Parsons and other Jesuits, which they represented as doing untold harm to the Catholic cause. They represented a substantial and responsible body of English clerical opinion, but they were no match for Parsons' international influence.

As soon as he was aware of their mission, Garnet wrote direct to the Pope, alleging that Blackwell's opponents in England were merely a handful of troublesome malcontents who should not be accorded a hearing. Consequently when they reached Rome at the end of 1598, the two emissaries were arrested, subjected to a form of trial and expelled from the city without being given any chance to discharge their mission. In April 1599 Blackwell's position and authority were confirmed by papal letter. Although the inexplicable injustice of Clement's action caused much indignation in England, there could be no question of defying his explicit command, and the quarrel might well have retreated again beneath the surface of public life. It did not do so because Blackwell, not content with receiving his opponents' submissions, demanded that they should acknowledge themselves to have been guilty of schism in their original defiance. In this he was supported by Garnet and other Jesuits, who published a justification of his attitude.[83] In January 1600 Blackwell forbade his opponents to reply to this work under threat of ecclesiastical penalties, and in October suspended two of his leading critics from their priestly functions. Such high-handed action invited a renewal of conflict, and within a month a petition against Blackwell's misgovernment was dispatched to the Pope bearing the signatures of thirty-three secular priests. So bitter were some of the Archpriest's enemies that they entered into secret negotiations with the English government. There had been isolated instances before of Catholics who had denounced their co-religionists for lending themselves to treasonable conspiracy, but this was a more deliberate and more constructive approach. The details of the discussions are not known, but probably the 'appellants', as they were soon to be called, agreed to work for the recall of the Jesuits from England, and perhaps the reopening of direct relations between England and Rome. In return they were certainly provided with money and other material assistance in forwarding their petition.[84]

This time, for a variety of reasons, their protest fared better. Clement responded to the petition of November 1600 by rebuking Blackwell, ordering him to withdraw his accusations of schism, and imposing silence on both sides. The appellant representatives were then received in Rome, and prolonged negotiations ensued, lasting from February to July 1602. Although they had compromised themselves by their relations with an heretical government, the appellants were strongly supported by French diplomatic influence. The Jesuits had committed themselves to a Spanish candidate for the English succession, and Henry IV naturally regarded such a prospect with deep disfavour. The outcome, a Holy Office decree of 20 July 1602, was not really a victory for either side. Blackwell was placed under the direct supervision of the Pope and the Cardinal Protector of England, and was explicitly forbidden to consult with the

Jesuits.[85] On the other hand he was continued in his existing office, and the appellants were sharply called to heel for 'dealings and communications with heretics to the prejudice of catholics'. In spite of some persuasive pleading, Clement had decided not to countenance negotiations with Elizabeth, and the possibility of reaching some *modus vivendi* on the basis of a limited toleration did not materialise. However, the situation did not remain altogether unchanged. An important royal proclamation of November 1602, while reaffirming in unequivocal words the policy of a single established religion, and making conventionally hostile noises against the Pope, nevertheless recognised that Catholics could, in a sense, be loyal subjects.[86] The laws against the Jesuits and their adherents were to be strictly enforced, but other priests (equally in danger of the law) were to be allowed two months to leave the realm. Moreover any who explicitly acknowledged the queen's temporal authority were to be given some special but unspecified immunity. No doubt the government hoped to split the Catholic clergy along the line of the existing dispute, but the outcome was rather less dramatic. In January 1603 thirteen secular priests signed a declaration of temporal allegiance to Elizabeth, acknowledging themselves bound to obey her civil laws, as being 'so grounded upon the word of God, as that no authority, no cause . . . can or ought . . . to be a sufficient warrant, more unto us than to any protestant, to disobey her majesty in any civil or temporal matter'.[87] This repudiation of the papal deposing power represented the *de facto* attitude taken by the Catholic laity for years, but it commanded the assent of only a handful of the 400 or so priests working in England. Weakened as they were by divisions, they saw this declaration as a mere device to divide them further and to cut them off from the papacy. The government, understandably, regarded their refusal to adhere as evidence of continued attachment to the deposing power. Had the queen not been visibly declining to her end the consequences might have been serious, both for those who signed the declaration and for those who refused. But in fact Clement took no action against the dissidents, and Elizabeth's death created new possibilities for a political and religious *rapprochement*.

In one sense the peaceful accession of the Protestant James was a death blow to Catholic hopes. The major Catholic powers, particularly Spain, finally concluded that English Catholicism was a broken reed for their political purposes, and lost all interest in forcible conversion. The Anglo-Spanish peace of 1604 was partly a reflection of this change of attitude. So, too, was the Gunpowder Plot, which probably represented a last despairing flicker of that political activism which had been expressed in theory by Allen and Parsons and in practice by Babington and Norton. In another sense, however, the new king could be looked to with hope and expectation. His queen, Anne of Denmark, was a Catholic convert, albeit of a rather feeble and ambiguous kind;[88] and he had given some assurances to his future Catholic subjects in the process of building up support in England. Clement seems to have entertained hopes of James' own conversion, and communicated with him through Sir James Lindsay, a Scottish Catholic exile. The king's response was courteous, but verbal and non-committal. In the summer of 1603, after his accession, the Pope tried again, this time through the agency of Sir Anthony Standen who was in Italy on a diplomatic errand from James to the Doge.[89] His intention was to use Standen to carry private letters and devotional objects to the queen, in the hope that her response might lead to an exchange of courtesies which would develop into a formal relationship. However, by the time Standen reached England again the irresponsible activities of the disillusioned appellant William Watson had revived fears of popish conspiracy. Standen's 'innocent plot' was detected and he was imprisoned in the Tower. James' position at this stage seems to have been that he was willing to extend considerable relief to the Catholic laity, including the remission of recusancy fines, but was determined to keep up his predecessor's pressure on the clergy. This illogical attitude may have originated in a misunderstanding of the declaration of January 1603. The signatories never had any intention of abandoning their priestly vocation, but the king may not have understood this, concentrating too exclusively upon their protestations of allegiance.[90] Mutual misunderstanding led to mutual disillusionment, and Watson's conspiracy convinced him that all priests were tarred with the same brush. Nevertheless the Pope's tentative overtures had given James some hope that Clement might prove an ally in resolving the problems of double allegiance. Towards the end of 1603 he had therefore dropped a hint to the papal nuncio in Paris that a willingness on Clement's part to excommunicate those clergy who sought to use their priestly functions for political purposes would help him to take a more lenient view of the Catholic church in England. The nuncio, Del Bufalo, forwarded this suggestion with some enthusiasm, but it met with a chilly response and the first year of the new reign ended without any significant progress towards a resumption of relations. Nevertheless the slight thaw discernible before Elizabeth's death had continued, and was accompanied by a gradual but marked change in the attitude of many of the leading clergy. The seventeenth century was to see many fluctuations before the papacy finally gave up trying to put political pressure on the English Crown, but there was to be no return to 'Regnans in Excelsis' – or to the restoration of Catholic allegiance.

Notes

1. G. de C. Parmiter, The King's Great Matter, London, 1967; M.A. Kelly, The Matrimonial Trials of Henry VIII, Stanford, California, 1976; [G. Bedouelle and P. Le Gal, Le 'Divorce' du roi Henry VIII, Geneva, 1987; Virginia Murphy and Edward Surtz, SJ, The Divorce Tracts of Henry VIII, Angers 1988;] C. De Frede, La Restaurazione Cattolica in Inghilterra Catholic sotto Maria Tudor, Naples, 1971; [G.R. Redworth, In Defence of the Church Catholic; a Life of Stephen Gardiner, Oxford, 1990] P. McGrath, Papists and Puritans under Elizabeth I, London, 1967.
2. L. Hicks, 'The Embassy of Sir Anthony Standen in 1603', Recusant History, VII, 1963, 50–81; J.P. Crehan, 'The return to Obedience: New Judgement on Cardinal Pole', The Month, n.s., XIV, 1955, 221–9; R.H. Pogson, 'Reginald Pole and the Priorities of Government in Mary Tudor's Church', Historical Journal, XVIII, 1975, 3–20; [idem 'The Legacy of the Schism; Confusion, Continuity and Change in the Marian Clergy', in The Mid-Tudor Polity, c.1540–1560, ed. J. Loach and R. Tittler, London, 1980;] T.P. Bostock, 'English Foreign Policy; the Diplomacy of the Divorce, 1528–1534', Illinois, Ph.D., 1967; [J.P. Marmion, 'The London Synod of Cardinal Pole', Keele, M.A., 1974; V.M. Murphy, 'The Debate over Henry VIII's First Divorce; an Analysis of the Contemporary Treatises', Cambridge, Ph.D, 1984.]
3. G.R. Elton, Policy and Police, Cambridge, 1972; J.J. Scarisbrick, Henry VIII, London, 1968; J.K. McConica, English Humanists and Reformation Politics, Oxford,

1965; [J.J. Scarisbrick, *The Reformation and the English People*, Oxford, 1984; S.E. Brigden, *London and the Reformation*, Oxford, 1989.]

4. D.M. Loades, *Two Tudor Conspiracies*, Cambridge, 1965; idem, *The Oxford Martyrs*, London, 1970; idem, *The Reign of Mary Tudor*, London, 1979; [J. Loach, *Parliament and the Crown in the Reign of Mary Tudor*, Oxford, 1986.]

5. J.A. Bossy, 'The Character of Elizabethan Catholicism', *Past and Present*, XXI, 1962; C. Cross, *The Puritan Earl; Henry Hastings Third Earl of Huntingdon, 1536–1595*, London, 1966; W.R. Trimble, *The Catholic Laity in Elizabethan England*, Cambridge, Mass., 1964; [C. Haigh, 'From Monopoly to Minority, Catholicism in Early Modern England', *Transactions of the Royal Historical Society*, 5 series, XXXI, 1981, 129–47.]

6. Bossy, London, 1975; Hughes, London, 1942.

7. These statutes, designed to submit papal jurisdiction in England to royal limitation, had culminated in an Act of 1393. For a brief but pertinent comment on Henry's relations with the papacy, see S.B. Chrimes, *Henry VII*, London, 1972, pp. 240–1.

8. W.E. Wilkie, *The Cardinal Protectors of England*, Cambridge, 1974, pp. 40–52, 105–10.

9. For example: *Oratio habita ad clerum in Convocatione*, by John Colet, London, 1511. [This view has more recently been challenged; see C.Haigh, 'Anti-clericalism and the English Reformation', *History*, LXVIII, 1983, 391–407.]

10. It was not until Henry and Wolsey began to move away from a pro-imperial alliance in 1525 that there was any noticeable cooling of relations, and that seems to have been caused more by Wolsey's complicated intrigues in the Curia than by any deliberate intention. Wilkie, *Cardinal Protectors*, pp. 141–9.

11. A.F. Pollard, *Wolsey*, London, 1929.

12. By Scarisbrick, *Henry VIII*, and others. It is more likely that Wolsey's diplomacy was motivated chiefly by the desire to gratify Henry and keep England at the centre of European affairs, R.B. Wernham, *Before the Armada*, London, 1966, pp. 89–110. [See also J. Guy, *Tudor England*, Oxford, 1989.]

13. Scarisbrick, *Henry VIII*, pp. 205–24.

14. *Letters and Papers, Foreign and Domestic, of the Reign of Henry VIII*, ed. Brewer et al., London, 1862–1910, IV, no. 3802.

15. Ibid., 4167 etc. See also Stefan Ehses, *Römische Dokumente zur Geschichte der Ehescheidung Heinrichs VIII von England, 1527–1534*, Paderborn, 1893, 23ff; H.A. Kelly, *The Matrimonial Trials of Henry VIII*, Stanford, California, 1976, pp. 54–74.

16. Ehses, *Römische Dokumente*, 44 ff., 54. Quoted in Scarisbrick, *Henry VIII*, p. 213.

17. By the Roman calendar, term ended on that day, and since the court was technically a papal one Campeggio seized this opportunity to adjourn for the summer vacation.

18. For example, Durham Place, in the Strand, which remained in the king's hands although it properly belonged to the see of Durham. C. Sturge, *Cuthbert Tunstall*, London, 1938.

19. S.E. Lehmberg, *The Reformation Parliament, 1529–1536*, Cambridge, 1970, pp. 76–182.

20. Over the notorious case of Richard Hunne, the London merchant who had been found murdered in the bishop's prison, see E.J. Davis, 'The Authorities for the Case of Richard Hunne, 1514–15', *English Historical Review*, XXX, 1915, pp. 477–88; also A. Ogle, *The Tragedy of the Lollard Tower*, Oxford, 1949.

21. Scarisbrick, *Henry VIII*, pp. 241–50. [This view has subsequently been generally accepted; see also Murphy and Surtz, (eds) *Divorce Tracts*.]

22. The idea of appealing to a General Council of the church against a papal decision was not a new one, and Luther had recently done the same. The renaissance popes generally were nervous of a Council, remembering the anti-papal record of the Councils of Constance and Basle. Clement was thought to be especially apprehensive

of a Council because of irregularities in his own election – and no papal initiative in that direction was taken until after his death, in spite of pressure from all sides. H. Jedin, *Geschichte des Konzils von Trient*, I. Freiburg im Breisgau, 1949.

23. Recent research has indicated that the source of the king's views at this time was a composite document ('Collectanea satis copiosa') in process of compilation by a group of divines supporting the divorce. J.A. Guy, *The Public Career of Sir Thomas More*, London, 1980, p. 131. [See also Murphy and Surtz, *Divorce Tracts*.]

24. D. Wilkins, *Concilia Magnae Britanniae et Hiberniae*, London, 1737, III, p. 725 ff.; G.R. Elton, 'The Commons Supplication of 1532', *English Historical Review*, LXVI, 1951; J.P. Cooper, 'The Supplication against the Ordinaries Reconsidered', *English Historical Review*, LXII, 1957; M. Kelly, 'The Submission of the Clergy', *Transactions of the Royal Historical Society*, 5 series, XV, 1965, 97–119.

25. 23 Henry VIII c. 20. Lehmberg, *Reformation Parliament*, pp. 135–8.

26. G.R. Elton, *The Tudor Revolution in Government*, Cambridge, 1953; idem, 'King or Minister? The Man Behind the Henrician Reformation', *History*, XXXIX, 1954; idem, *Thomas Cromwell, Reform and Renewal*, Cambridge, 1972.

27. This was a line which had been taken as early as 1529 by the radical Simon Fish in his *A Supplication for the Beggars*; by 1534 it had been taken up by less extreme publicists, such as Robert Crowley, Christopher St German and Richard Sampson.

28. *Letters and Papers*, VIII, 805–7. Scarisbrick, *Henry VIII*, pp. 333–4.

29. For a full discussion of this abortive negotiation which involved Campeggio and his brother Marcantonio, see Wilkie, *Cardinal Protectors*, pp. 226–33.

30. A son of Margaret, Countess of Salisbury, and thus a grandson of George, Duke of Clarence, the younger brother of Edward IV. Having at first co-operated in the king's plan to obtain the opinions of the universities concerning the marriage, Pole became increasingly hostile to Henry's actions, and withdrew to Italy in 1530. There, in 1535, he wrote 'Pro Ecclesiasticae unitatis defensione', a manuscript of which he sent to the king. It was published in Rome, without his consent, in 1537.

31. In the aftermath of the so-called 'Exeter conspiracy' of 1538. His mother, his brother, Lord Montague and his cousin the Marquis of Exeter were all beheaded for treason.

32. In January 1539 Christopher Mont had been sent as envoy to the Duke of Saxony and the Landgrave of Hesse, to negotiate both for a relationship with the Schmalkaldic League and for the Cleves marriage. The marriage was completed by January 1540, and repudiated within six months. *Letters and Papers*, XIII (i) 1189; XIV (i) 103; Scarisbrick, *Henry VIII*, pp. 368–75.

33. Notably Richard Coxe and John Cheke. For a full discussion of the composition of this household and its significance, see McConica, *English Humanists*, pp. 214–34. [See also D.M. Loades, *The Tudor Court*, London, 1986, pp. 121–2.]

34. D.M. Loades, *The Oxford Martyrs*, London, 1970, pp. 55–7. Gardiner set out his arguments against the Protestant trend of ecclesiastical policy in a series of letters to Protector Somerset. J.A. Muller, *The Letters of Stephen Gardiner*, Cambridge, 1933, 316, 379, 405, etc.

35. Articles of the western rebels, no. 12, in: *A Copy of a Letter*, London, 1549, reprinted in F. Rose Troup, *The Western Rebellion of 1549* (London, 1913) pp. 485–95.

36. W.K. Jordan, *Edward VI; the Young King*, London, 1968, pp. 206–9; idem, *Edward VI; the Threshold of Power*, London, 1970, pp. 256–65, [D.M. Loades, *Mary Tudor; a Life*, Oxford, 1989.]

37. *Letters and Papers*, X, 1137.

38. *Calendar of State Paper, Spanish*, xi, 419. [*Cal. Span.*]

39. D.M. Loades, *The Reign of Mary Tudor*, London, 1979, pp. 112–14.

40. *Cal. Span.*, xi, 194.

41. *Calendar of State Papers, Venetian*, v, 398. [*Cal. Ven.*]
42. R.H. Pogson, 'Cardinal Pole, Papal Legate to England', Cambridge, Ph.D., 1972, 105–10.
43. D. Fenlon, *Heresy and Obedience in Tridentine Italy*, Cambridge, 1972, pp. 100–15.
44. *Cal. Ven.*, v, 398.
45. Ibid., 429.
46. British Museum [BM] Add. MS 25425 fols 285–6.
47. Pole opened his Legatine Register in March 1554, six months before he landed in England. C.H. Garrett, 'The Legatine Register of Cardinal Pole', *Journal of Modern History*, XIII, 1941, 189–94; Loades, *Oxford Martyrs*, pp. 113–16.
48. BM Add. MS 41577 fol. 161. Crehan, 'The Return to Obedience'.
50. Pogson, 'Cardinal Pole', 116 ff.
51. J.P. Marmion, 'The London Synod of Reginald, Cardinal Pole', Keele M.A., 1974. The decrees are printed in Wilkins, *Concilia*, IV, p. 126 ff. An expanded version of these decrees was published in Rome in 1564, under the title *Reformatio Angliae ex decretis Reginaldi Poli Cardinalis*.
52. Pogson, 'Cardinal Pole', and idem, 'Reginald Pole and the Priorities of Government in Mary Tudor's Church', *Historical Journal*, XVIII, 1975, 3–20.
53. Public Record Office [PRO] SP 69/10 f. 57.
54. Loades, *Reign of Mary*, pp. 428–39.
55. Loades, *Oxford Martyrs*, pp. 256–8. Richard Sampson to Bullinger, *Original Letters, Relative to the English Reformation*, ed. H. Robinson, I, 177, (London 1913, reprinted 1968).
56. C.G. Bayne, *Anglo-Roman Relations*, Parker Society, 1856, 10.
57. Notably by J.E. Neale, 'The Elizabethan Acts of Supremacy and Uniformity', *English Historical Review*, LXV, 1950, 304–32; and W.P. Haugaard, *Elizabeth and the English Reformation*, Cambridge, 1968. More recently N.L. Jones, has extensively and convincingly challenged certain aspects of Neal's interpretation. N.L. Jones, 'Faith by Statute', Cambridge, Ph.D., 1977. [Published in 1982, by the Royal Historical Society, with the same title]
58. In fact Carne remained in Italy, protesting that he was detained against his will, but it later transpired that he had arranged his own 'detention' in order to avoid subscribing to the changes in England. Bayne, *Anglo-Norman Relations*.
59. The Convocations which assembled in January 1559 unequivocally reasserted Catholic doctrine and the papal authority, and the depleted bench of bishops consistently opposed the royal supremacy in the House of Lords. Haugaard, *English Reformation*, pp. 87–8.
60. Bayne, *Anglo-Norman Relations*.
61. Several bishops and other reformed clergy expressed their unease in letters to Bullinger, which form one of our chief sources for the interpretation of this period. *Zurich Letters*, ed. H. Robinson, Parker Society, 1842.
62. W. MacCaffrey, *The Shaping of the Elizabethan Regime*, London, 1969, pp. 75–80.
63. It is clear that Cecil planned this stroke carefully for the purpose of frustrating the negotiations, or, as he put it 'for the rebating of the papists humours, which by the Queen's lenity grow too rank . . .'. PRO, SP12/16/55, 66–8; SP12/18/7, 8, 19.
64. Opinions differ as to the effectiveness of these Marian priests. Bossy (*English Catholic Community*) regards them as little more than an appendix to the history of the medieval church, but Haigh ('The Fall of a Church or the Rise of a Sect? Post Reformation Catholicism in England', *Historical Journal*, XXI, 1978, 181–6) argues that they represented a real element of continuity, and that their effectiveness has been much underrated.
65. Notably Thomas Stapleton, Thomas Harding, Richard Smith, William Soane and Richard White. See A.C. Southern, *Elizabethan Recusant Prose*, London, 1950; and

P. McGrath, *Papists and Puritans under Elizabethan I*, London, 1967, pp. 57–65.

66. This money still technically belonged to the Genoese bankers when the ships carrying it were driven to seek shelter in Southampton. Cecil, with the queen's approval, borrowed it for English purposes. MacCaffrey, 183–95.

67. The best recent accounts are ibid., *Elizabethan Regime*, pp. 221–46; Anthony Fletcher, *Tudor Rebellions*, London, 1968, pp. 91–106; and M.E. James, 'The Concept of Order and the Northern Rising of 1569', *Past and Present*, LX, 1973, 49–83.

68. *Cal. Span.*, 186, 217, 224. MacCaffrey, *Elizabethan Regime*, pp. 232–3.

69. This is the normally accepted view, expressed most recently and fully by Bossy, *English Catholic Community*. Haigh, both in 'The Fall of a Church?' and in a paper as yet unpublished, has argued that the missionaries did a major disservice to English Catholicism by abandoning the geographical areas where the old faith was strong, and coverting it into a 'seigneurial religion' of aristocratic households to suit their own convenience. [C. Haigh, 'From Monopoly to Minority, Catholicism in Early Modern England', *Transactions of the Royal Historical Society*, 5 series, XXXI, 1981.]

70. Richard Challoner, *Memoirs of Missionary Priests*, London, 1741–2, p. i, p. 12 ff. A.L. Rowse, *Tudor Cornwall*, London, 1941, pp. 344–54. McGrath, *Papists and Puritans*, pp. 117–18.

71. This declared that the sentence against Elizabeth 'in no way bound the catholics, things being as they are, but then only when the public execution of the said Bull can be carried out'. In other words Catholics were not necessarily bound, in all circumstances, to seek to carry the sentence into effect. A.O. Meyer, *England and the Catholic Church under Queen Elizabeth*, London, 1913, p. 246.

72. Ibid., pp. 143–4.

73. *The Execution of Justice in England*, by William Cecil, London, 1584; a propaganda work intended to justify the severe measures which the government was then taking against Catholics.

74. *A True, Sincere and Modest Defence of English Catholics*, by William Allen (probably Rouen), 1584.

75. P. Hughes, *Rome and the Counter Reformation in England*, London, 1942, p. 214.

76. J.H. Pollen, *English Martyrs, 1584–1603*, Catholic Record Society, 1908, V, p. 314.

77. W.S. Maltby, *The Black Legend in England*, Duke University Press, Durham, North Carolina, 1971.

78. *Letters and Memorials of Cardinal Allen*, ed. T.F. Knox, London, 1882, p. 272 ff. McGrath, *Papists and Puritans*, p. 200.

79. This 'Declaration' was printed by M.A. Tierney, *Dodd's Church History of England*, London, 1839–42, III, Appendix XII.

80. *Letters and Memorials of Cardinal Allen*, p. 378. McGrath, *Papists and Puritans*, p. 276.

81. The brief is printed in *Dodd's Church History*, III, p. cxix ff. See also J.H. Pollen, *The Institution of the Archpriest Blackwell*, London, 1916.

82. William Watson, *A sparing discoverie of our English Iesuits and of Fa. Parsons proceedings under pretence of promoting the Catholick faith in England*, 1601. Quoted in McGrath, *Papists and Puritans*, p. 286.

83. Thomas Lister, *Adversus factiosos in ecclesia*, (unknown) 1599.

84. Meyer, *England and the Catholic Church*, p. 246; McGrath, *Papists and Puritans*, p. 291. The agent was Richard Bancroft, Bishop of London.

85. Meyer, *England and the Catholic Church*, p. 446; McGrath, *Papists and Puritans*, p. 293. See also T.G. Law, *The Archpriest Controversy*, Camden Society, 1808, II; A Historical Sketch, Introduction, p. 7.

86. P.L. Hughes and J.F. Larkin, *Tudor Royal Proclamations*, III, New Haven, Conn.,

and London, 1969, pp. 250–5.

87. *Dodd's Church History*, III, p. clxxxviiiff. Meyer, *England and the Catholic Church*, p. 456 ff.

88. There is no doubt about her conversion, but her persistence in the faith is still a matter of some doubt. A.W. Ward, 'James VI and the Papacy', *Scottish Historical Review*, II, 1905, 249–52; A.O. Meyer, *Clemens VIII und Jacob I von England*, Rome, 1904; G. Albion, *Charles I and the Court of Rome*, London, 1935, p. 194.

89. L. Hicks, 'The Embassy of Sir Anthony Standen in 1603', *Recusant History*, VII, 1963, 50–81.

90. J.A. Bossy, 'The English Catholic Community, 1603–1625', in *The Reign of James VI and I*, ed. A.G.R. Smith, London, 1973, pp. 93–4.

Part II: Censorship

7 The Authorship and Publication of *The copye of a letter sent by John Bradforth to the Right Honorable Lordes the Erles of Arundel, Darbie, Shrewsbury and Penbroke*

Among the large number of polemical tracts produced in Mary's reign, this *Letter* is remarkable in that it is an attack on the queen's policies from a Catholic rather than a Protestant point of view. Unlike most similar works of the period, therefore, it is a political rather than a religious pamphlet. First the proposal, and then the fact, of Mary's marriage to Philip of Spain divided and weakened that wave of loyalty which had carried her to the throne in the summer of 1553. The hostility of the Protestants to the match needs neither explanation nor emphasis. It found violent expression at the time, and has left many memorials behind it. Many who were not Protestants, however, disapproved with almost equal violence, and their viewpoint has left far fewer traces. Perhaps this is because they were largely humble people, who are inarticulate in all ages; and perhaps also because they did not command the facilities of either the officially sanctioned press or the well-organised Protestant channels. As an expression of the Catholic anti-Spanish sentiment, this *Letter* is, therefore, both rare and interesting.

In form it is an open letter to the four Lords of the Council named, urging them not to co-operate in any scheme for the coronation of Philip as king of England. This coronation was an event greatly desired both by the queen and by the Spaniards, and opposed by Englishmen of all ranks, even those who were prepared to acquiesce in the marriage. Not only was it looked upon as a symbol of foreign domination, but it carried a real threat of continued Spanish rule in the event of the queen's death. In her anxiety to create a party in her husband's interest, Mary privately canvassed a number of leading noblemen in May 1556, attempting to win their individual consents to the coronation. Derby, Shrewsbury and Pembroke were certainly among those approached, and Arundel may have been. News of this activity soon leaked out, and the rumour rapidly spread that Pembroke was going 'to fetche the crowne from the Erle of Shrewsbury to crowne the Kyng withal'.[1] It is reasonable to assume that these rumours, which were current for most of the summer, inspired the writing of this *Letter*. Otherwise it would be hard to see why an exhortation of this kind should have been addressed to these particular men.

The date, 1555, which is tentatively ascribed to it by the *Short Title Catalogue* is based on the mistaken assumption that the author was the same man as John Bradford, the Protestant divine, who was burned at Smithfield on 30 June in that year. [An error corrected in the revised edition of 1986.] The Bradford of the *Letter* was a very different person. At one point he says of himself: 'for the space of ii or iii yeres my frendes put me to lerne their (i.e. the Spaniards') language, and compelled mee to be amongst them . . .', and again later in the text 'I served in King Edwards time the right worshipfull and my good master Sir William Skipwithe, in Lincolnshire'. These details of autobiography, which could certainly not be applied to the Prebendary of St Paul's, identify him with that John Bradford of Nantwich in Cheshire who was insinuated as a spy into the household of the Duke of Medina Celi between 1554 and 1556. He was involved in the Dudley conspiracy,[2] which was broken up in February and March 1555–6, and was finally executed at Tyburn for taking part with Thomas Stafford in his ill-fated raid on Scarborough in 1557.[3]

Bradford, although described as a gentleman, seems to have been little more than a servant, and justly confessed himself to have been 'without all knowledge and learning'. The main theme of his *Letter* is the sexual irregularity of the Spaniards in general and the king in particular, and the whole work is written in a tone of bitter scurrility. There would be nothing remarkable in this, coming from a Protestant pen; but Bradford is almost as bitter against 'heretiks' as against Spaniards. In his preface he justifies his book by claiming that previous attacks upon the Spaniards are vitiated because written 'by the develishe device of certayne heretickes, thinking thereby to grounde in the hartes of all people . . . many abominable heresies . . .', and he goes on to say that he will 'write nothing to disturb the true and most godly state of oure religion, which the Queenes Majestie moste graciously setteth oute at thys present, and wherein god hath preserved me . . .'. Christina Garrett, in her notice of Bradford published in *The Marian Exiles*,[4] assumed that such remarks were a conscious disguise adopted by the Protestant author to give his work greater currency. While it is not possible to prove conclusively that this was not so, further evidence makes it appear improbable. Christina Garrett noted that the version of the *Letter* in Strype (*Ecclesiastical Memorials*, III, No. xlv) differed considerably from the only known contemporary edition in the British Museum (C.8. b.8), but was undecided whether Strype had transcribed from a different edition, or modified it to suit his own taste. It now seems certain that another version did exist.

In the course of its strenuous battle against hostile pamphleteers, the council examined a number of men in early March 1556–7.[5] One of these, Gilbert Gennyns of Ware, confessed to having written a 'lewde seditious booke', which he claimed to have received from another, Anthony Burton. Burton was also accused of writing a second book in association with one John Capstocke; and a fourth man, Thomas Penny, described as a servant of Sir Walter Mildmay, was charged with a similar offence. This was clearly one of those groups of associates engaged in the production and circulation of seditious literature, who appear in the council records from time to time. Burton was a Cambridge man, who was to graduate B.D. in 1562, and Penny can perhaps be identified with that Thomas Penny of Trinity who held a succession of offices in the College from 1559 to 1565,[6] and was deprived of a prebend in St Paul's for Puritan activities in 1570. The existence of such groups in Marian London is a well-known fact, but little is yet known about their composition and activities. This particular group was sent to Newgate, and its examinations forwarded, together with the offending works, to the Mayor and Recorder of London on 9 March. It was an offence at common law, under the Statute of 1 and 2 Philip and Mary, cap. 3, to 'devise write print or set forth any manner of Book Rime Ballad Letter of Writing conteining any false matter clause or Sentence of Sclander Reproche, or Dishonor of the King and Queens Majesties or of either of them . . .', but despite a hastener from the council on 7 August, only one member of the group seems to have been indicted. The remainder were bound under recognisances of £40 and £100 to keep the peace and be forthcoming when commanded. Unfortunately only one side of the correspondence relative to these men can now be traced, as there is no record in the Letter Books or Repertories of the City.

The man indicted was John Capstocke, 'yeoman alias servingman', and he did not suffer for his indiscretion as he received the royal pardon on 5 December 1557.[7] In the record of his pardon it is stated that he was indicted for that '. . . on 27th December 3 & 4 Philip and Mary, in the Parish of St Peter le Poore, London, (he) wrote a malicious false and scandalous book entitled "The copie of John Brodfords letter to the Queene and to the lordes and estates of the realme of England . . ." '. This was clearly the 'lewde seditious booke' for which he and Burton had been committed in March, but the wording of the record presents some difficulties. The title is not the same as that of the British Museum text, which specifically mentions the four earls. If Capstocke was the publisher, why is there no mention of printing? If he was the author, as seems to be implied, was the use of Bradford's name spurious? Also, if we are correct in our identification of Burton and Penny, their participation in the production of such a work is certainly remarkable. Fortunately the indictment goes on to quote an offensive passage from Capstocke's book:

> Peradventure her grace thinketh that the King will keep her more company and love her the better if she give him the crowne; ye will crowne him to make him live chaste and contrary to his nature, for peradventure after he were crowned he would be contented with one woman, but in the meane space he would have three or foure in one night to prove which of them he liketh best, not of ladies and gentlewomen but of bakers daughters and such poore whores.

Now this extract differs in several verbal points from the BM text, but is exactly the same as that in Strype, so it is clear that the copy among John Foxe's MSS in the Harleian collection which Strype used was the same as that which Capstocke was prosecuted for producing. We have already noted that Strype's version is considerably less Catholic than the BM text, and we may, therefore, deduce that this was a Protestant edition, preserving the attack upon the Spaniards while removing the more offensive references to the exponents of the gospel.

If we accept that Capstocke was responsible for the considerable differences between the Foxe and the BM texts, then the imputation of authorship contained in his accusation can be explained without assuming that the use of Bradford's name was false. Such an explanation would also account for the difference in title, and for the late date mentioned in the indictment. By the end of December the particular circumstances of the early summer would have faded from memory; so naturally a later edition would carry a more general title, retaining the old address as a subtitle. It therefore seems probable that the BM text represents Bradford's original work, and the Foxe text Capstocke's amended production. Quite apart from internal evidence, the fact that the Protestants considered it necessary to publish an expurgated edition is a strong indication of the validity of Bradford's Catholicism.

From the surviving evidence we cannot be sure whether the second edition was ever printed, or whether it survived in MS only. The relationship between Capstocke's group and the printing trade is obscure. The obstinate omission of any reference to printing in either the council records or the surviving indictment is baffling, for it cannot at this date be assumed that 'writing' was used as a generic term to include printing. Yet they must certainly have intended their products to be printed, as nothing longer than a ballad could conveniently be circulated in MS. Either the group was itself operating a press which the authorities failed to locate, or else it was passing on its work to other associates who succeeded in avoiding detection. None of those examined had any traceable connection with the trade, and it is probable that the actual printing was done by journeymen or apprentices. In view of the suspicion with which the council regarded all recognised printers and the closeness of the surveillance over them, it is unlikely that any established tradesman would have handled such material. The location of the group in the parish of St Peter le Poore, near the Dutch church, is not, therefore, any real help in establishing the identity of the printer. Nor do we have any contemporary work which can unhesitatingly be ascribed to their press. The possibility of some connection with John Day, who was imprisoned by the council in 1554 for 'printing noythy bokes'[8] and began business again by printing for the Dutch church in 1557, cannot be excluded, but it is unlikely. Until more evidence is forthcoming we can do no more than claim to have identified one of the Protestant propaganda cells in Marian London.

The BM text of the *Letter* presents the opposite problem. It is a small octavo book, very badly printed in a 77 roman type, interspersed with occasional letters of a similar-sized textura. The 'w' and 'h' are in textura throughout, and a textura long 's' also occurs. The contrast between its very poor workmanship and the competent products of the foreign presses indicates that it was produced in London. Equally, it bears no resemblance to the work produced secretly in London by established tradesmen such as 'Nicholas Dorcaster', whom Frank Isaac tentatively identified with Day.[9] The worn state of the type, lack of ornament, and the absence of even a deceptive colophon, suggest the work of the half-skilled amateur, probably using whatever cast-off equipment he could procure. Who would have handled Bradford's book in its original form it is hard to say. Neither the official printers nor the Protestant cells would have touched it. Perhaps some pirate who valued his profits more highly than his safety took the risk. We can be sure that at the time when it must have come out, between June and December 1556, there would have been a ready market for such a philippic.

In the course of his *Letter* Bradford struck a note which was to be echoed repeatedly in the next hundred years: 'we must obey her (the Queen) surely in those actes that be paste by parliament and confirmed by the whole realme . . . but I think there is no lawe confirmed and paste by which the Queene may lawfully disinherit the realme of the crowne'. In his time he was unusual in allowing such considerations rather than religious alignments to determine his course of action, but such a sentiment explains, without recourse to hypocrisy, how a man could be at the same time a Catholic and a persistent opponent of the Catholic government. This is the other, and less familiar side of the opposition to Mary's government. The two editions of this pamphlet demonstrate at once the similarities and the differences of the two points of view. The same work could serve the purposes of either party, but it would not be produced in both forms by the same people. The printers of Bradford's *Letter* remain in obscurity, and we are left with no certainty that they normally functioned as printers at all. Both the BM text and the Foxe text present many unsolved problems; but the relationship between them and the circumstances of their production provide an interesting basis for further investigation.

Notes

1. Examination of William Crowe, 11 May 1556. *State Papers, Domestic, Mary*, SP11/VIII/70. *Ambassades de Messieurs de Noailles* (ed. Vertot, Leyden, 1763), 365. [For a consideration of the Earl of Shrewsbury's role in this situation, see George Bernard, *The Power of the Early Tudor Nobility; a Study of the Fourth and Fifth Earls of Shrewsbury* , Brighton, 1985.]
2. Baga de Secretis, published in the *Appendix to the Fourth Report of the Deputy Keeper of the Public Records*, (London, 1844) p. 285.
3. Ibid.
4. *The Marian Exiles*, Cambridge, 1938, pp. 96–7.
5. *Acts of the Privy Council*, VI, ed. J.R. Dasent (London, 1890–1964), 8 and 9 March 1556–7, 17 April and 7 August 1557.
6. *Dictionary of National Biography*. The fact that Penny's wife was buried in the church of St Peter le Poore in 1587 indicates some earlier connection with the parish.
7. *Calendar of the Patent Rolls, Philip and Mary*, London, 1939, IV, 150. Also, T. Rymer, *Foedera, conventiones, litterae, et . . . acta publica*, London, 1704–35, XV, p. 480.
8. *The Diary of Henry Machyn 1550–1563*, ed. J.G. Nichols, Camden Society, XLII, 1848, p. 72.
9. F.S. Isaac, *English Printers' Types of the Sixteenth Century*, Oxford, 1936, p. 47. [See also below, Chapter 10, 'Books and the English Reformation prior to 1558'.]

8 The Theory and Practice of Censorship in Sixteenth-Century England

A student of the sixteenth century is always tempted to represent the period as one of unprecedented change and new departures. In the case of my present subject the temptation is particularly strong, because printing was a new invention, and the technical problems and opportunities it presented to governments were also new. Nevertheless it would be most misleading to begin a discussion of Tudor censorship with Sir Thomas More's restrictive proclamation of 1530, or even with the introduction of printing to England in 1476. The concept of society, and of the duties and responsibilities of government, which censorship was to reflect was deeply rooted in the past, and was not fundamentally challenged until the puritan revolution of the seventeenth century.

The image used was that of an organism. Society was a 'body politic', each of whose members existed in a fore-ordained and permanent relationship with the rest. This situation expressed the will of God, and its preservation represented that *pax terrena* which St Augustine had described as the highest achievement of temporal government. To sow discord in society – to set one member against another or any member against the head – was thus not merely a crime but an offence against God. This ideal of harmony, and of unquestioning acquiescence in the will of the ruler and the status quo, enjoyed universal currency largely because the attainment fell so far short of the aspiration. All medieval societies were in process of being slowly won from narrow allegiances to wider, from violence to litigation, and from self-help to dependence upon public authority. In this process the concept of the 'body politic' was both an inspiration and a help. Tudor England was still in the throes of this development when the controversial policies of Henry VIII and his children added a new emphasis to the traditional insistence upon the solemn duty of obedience. It would hardly be an exaggeration to say that the whole success of their revolt against the papacy depended on their ability to persuade their subjects to accept this adaptation of the ancient theory. Tudor propaganda derived much of its effect from deep-rooted fears of lawlessness and strife which owed little to the immediate issues of controversy. The official attitude was well expressed by the Lord Keeper, Sir Nicholas Bacon, in 1567:

It it given to the Queen's Majesty to understand that divers her subjects by their evil dispositions do sow and spread abroad divers seditious errors and rumours to the derogation and dishonour first of Almighty God in the state of religion established by the laws of this realm, and also to the dishonour of her highness in disproving her lawful right to supremacy amongst her subjects. And this that they do is not done secretly or by stealth, but openly avouched . . . as for example by bringing in and spreading abroad divers seditious books and libels from beyond the seas . . . if such disorders be not redressed by law, then must force and violence reform . . . then you well know that law is put to silence and cannot be executed which should only maintain good order . . .[1]

Censorship was thus an inevitable consequence, not only of an insecure regime but also of the responsibility which had rested upon the monarchy time out of mind to protect society from its own disruptive instincts, and to defend the people of God against the wily onslaughts of the devil in whatever form he was then supposed to appear.

bringing in of these books and seditious libels (Bacon continued) maketh mens minds to be at variance one with another, and diversity of minds maketh seditions, seditions bring in tumults, tumults make insurrections and rebellions, insurrections make depopulations and bring in utter ruin and destruction of mens bodies, goods and lands.

The roots of censorship lay far back in the Middle Ages, in two separate but related codes. On the one hand, the law of the church forbade the teaching of heretical doctrine, and in England this law had been reinforced by the early fifteenth-century statutes against Lollardy. In 1408 Convocation had prohibited the reproduction of English translations of the scriptures, unless such translation was specifically authorised, and in 1414 parliament had confirmed the legal right of ecclesiastical officials to proceed against the makers and writers of heretical books.[2] On the other hand stood the law of treason, and that small group of statutes sometimes collectively known as *Scandalum Magnatum*. Open abuse of the king, whether in speech or writing, was an ancient offence and could be construed as treason under the Act of 1352. For example in 1450 a certain William Dalton of Ipswich was indicted for declaring 'that he would that our sovereign lord the king . . . were as cold at his heart root as the stone under his foot be so we had another king that could better rule this land . . .'.[3] Similarly, defamation of the king's officers and of the 'great men of the realm' was already an offence before the first Statute of Westminster in 1275. The thirty-fourth chapter of that statute provided that anyone who should 'tell or publish any false news or tales whereby discord or occasion of discord or slander may grow between the king and his people, or the great men of the realm . . .' should be imprisoned 'until he hath brought him into the court which was the first deviser of the tale'.[4] It thus became an offence to spread or repeat such gossip as well as to originate it. Two statutes of Richard II repeated the substance of this chapter, adding only that the spreaders of tales whose devisers could not be found were to be punished at the discretion of the council.[5] These acts remained the basis of the law until the legislation of the Reformation parliament, and were confirmed by statute as late as 1555, when the government of Mary was faced with a fresh upsurge of criticism and hostile comment.[6]

How often this law was invoked we do not know, but the connection between agitation and action was real enough. In 1450 rumours that the court was planning a ferocious revenge for the death of the Duke of Suffolk helped to launch the rebellion of Jack Cade. Twenty years later Sir Robert Welles confessed that the Lincolnshire rising of 1470 'was grounded upon this noise raised among the people that the king was coming down with a great power into (the county) where the king's judges should sit and hang and draw great numbers of the commons' – a rumour which Sir Robert himself seems to have invented for the purpose.[7] Recent research has also shown that similar 'tales' played an important part in launching the Pilgrimage of Grace and the Wyatt rebellion of 1554.[8] In the latter year the council, alarmed by the rising tide of disaffection, wrote around to the justices of the peace, urging them to renewed efforts because 'vain prophecies and untrue bruits (are) the very foundation of all rebellion'.[9] Recent studies have tended to show that the connection between words and deeds in the mid-sixteenth century was less immediate than many contemporaries feared, and probably less immediate than it had been in the previous century, but it was close enough for alarm and corresponding precautions to be justified. 'In our country', wrote Sir John Mason in 1554, '. . . talking is preparatory to a doing'.[10]

Seditious talk was both a symptom and a cause of disaffection, and was a constant preoccupation of Tudor governments, particularly after the royal supremacy had subordinated ecclesiastical jurisdiction to the Crown. The law expanded and became very much more precise. It became treason to call Henry VIII 'schismatic' or 'heretic' as well as 'tyrant', or to reject his various rearrangements of the succession. It became treason to pray that Queen Mary's heart might be turned from popery, or to call Elizabeth 'bastard' or 'usurper'. Where we have only isolated examples of proceedings against offenders before 1530, after that date we have plentiful material for a study of the law and its enforcement.[11] However, the basis upon which the law rested did not change. Cromwell and Cecil were more diligent and effective administrators than their predecessors, and could use lay and ecclesiastical officials interchangeably, but their reasons for punishing the authors and spreaders of 'lewd and seditious tales' would have been perfectly comprehensible to the framers of the Statute of Westminster.

Censorship was the extension of this principle to the expression of similar sentiments in writing or in print. Consequently the three methods of communication were frequently linked together. A typical example is a statute of 1563, 'against fond and fantastical prophecies', which stood in the direct tradition of Scandalum Magnatum. This prohibited the 'publishing and setting forth' of such prophecies concerning the queen 'and other noble persons' by 'writing, printing, singing or other open speech or word'.[12] The author of a seditious writing, like the originator of a seditious rumour, might, if caught, be proceeded against for misdemeanour, felony or treason according to the seriousness of the offence. Possessors and distributors of such writings, like the spreaders of rumours, normally stood in danger only of the lesser penalties. But, of course, writings were tangible objects, and printed books and pamphlets went through a sophisticated process of production. So although the principles behind censorship and the suppression of seditious speech were the same, and the laws extremely similar, the techniques of enforcement naturally differed.

Printing was first and foremost a business – a group of crafts by which men maintained themselves and their families. This undoubtedly assisted the process of censorship, but it also brought into existence a complex structure of ordinary trade control similar to that which regulated the production of woollen cloth, pins, or any other manufacture.[13] Consequently there were almost from the beginning two distinct but overlapping systems of regulation, and this fact has to some extent confused the study of government attitudes towards the press. For the half-century after its introduction into England, printing was treated simply as a new and ingenious form of manufacture. Edward IV and Henry VII both patronised printers, and the latter appointed the first Royal Stationer.[14] The main bone of contention was the early domination of the trade by aliens, a domination which was expressly permitted by a statute of 1484 which gave aliens full freedom to practise the craft. This freedom was systematically attacked and undermined by the London Stationers, and a series of statutes in 1515, 1523, 1529 and 1534 whittled away and finally abolished the privileges of the foreign printers. The form of all these Acts, even the last, strongly suggests that they were trade measures in which the government was yielding to the demands of the Stationers, rather than security measures initiated by the Crown.

The monopolistic position of the Stationers was strongly consolidated in 1557 by the grant of a royal charter to the company, and for the remainder of the century the wardens operated their own licensing system. As we shall see, this was closely related to government censorship, but it was by no means identical with it. Nor was the Crown's direct concern with the press always of a restrictive nature. The continuous sequence of royal printers had begun in 1503,[15] and in 1544 Henry VIII had granted the first patent monopoly, to Grafton and Whitchurch for the printing of service books. Royal patronage of this kind was naturally regarded with suspicion by the Stationers, and the company tried extremely hard to persuade Elizabeth to give up the granting of patents which diminished its own control. The major part of the correspondence and litigation connected with printing and bookselling in the second half of the sixteenth century relates to the enforcement of the Stationers' own licensing system, or to quarrels between privileged and unprivileged printers. The most celebrated such case is that between the company and John Wolfe, which provoked a petition from the wardens to the Privy Council in 1583, and dragged on in Star Chamber for several years before being resolved by compromise. Wolfe's protest touched the prerogative because he challenged the granting of patent monopolies, but there was never any suggestion that the content of his work was seditious.[16]

There would have been a Stationers' Company with exclusive policies, a licensing system and a great deal of litigation even if the Tudors had never evinced any serious interest in the propaganda functions of printing – just as it would have been an offence to write seditious or heretical words had the art of printing never been invented.

Nevertheless, the development of the press did present both church and state with a security problem of unprecedented dimensions. John Foxe put his finger on the point very accurately when he contrasted the effectiveness of Protestant teaching in his own day with the earlier impact of Wycliffe and Huss: 'although through might be stopped the mouth of John Huss . . . God hath opened the press to preach, whose voice the Pope is never able to stop with all the puissance of his triple crown . . .'.[17]

In England the first awareness of this danger dawned with the appearance of early Lutheran tracts, and of Tyndale's English New Testament in the mid-1520s. The ecclesiastical machinery, which had dealt so effectively with Lollard writings in the previous century, was soon seen to be hopelessly inadequate in this new situation. In 1524 Cuthbert Tunstall, the Bishop of London, issued the first regulations that recognised the distinctive importance of the new medium. No books were to be imported without episcopal permission, and no new works were to be printed without licence from the same authority. The effect of these orders seems to have been negligible, and it was not until Sir Thomas More as Lord Chancellor entered the fray in 1530 that any effective action could be taken. A royal proclamation of that year 'for the resisting and withstanding of most damnable heresies sown within this land by the disciples of Luther' condemned fourteen named books and ordered that those possessing them should give them up to the ordinary.[18]

This proclamation did not add anything to the existing law, provide any extra administrative machinery, or decree any secular penalties, but it did mark the first attempt by the Crown to limit and control the production and circulation of books. With More's energy behind it, it also resulted in a period of close co-operation between royal and ecclesiastical officials, which produced a number of arrests during 1531. In December of that year Richard Bayfield, one of the apprehended traffickers, was burnt for heresy.[19] After this, events moved rapidly, and in the crisis of his 'great matter' Henry's concern over the expression of criticism and opposition reached a new level of sensitivity. It cannot be my concern here to deal with the positive side of government propaganda, but this was the period in which Thomas Cromwell enlisted the services of scholars, publicists and printers on a grand scale to defend and explain the king's proceedings. It was also a period in which prosecutions for treasonable and seditious words reached a new level of intensity and effectiveness.[20] By the first Act of Succession it became high treason to 'do or procure to be done by act of deed or word written or printed, anything to the prejudice of the king, against his marriage with Queen Anne . . .'. Also in January 1536 a new proclamation denounced

> divers and sundry writings and books, as well imprinted as other in which such writings and books many open and manifest errors and slanders are contained, not only in derogation and diminution of the dignity and authority royal of the king's majesty and of his Imperial Crown, but also directly and expressly against the good and laudable statutes of this realm . . .[21]

Such works were to be given up within forty days, not to the ordinary but to the Lord Chancellor or Thomas Cromwell. *Scandalum Magnatum* as well as heresy had now brought the printers into the forefront of controversy.

In spite of this, there was as yet no system of royal licensing. The phrase 'cum privilegio regali' which appears in a number of variants in the colophons of numerous works printed from 1518 onwards seems to have signified a form of copyright rather than an imprimatur.[22] Such privileges could be granted by authorities other than the king, for example the chancellors of the universities, and were the predecessors of the patents of monopoly which began to appear in the 1540s. It was not until 1538 that the old system of episcopal licences was superseded. In November of that year an important proclamation 'for expelling and avoiding the occasion of . . . errors and seditious opinions by reason of books imprinted in the English tongue' laid down fresh regulations for the trade.[23] No English books were to be imported without the king's special licence, on pain of imprisonment during pleasure and forfeiture of goods; and no English book was to be printed within the realm unless licensed by members of the Privy Council or other appointed, on pain of imprisonment and fine at the king's discretion. Every duly licensed book was to contain the full effect of the licence 'plainly declared and expressed in the English tongue'. Although the bishops retained certain functions, the main burden of inspection and control had now been assumed by the Crown, which already bore the burden of punishing breaches in the existing laws.

Thomas Cromwell's campaign against sedition in the 1530s enjoyed, as we know, a considerable measure of success, but seditious printing was one of his lesser problems. The government brought off a notable coup in confiscating all 700 copies of *The Nun's Book* before they could be distributed, but references to publishing or distributing undesirable books are few among the surviving records and punishments. Prevention was better than cure, and it was no doubt the need to systematise prevention which led to the introduction of royal licensing. The system seems to have had some effect. The council acted against offending or suspect printers on a number of occasions, and in the early 1540s clandestine publications began to appear. These were books which can be shown on typographical evidence to have been printed in England, but which bore colophons ascribing them to Leipzig or Wesel.[24] An underground press was the natural consequence of more stringent official surveillance. In 1543 the government intensified its pressure. For the first time specific penalties for unlicensed printing appeared on the statute book.

> if any printer, bookbinder, bookseller, or any other person or persons . . . print or cause to be printed, or utter, sell, give or deliver within this realm or elsewhere within the king's dominions of any of the books or writings before abolished or prohibited . . .

the offender was to be imprisoned for three months and fined £10 for each book.[25] If he repeated the offence a second time he was liable to forfeiture of goods and perpetual imprisonment. These penalties could be inflicted irrespective of the content of the books concerned, and quite independently of any other penalties which might have been incurred by their authors. This statute therefore clearly marks a new stage in the development of royal policy, a stage perhaps necessitated by the growth of clandestine publishing or perhaps by a decline in the efficiency of less formal conciliar methods after Cromwell's death.

The death of Henry himself in 1547 brought about a relaxation of the treason laws, and a sharp increase in all forms of religious controversy. Somerset and Cranmer, moving cautiously towards a Protestant establishment, found themselves caught between two fires. The latter, like other Protestant divines, was inclined to see 'truth' as possessing an irresistible persuasive force. By allowing Reformed ideas a much greater liberty of expression, he seems to have hoped to bring about a rapid and peaceful conversion of the country. If such was his hope, it was speedily disappointed, and within a few weeks he found himself denounced with equal vigour by radicals who were disappointed with his caution and conservatives who were disgusted with his heresy. To such traditionalists as Stephen Gardiner, Protestantism was the religion of 'liberty', and liberty was the solvent of the whole social order. Damage the fabric of reverence and obedience in one place, he argued, and the whole structure was in danger. '. . . by his reasoning', he wrote in an attack on William Turner, '. . . it were idolatry for the servant to make courtesy to his master, wherein he should bow the knee, or the goodman to kiss his wife; but to kneel and kiss his superior's hand were by him foul and filthy abomination . . .'.[26] 'O devilish liberty', wrote the similarly minded Miles Huggarde, 'I would to God Germany might have kept thee still . . . .'[27]

Such arguments carried considerable weight and the English Protestant leaders shared their opponents' belief in the need for uniformity. In the late 1540s they had had no experience in the formulation of policy, and soon became alarmed and disillusioned by the outburst of preaching and pamphleteering which greeted their early leniency. 'I never saw so little discipline as is nowadays', lamented Hugh Latimer in 1549, and he was soon preaching that '. . . the wicked preachers . . . the gainsayers' must 'have their mouths stopped'.[28] Consequently the Protestant establishment which was set up between 1549 and 1553 was no more tolerant of dissenting opinions than the regime of Henry VIII. It was, however, rather less successful in making its will effective. This was partly because of the inevitable difficulties attendant upon a royal minority, partly because of dissensions within the council, and partly because impatient radicals like Hooper were valuable allies in combating the immense, if somewhat inert, weight of conservatism. The law was not changed during the reign of Edward VI, and the proclamations for its enforcement did not bring about any significant developments. On 13 August 1549 the sole licensing authority of the council was reiterated, this aspect of its work being placed in the hands of 'Mr Secretary Peter, Mr Secretary Smith and Mr Cicill, or the one of them . . .'.[29] A further proclamation of 1551 concerning the control of imported books, and of plays and interludes, spoke more generally of '. . . writing signed with his Majesty's most gracious hand, or the hands of six of his said Privy Council'.[30] Such evidence as we have for the effectiveness of this control comes mostly from the records of the council, and is not extensive. A small number of printers and others were interrogated and bound by recognisances not to offend again. In March 1551 William Seth was arrested on a charge of importing popish books, and his examination gives an illuminating glimpse of what was clearly a well-organised smuggling business.[31] At least one London printer, Robert Caly, fled abroad during this period and played a part in producing English Catholic propaganda; but the major challenge seems to have come from a great increase in the home production of ballads, broadsides and other ephemera, and in this direction the government's censorship efforts very largely failed.

The advent of the Catholic Mary in 1553 led to a further aggravation of the problem. From the beginning the printers and stationers of London seem to have included a disproportionate number of Protestant sympathisers, and Protestant propaganda had a panache and an edge lacking in the writings of conservatives. The queen's first reaction was to see the large output of heretical literature simply in terms of gratifying a demand for novelty and scurrility. Her initial proclamation on religious matters denounced the

> printing of false fond books, ballads, rhymes and other lewd treatises in the English tongue concerning doctrine now in question and controversy . . . which books, ballads, rhymes, and treatises are chiefly by the printers and stationers set out to sale to her graces subjects of an evil zeal for lucre and covetousness of vile gain.[32]

The same proclamation also made reference to 'her grace's special licence in writing', but gave no indication of how this licence was to be bestowed, and threatened simply 'due punishment' according to the order of the existing law for those who should fail to obtain it. It is not clear how Mary's licensing system worked at any stage of her reign. Perhaps the power remained vested in the Privy Council, but more probably it was returned to the church, particularly after Cardinal Pole took up his legatine responsibilities in England at the end of 1554. Significantly, we know very much more about the government's attempts to suppress heretical and seditious literature already in circulation than we do about any system of search and prevention.

It is not my purpose here to discuss the propaganda campaign against Mary. Its general features are sufficiently familiar. Large quantities of Protestant polemic, exhortation and spiritual guidance were printed in such places as Strasburg, Basle and Emden, and smuggled into the country by numbers of bold and determined men and women. Within England, clandestine presses produced some similar works, and also ballads, broadsheets and books of a more frankly political and subversive nature, such as *The copy of a letter sent by John Bradford*, which was a violent and libellous attack on Philip.[33] Against this attack the government defended itself for the most part by traditional means, proclamations and council letters urging officials to do their duty and enforce the law. The law itself was also twice extended. In January 1555 it became a felony to publish slanders against the king and queen which could not be construed as treason, the penalty being the loss of the right hand. Another statute of the same session also made it treason to preach or write against King Philip's title, or to conspire his death by such means.[34] In June of 1555 an index of prohibited authors was proclaimed, and towards the end of the reign, in June 1558, martial law was extended to cover the possession of any heretical or treasonable book, wherever published.[35]

Enforcement, as usual, fell far short of intention. In spite of the revived jurisdiction of the church, special royal commissions were set up 'to inquire concerning all heresies, heretical and seditious books . . . (within a given area) with power to seize all such books and writings . . .', but they do not seem to have been very effective.[36] Fewer than twenty individuals are on record as having been proceeded against for offences of this kind, and the majority of those escaped any serious penalty. John Day, swiftly detected and apprehended in October 1554, escaped from custody and got away to the continent. Of the six men arrested in March 1557 for producing a number of clandestine books, three were eventually released upon recognisances of £40, one was indicted and almost immediately pardoned, and the other two disappear from the records.[37]

William Rydall, William Copland, John Kingston and Thomas Marsh were all censured by the council, although no worse penalties seem to have been imposed.[38] Probably there were prosecutions at the assizes, which cannot now be traced, but on the surviving evidence the discrepancy between the anxiety displayed and the level of effective action is very marked.

It is against this background that the incorporation of the Stationers' Company in March 1557 should be seen. The company already had a long history but the grant of a royal charter increased its prestige, and gave it the right, and power, to defend its own monopolistic interests. These interests could readily be made to serve the policy of the Crown. When the master and wardens of the newly chartered company were given the right to search out and destroy books which infringed their own regulations, they were also empowered to '. . . make search in any place, shop or building of any printer, binder or seller of books printed contrary to statute or proclamation, and . . . seize or burn the same'.[39] Thereafter, it is clear that the government depended heavily on the co-operation of the company in controlling subversive publication. The wardens were concerned to protect the interests of their members, and their licensing system overlapped with that of the Crown without being dependent upon it. It was not until after the Star Chamber decree of 1586 that a record of the government licence normally accompanied the registration of a new work in the company's own records.

The well-documented and complex Elizabethan system was thus built on a substantial foundation of practical experience, as well as on a more general basis of accepted political and social theory. There is neither space nor need for me here to discuss the progressive elaboration of those treason laws with which the government protected itself against Catholic intrigue and ideology. The vast majority of those who fell foul of the government for writing, printing, importing or distributing seditious books did so in the service of the Catholic church. Men like William Carter and Richard Verstegan were persistent and courageous, and kept the council in a perpetual state of anxiety. Indeed the Catholics were well served by their press, which never wholly succumbed to official pressure, and it was not the fault of its literary agents that the Roman church failed to recover England for the Counter-Reformation. At the opposite extreme, although on a much smaller scale, the government also suffered intermittent anxiety about puritan attacks on the queen's management of the church. 'Papists and precisians have one mark to shoot at', wrote Parker in 1573, 'plain disobedience'; and Cecil, who was sympathetic to their cause, observed that 'to think it a burden of conscience to observe the orders and rites of the church established by law (is) a matter pernicious to the state of Government'.[40]

Consequently penalties were inflicted upon the protagonists of both sides at all levels, from fining and imprisonment to mutilation and death. Against Catholic sympathisers the censorship laws operated mainly at the lower level. William Carter was one of very few whose treason consisted principally of clandestine printing.[41] Against some puritans however, such as Stubbs and Penry, seditious writing was the only charge. The latter was convicted and hanged for felony in 1593 for writing on open letter to the queen, part of which ran:

Therefore, Madam, you are not so much an adversary unto us poor men as unto Christ Jesus and the wealth of his kingdom. But, Madam, this much we must needs say. That in all likelihood if the days of your sister Queen Mary and her persecution had continued to this day, that the church of God in England had been far more flourishing than at this day it is.[42]

If his share in the Marprelate publications played any part in persuading the authorities to act against him, it did not appear at his trial.

It is understandable in the circumstances that such 'derogation of the Queen's authority' should be taken seriously, but on the whole the government seems to have been reluctant to take extreme measures. In his explanation for the necessity of censorship laws in 1567, Bacon justified the sharp application of lesser penalties on just these grounds: 'when execution thereof . . . by touching half a dozen offenders may sufficiently warn half a hundred, I think those laws nor the execution of them may justly be called extreme . . . '.[43] Moreover '(when) by whipping a man may escape hanging . . . it were better to be twice whipped than once hanged . . .'. As in the 1530s, it was clearly recognised that prevention was better than cure and Cecil, like Cromwell, was a master in the management of positive propaganda. He was forced, however, by technical developments to excel his predecessor in his painstaking supervision of the press. The Royal Injunctions of 1559 made comprehensive provision for licensing: 'because there is great abuse in the printers of books, which for covetousness chiefly regard not what they print so they may have gain . . . '.[44]

Licences could be granted by the queen herself, six of her Privy Council, the two archbishops and the bishop who was ordinary of the place of publication, or by any two of them, provided that the ordinary was one. At the same time, to prevent the publication of pamphlets, plays or ballads, 'heretical, seditious or unseemly for Christian ears', such works must be licensed by three members of the newly established ecclesiastical commission. The same commissioners were also made responsible for overseeing all other matters concerning the printing or importation of books, '. . . to which her Majesty straightly commandeth all manner her subjects, and especially the Wardens and Company of Stationers, to be obedient'.[45] These regulations were supplemented in 1566 by a council decree laying down a scale of penalties for unlicensed printing (irrespective of content), which involved exclusion from the trade, fines and imprisonment. Twenty years later the whole system was drastically simplified by a well-known Star Chamber edict which placed all licensing (except that of law books) in the hands of the Archbishop of Canterbury and the Bishop of London;[46] and in the closing years of the century those perpetual gadflies, the actors and players of interludes, were curbed by the evolution of a subsidiary licensing system operated by the Lord Chamberlain and his assistant the Master of the Revels.[47]

The enforcement of these regulations lay first and foremost in the hands of the Stationers' Company, and its registers provide the best evidence for the working of the system.[48] The company organised weekly searches, and the Court of Assistants destroyed illicit books, defaced illegal type, fined, excluded and occasionally imprisoned offending printers on its own authority. Co-operation with the ecclesiastical commissioners was close, if not always enthusiastic. In 1582 the company complained of the charges · it had undergone through searching for and suppressing popish books by warrant of the commission.[49] The commissioners never seem to have hesitated to issue instructions to the wardens, and these were almost invariably obeyed. From 1588 onwards the licensing function of the Archbishop of Canterbury and the Bishop of London was regularly delegated to a group of deputies, and the names of these men constantly appear authenticating licences in the Stationers' Register. By the end of the century the appointment of master printers was tightly controlled by High Commission,[50] and it is probable that that court dealt with a proportion of the more serious offences against the licensing laws.

The part played by Star Chamber is rather less clear. It certainly handled patent and privilege cases and concerned itself with the issuing of regulations, but does not seem to have dealt with penal offences. In 1593 the pursuivant Richard Topcliffe sent what he described as 'a lewd traiterous book' to Lord Keeper Puckering, commenting that he did not know how soon there might be proceedings 'in Star Chamber or elsewhere',[51] but the jurisdiction of Star Chamber did not extend to treason, and major disciplinary cases seem to have been dealt with exclusively by the courts of common law. A systematic search of the assize records would probably reveal many such cases. It is well known that John Udall was so handled, and glimpses can be caught of proceedings against more obscure men, such as Robert Sutton of Aylsham, indicted at the Norfolk assizes in 1584 for distributing and defending a book containing the words 'not to be with the pope is to be with anti-Christ'.[52] It may well be that the bulk of those who disappear from the records after imprisonment and interrogation by the council were committed to the assizes, but for the moment their fate remains unknown.

The council, of course, bore the overall responsibility for enforcement, and it might use other agents than the Stationers or the Ecclesiastical Commission. Outside London the Lord-Lieutenant or justices; inside London the Lord Mayor, as when the latter acted in 1568 to arrest the author of a pamphlet against the Duke of Alva. Occasionally the council even acted directly, as it did in 1570 to suppress William Elderton's ballad *Dr. Story's stumbling into England*.

The impression created by a study of Elizabethan censorship is one of great assiduity and relative effectiveness. Techniques of suppression had kept pace with the techniques of sedition, and it is hard to imagine any sixteenth-century government doing better. Yet it was, in an important sense, a barren achievement. With its emphasis on uniformity and strict repression of criticism, official thinking had not advanced beyond the Lollard laws, and *Scandalum Magnatum*. At the same time political and social developments had created a much more stable and governable community than that which the Tudors had won in 1485. Censorship had played its part in helping to bring this about, but by 1600 the time had come for a more mature and discriminating philosophy, which could take account of informed criticism and comment. When this did not happen, the whole concept of the 'body politic' began to seem an oppressive mechanism, and the next generation of critics was driven to seek an alternative image of society. It found it in the puritan 'ship of state', which implied a very different theory of the role of the subject in government.[53]

Notes

1. Public Record Office [PRO], State Papers Domestic, Elizabeth, SP12/4/52.
2. D. Wilkins, *Concilia Magnae Britanniae et Hiberniae*, London, 1737, III, p. 317: 2 Henry V, I, c.7.
3. PRO, King's Bench Plea Rolls, KB27/760, r. Rex 3.
4. 3 Edward I c. 34; *Statutes of the Realm*, London, 1810–28, p. 35.
5. 2 Richard II st. I c.5: 12 Richard II c. 2.
6. 1 and 2 Philip and Mary c.3.
7. 'Chronicle of the Rebellion in Lincolnshire, 1470', ed. J.G. Nichols, *Camden Miscellany*, I, London, 1847, 22.
.8 M.E. James, 'The Lincolnshire Rebellion of 1536', *Past and Present*, XLVIII, (1970), 1–70; D.M. Loades, *Two Tudor Conspiracies*, Cambridge, 1965.
9. British Museum, Cotton MSS, Titus B. 11, fol. 104.
10. *State Papers, Foreign, Edward VI and Mary*, London, 1861, II, 119.
11. See particularly G.R. Elton, *Policy and Police*, Cambridge, 1972, concerning the activities of Cromwell and his agents.
12. 5 Elizabeth c. 15. An interesting example from the previous reign is that of William Oldenall, tried in King's Bench in 1557 for declaring, 'That the Queen's Majesty was baseborn, and that in St Paul's Churchyard a twopenny book might be had which would prove his saying to be true'. PRO, KB27/1184 r.Rex. 12d.
13. H.S. Bennett, *English Books and Readers, 1475–1557*, Cambridge, 1952.
14. Peter Actors, 'Stationer to the King' from 1485.
15. The first man to take that title was William Faques. The Royal Printers were the official agents of government propaganda.
16. W.W. Greg, *A Companion to Arber*, Oxford, 1967, pp. 28–9: PRO, State Papers Domestic, Elizabeth, SP12/15/38–40.
17. John Foxe, *Actes and Monuments*, eds. S.R. Cattley and G. Townsend, London, 1837–41, III, p. 720.
18. P.L. Hughes and J.F. Larkin, *Tudor Royal Proclamations*, I, New Haven Conn. and London, 1964, pp. 181–6; for the date, see Elton, *Policy and Police*, p. 218, n. 5.
19. D.M. Loades, 'The Press under the Early Tudors', *Transactions of the Cambridge Bibliographical Society*, IV (i), 1964, 32.
20. Elton, *Policy and Police*.
21. Hughes and Larkin, *Tudor Royal Proclamations*, I, pp. 235–7.
22. F.S. Siebert, *The Freedom of the Press in England, 1476–1776*, Urbana, I11, 1952, pp. 35–6.
23. Hughes and Larkin, *Tudor Royal Proclamations*, I, pp. 270–6. It is clear from the original draft of this proclamation, amended in the king's hand, that many of the important changes introduced were Henry's own ideas. Elton, *Policy and Police*, p. 256 n.1.
24. *Transactions of the Cambridge Bibliographical Society*, IV (i), 33 and n.
25. 34/35 Henry VIII c. 1.
26. Gardiner's tract against William Turner; *The Letters of Stephen Gardiner*, ed. J.A. Muller, Cambridge, 1933, p. 480.
27. Miles Huggarde, *The Displaying of the Protestants*, London, 1556, f. 114^v.
28. Hugh Latimer, *Sermons*, ed. G.E. Corrie, Parker Society, 1844, p. 132.
29. *Acts of the Privy Council*, ed. J.R. Dasent, London, 1890–1964, II, 312.
30. Hughes and Larkin, *Tudor Royal Proclamations*, I, pp. 514–18.
31. *Historical Manuscripts Commission, Hatfield*, i, 83–4.
32. Hughes and Larkin, *Tudor Royal Proclamations*, II, New Haven and London, 1969, pp. 5–6.

33. For the consideration of this work see my notes in the *Transactions of the Cambridge Bibliographical Society*, III (ii), 1960, 155–60. [For a full catalogue of this polemic, and the conservative response, see E.J. Baskerville, A *Chronological Bibliography of Propaganda and Polemic Published in English between 1553 and 1558*, American Philosophical Society, Philadelphia, 1979.]

34. 1 and 2 Philip and Mary c. 3: 1 and 2 Philip and Mary c. 10.

35. Hughes and Larkin, *Tudor Royal Proclamations*, II, p. 90.

36. *Calendar of the Patent Rolls, Philip and Mary*, London, 1936–9, III, 24.

37. *Transactions of the Cambridge Bibliographical Society*, IV (i), 44.

38. Ibid., 45. All these men were established printers and among the original 97 members of the chartered company.

39. *Cal. Pat. Rolls, Philip and Mary*, III, 480.

40. British Museum, Cotton MSS, Titus B.II, fol. 249; quoted by Conyers Read, *Queen Elizabeth and Lord Burghley*, London, 1960, p. 117.

41. Carter was a persistent offender, but the government had some difficulty in securing his conviction; Siebert, *Freedom of the Press*, pp. 89–90.

42. PRO, King's Bench Plea Rolls, KB27/1325 r. Rex 3.

43. PRO, State Papers, Domestic, Elizabeth, SP12/44/52.

44. *Visitation Articles and Injunctions*, ed. W.H. Frere and W.P.M. Kennedy, Alcuin Club, London, 1910, III, p. 24.

45. Ibid., p. 25.

46. PRO, State Papers Domestic, Elizabeth, SP12/190/48.

47. E.M. Albright, *Dramatic Publications in England, 1580–1640*, New York, 1927.

48. A Transcript of the Registers of the Stationers' Company, 1554–1640, ed. E. Arber, London and Birmingham, 1875–94.

49. British Museum, Lansdowne MSS, 48/83 fol. 195; Greg, A *Companion to Arber*, p. 91.

50. This was also laid down in the Star Chamber decree of 1586. Siebert, *Freedom of the Press*, p. 70.

51. PRO, State Papers, Domestic, Elizabeth, SP12/244/4.

52. Ibid., 170, 48.

53. For a full examination of the implications of this image, see M. Walzer, *The Revolution of the Saints*, London, 1966.

9 Illicit Presses and Clandestine Printing in England, 1520–90

In 1587 Sir Thomas Mostyn, acting on a 'tip off', as we would now say, raided a cave in the remote sea cliffs of Creuddyn on the north coast of Wales. By the time he arrived its occupants had fled, but they left behind evidence of long use as a chapel, meeting place and workshop. Among the debris partly jettisoned into the sea was a set of printers' type, which, although valuable, had been too heavy and bulky to remove at short notice. Mostyn had come upon the press of the mysterious – and probably pseudonymous – Roger Thackwell, who, according to Martin Marprelate 'printed Popishe and traiterous Welshe books in Wales'. It was probably from this press, although not necessarily in this location, that Gruffydd Robert had issued his *Y Drych Christianogawl* and perhaps also *Ynglynion ar y Pader y Credo*.[1] Thackwell's was neither the first nor the last secret press in Britain to publish Catholic books, but it provides me with a convenient starting point for a number of reasons. Firstly Marprelate, in lamenting Thackwell's success, contrasted him with his own printer, Robert Waldegrave, who had been twice imprisoned and was finally driven into exile for illicit publishing in the puritan interest; thus neatly illustrating the common ground shared by the two extremes of the Elizabethan religious spectrum. Secondly, no location could be more clandestine than a cave on the Little Orme, in the sixteenth century several miles from the nearest settlement, at Deganwy; and thirdly, I am actually looking across the Llaven Sands to the Little Orme as I write these words.

By 1587 illicit presses were a familiar concept. As we shall see, several had been detected and broken up over the previous twenty years. Nevertheless, it had taken some time for them to evolve from the more confused and ambiguous evasions which had been practised in earlier generations. Before 1520 there had been no clandestine printing in England, for the simple reason that there had been no constraints or restrictions to avoid. For many years the words of William Caxton, written in the epilogue to his first book *The recuyell of the Historyes of Troye*, summed up the innocuous merits of the art:

> I have practysed and lerned at my grete charge and dispense to ordeyne this said book in prynte after the manner and forme as ye may here see. And it is not wreton with penne and ynke as other bokes ben, to thende that every man may have them attones, for all the bookes of this storye . . . were begonne in oon day, and also fynyshid in oon day . . .[2]

In other words printing was simply an ingenious technical device to enable the scrivener to increase and speed up his output. The fact that it also enabled scholars to eliminate scribal errors, and produce a large number of identical texts, was warmly appreciated by the humanists but not, at this stage, of much significance to the printers themselves. Censorship had a long history, going back to the first Statute of Westminster in 1275, and possibly beyond, but there was no sign before 1520 of any perception that printing had created a new problem in that connection.[3] In 1408 Convocation, worried by the development of Lollardy, had prohibited the reproduction of English translations of the scriptures, and in 1414 parliament had confirmed the legal right of ecclesiastical officials to proceed against the makers and writers of heretical books.[4] At the same time, open abuse of the king, whether verbally or in writing, was an ancient common law offence, and could be construed as treason under the statute of 1352. Sowing discord or slander, and bringing the great men of the realm into disrepute by such means, was also an offence under the Statute of Westminster, punishable by imprisonment. *Scandalum Magnatum* was somewhat elaborated by further statutes in the reign of Richard II, but neither its scope nor its nature was changed.[5] The late fifteenth-century printer was therefore operating within a legal and customary framework which had been well known for many years, and there is no sign that any of them fell foul of it. No Lollard texts crept off the presses of Caxton, Pynson or Wynkyn de Worde, and although one celebrated lampoon against Richard III cost its author his life, no attempt was made to print it, either at the time or subsequently.[6]

One of the reasons for this was that most of the early London printers were Frenchmen or Flemings, with no particular interest in England's domestic affairs, and heavily dependent on royal favour. Any Englishmen wishing to practise any of the crafts connected with book production in London had to join a recognised livery company. Since the most strongly established scribal company – the Scriveners – proved unwelcoming, most of the printers became members of the Stationers, a company which already included booksellers, bookbinders, limners, and writers of text hand.[7] The Stationers were well organised, with their own wardens, hall and court, although they did not receive a royal charter and a grant of arms until 1557. The 'strangers', however, did not need such an organisation. A statute of 1484 had explicitly exempted printers and booksellers from the ban that prohibited other alien craftsmen from working in the city, and although the Stationers persistently attacked this privileged position, it was not until 1534 that they eventually succeeded in getting the exemption clause repealed.[8] There was nothing to prevent English printers from working in the provinces, and there were presses in Oxford and St Albans before 1513, but despite the steadily growing and diversifying book market, English printing was still heavily dominated by foreign craftsmen when the onset of the Reformation thrust it into the political and ecclesiastical firing line.

Lutheran books had already begun to appear in England before the end of 1520, in sufficient numbers to cause alarm to the authorities, and on 14 May 1521 Cardinal Wolsey issued a legatine commission which was the first specific act of censorship. Directed to all bishops, and commanded to be read in every church at mass time, it warned of the dangers of 'multos et varios articulos sive errores cuisdam Martini Lutheri pestiferos et perniciosos, ac Graecorum haeresim et Bohemican expresse continentes . . .', and ordered that all books containing these errors should be given up to the bishop or his commissary within fifteen days, under pain of judgment as a heretic. In order to avoid misunderstanding, a list of forty-two alleged errors, taken from the papal condemnation of Luther, was promulgated at the same time. The response to this edict was sufficient to enable Wolsey to stage a number of book burnings, including the celebrated one at Paul's Cross, before the end of the year, but quite inadequate to stem the flood of imports. Wolsey was not a persecutor by conviction, and had many other things on his mind, so having set an example, he left it to others to follow up his initiative. Cuthbert Tunstall, the Bishop of London, was forced to take the lead by virtue of his exposed position, and in 1524 he summoned the printers and booksellers of London to meet him, and having warned them afresh of the consequences of handling heretical books, issued the first licensing order.[10] No book was to be imported without episcopal licence, and no new work was to be published without the sanction of a board of censors consisting of himself, Wolsey, Warham and Fisher. Whether the latter order was merely a precaution, or whether suspect books were already being printed in the city is not clear. The record of Tunstall's visitation of 1527 suggests that some works which were then circulating, but of which no copy now survives, may have come into that category.[11] The main problem was clearly smuggling, and this continued to be the case for the next fifteen years.

After 1526 the situation, from the bishops' point of view, began to deteriorate alarmingly. This was principally on account of the publication in that year of William Tyndale's translation of the New Testament, printed in Germany. This was the first English 'bestseller', and went through a number of editions of about 1500 copies each over the next few years. Tunstall battled hard against this avalanche, and enjoyed some success. One consignment of 500 copies was seized, another was bought up and destroyed; the principal financial backer, Humphrey Monmouth, was arrested and interrogated in 1528;[12] and a solemn warning was issued (in German) to the merchants of the Steelyard.[13] But these achievements were not followed up. Van Ruremond the colporteur was released after doing penance, and Monmouth had influential friends in the city who got him off. The bishop's alarm can be clearly detected in the language of his proclamation of 23 October 1527, issued as soon as the scale of the problem became apparent;

> many children of iniquity, maintainers of Luther's sect, blinded through extreme wickedness and wandering from the way of truth and the catholic faith, craftily have translated the new testament into our English tongue, intermeddling therewith many heretical articles and erroneous opinions . . .

All copies were to be surrendered to the archdeacons within thirty days.[14] Over the next two years, Tyndale followed up his New Testament with a number of controversial vernacular works, all printed abroad: *A Compendious Introduccion Prologue or Preface to the Pistle of Paul to the Romans*, which probably came from the press of P. Schoeffer at Worms, the same man who had first printed the New Testament;[15] *The Obedience of a Christen Man*, and *The Parable of the Wicked Mammon*. The latter two were ascribed to the press of one Hans Luft, of 'Marlborow in the land of Hesse', but almost certainly came from Jan Hoochstraten of Antwerp.[16] Also in 1528, William Roy's *Burial of the Masse* was printed in an edition of 1000 in Strasburg. Not only zeal for the Reformation tempted the smuggler of these books. When a colporteur named Robert Necton was apprehended in 1530, his confession uncovered a fascinating corner of this forbidden trade. Necton had numerous contacts, and disposed of his books in small numbers all over the south and east of England, charging between 2s.4d. and 2s.8d. each. At the same time his supplier, an anonymous Dutchman, had offered him 300 for £16.5s., or about 13d. each, and since Necton had temporised over the offer, he had probably expected to get them for less.[17] The business was risky, but clearly commanded a high profit, and Tunstall would no doubt have agreed with his arch-enemy John Bale, who later wrote, 'suche is the insatiable thirst of them that are covetous that they care not what mischief they may do to get money . . .'.[18]

After Wolsey's fall in 1529, and Tunstall's departure for the distant northern see of Durham, the battle against heretical books was taken up directly by the royal government. The initial reason for this was not so much the failure of the ecclesiastical authorities as the zeal of the new Lord Chancellor, Sir Thomas More. It was he who was responsible for the comprehensive proclamation of March 1530, which established the first index of fourteen prohibited books, and mobilised the justices of King's Bench, justices of the peace, and justices of assize in support of doctrinal orthodoxy.[19] Later in the same year a further proclamation added five more books to the list, and warned against 'divers other books made in the English tongue and imprinted beyond the sea'. Almost as an afterthought, it was also ordered that works 'concerning Holy Scripture', and not before printed in England, were to be licensed by the ordinary, and the licence recorded on the title page, although no specific penalties were prescribed for default.[20] By this time political developments were rapidly complicating the situation, and the very next proclamation issued was against the importation of papal bulls. Shortly after, the appearance of Fisher's *De causa matrimonii serenissimi Regis Angliae*, published at Alcalá in Spain, indicated the dangerous cross-currents ahead.[21] More's strenuous campaign was running into serious difficulties, not because the king was becoming sympathetic to heretics, but because his 'great matter' was making enemies of his doctrinal friends, and friends of his enemies.

The London printers were not, as yet, very seriously affected by these developments. Their numbers were growing, and the privileges of the aliens were steadily being whittled away, but what control (if any) the Stationers' Company exercised over the products of its members is unknown. John Gough, Robert Redman and Thomas Berthelet had all been briefly in trouble with the Bishop of London in 1526 and 1527 for printing without ecclesiastical licences, but they were not punished, and their offences may have been purely technical.[22] It seems that the government was not very interested in printers or bookbinders, even when the books in question were clearly offensive, regarding them simply as craftsmen, who were not responsible for the contents of the works which they processed. Even John Scot the printer of *The Nun's Book*, escaped with a brief period of imprisonment, while the author, Edward Bocking, was executed.[23] The period of Cromwell's ascendancy, from 1533 to 1540, was one of very strict surveillance, but also of considerable opportunities. The demand for traditional service books rapidly disappeared; over sixty breviaries had been printed before 1535; thereafter, until the accession of Mary, there was just one, in 1543. On the other hand, there were new service books to be printed, and primers, and considerable quantities of royal propaganda. The virtual disappearance of independent alien printers after 1534 also encouraged members of other companies to try their hand at the craft. Richard Grafton, John Mayler and Edward Whitchurch were all substantial merchants drawn into printing by Cromwell's patronage, and particularly by his project for a translation of the Bible, which finally bore fruit in 1538.[24] Cromwell also seems to have been in the habit of distributing his favour in the form of verbal guarantees, or patents, to individual printers for particular kinds of work. This could cause considerable problems, as was demonstrated by the case of John Wayland who, having been granted a vebal patent for Hilsey's Primner, then sold his rights to John Mayler in 1539. Mayler unwisely did not check up on the nature of the rights which he had purchased, was subsequently prosecuted after Cromwell's fall, and endeavoured to sue Wayland for fraud.[25]

Cromwellian censorship was strict, and at least as much political as religious, being reinforced by successive treason laws. It was also remarkably successful. Despite the ritual lament contained in a proclamation of January 1536 about 'divers and sundry writings and books, as well imprinted as other . . . in derogation and diminution of the dignity and authority royal of the king's majesty . . .',[26] the quantity of 'street literature' was small, and mostly hand-written. A few serious works challenging the king's policies were imported from abroad, but very little was produced in England. A further proclamation of November 1538, although evincing renewed concern about erroneous doctrine, shifted the whole responsibility for controlling the press and the book trade on to 'some of his Grace's Privy Council, or such other as his highness shall appoint', and introduced for the first time a royal, as opposed to an episcopal, licensing system.[27] This was developed further in 1543, when penalties of three months' imprisonment and a £10 fine for each unlicensed book were specified, irrespective of any further penalties that might be incurred by virtue of the contents.[28] A second offence could result in the forfeiture of all goods and perpetual imprisonment. By 1543 the Act of Six Articles and the disappearance of Cromwell had wrought a dramatic change. In place of cautious and firmly controlled reform came uncertainty, and divided counsels. The production of the newly authorised Bible and service books continued, with formal patents now being issued to Cromwell's former protégés, such as Grafton, Whitchurch and Mayler. On the other hand, the production of overtly Lutheran books was sharply curtailed; Grafton was imprisoned in 1541 for printing Melanchthon's letter against the Six Articles, and several other publishers were interrogated by the Privy Council, and placed under recognisances two years later.[29] Character-istically, Grafton did not lose his patent, and none of the other printers seems to have been further punished.

There was also a rapid upsurge in the production of controversial ephemera after 1540. Broadsheets and ballads defending Cromwell, and others attacking him; lampoons against Stephen Gardiner, the Bishop of Winchester and a leading conservative; scurrilous attacks on the clergy and the mass; all coming anonymously or under false colophons from the presses of London. It has been suggested that one of the reasons for this was that the development of the patent system had concentrated so much lucrative work in the hands of a few substantial printers that younger and less well established men were forced to take risks in order to make a living.[30] However, since Grafton himself was one of the main offenders, this must be a doubtful hypothesis, and when we realise that Grafton was already royal printer to Prince Edward before Henry's death, the suspicion arises that these printers were being encouraged and protected by the rival parties in the council.[31] At the same time the word 'book', frequently used in contemporary accounts, did not necessarily mean a printed work. The 'divers books of heresies . . . against the sacrament of the altar' which were 'cast abroad by night' in May 1544, or the 2000 books against the mass which Sebastian Newdigate boasted of having placed in the hands of the citizens of London, were probably handwritten broadsheets,[32] which were even more difficult to trace to a source. Both sides, of course, fell foul of official policy. John Bale complained bitterly of the popularity of the *Genealogy of Heresy*, and of Eck's *Enchiridion*, but his own *Elucidation of Anne Askew's martyrdom*, secretly imported from Wessel, was even less acceptable, and the conservatives scored a number of minor victories against radical publishers in the last months of the reign.

By 1547 there were twenty–five recognised presses in London, and a handful elsewhere. At the same time the Stationers' Company probably numbered about eighty members, most of whom would have been primarily bookbinders or retailers. Several of the most successful presses were operated by patentees who were not members of the company. Richard Grafton was (and remained) a grocer, while Edward Whitchurch was a haberdasher. Apart from Reynold Wolfe, Anne Boleyn's protégé, who had managed to overcome the hostility of the Stationers, the only foreign workmen were journeymen and employees of the English masters, many of whom also had numerous native workmen and apprentices. Clandestine and unlicensed printing was common, and was extremely difficult to detect, partly because of the ease and frequency with which workers, editors, and even typeface, moved from one press to another.[33] The appetite of Londoners for controversial ephemera was enormous, and since most printers were men of trade first, and proselytisers second (if at all), they took their profit and let the authors shoulder the main burden of risk. At the same time false colophons were beginning to appear, and books purporting to come from Wittenberg, of from 'Ubryght Hoff at Lipse' were being printed within the shadow of St Paul's. No secret press, as opposed to a press put to secret use, had yet appeared, and with the death of Henry VIII many of the conflicting pressures which had been bearing on the trade over the previous twenty years were reduced, or temporarily disappeared. The first and most obvious change that took place was the 'sudden relaxation of censorship against overtly Protestant works, both pastoral and polemic.[34] Scores of such works, by a wide variety of authors, appeared between 1547 and 1549, and the total number of titles went up from about 100 in the former year to 225 in the latter.[35] During the same period the number of presses rose to thirty-nine. New patents for service books, bibles, primers, catechisms and other religious books were granted to Walter Lynne, John Oswen, Humphrey Powell, John Day, Thomas Gualthier and Richard Jugge. It was a period of unprecedented relaxation and prosperity, assisted by the repeal of Henry's draconian treason laws in the autumn of 1547.

Catholic works did not disappear, nor were they banned unless explicitly papalist. Richard Smith was forced to recant papalist doctrine at Paul's Cross in May 1547, and to burn two of his printed books, *A Briefe treatise settinge forth divers truthes*, and a *Defence of the blessed masse*,[36] but other conservative tracts continued to circulate without penalty. Protector Somerset may well have felt that he could afford to be lenient in that direction, since the overwhelming majority of the printers seem to have been sympathetic to reform, and the scale of written and printed Catholic polemic was small. Neither the Stationers, who were a highly educated elite, nor the literate population of London which provided their main market, were at all typical of the country at large in their religious opinions, but they have naturally exercised a disproportionate influence over historical interpretation. In spite of the reforming policies of Edward's council, radical printing continued to be a bigger problem than Catholic, for social and political as well as religious reasons. Before the end of 1547 Day and Sheres were producing scurrilous tracts such as *The upchering of the masse* and *A dyalogue betwene a gentylman and a preest* with the colophons of 'H. Lufte, Wittenberg' or 'Hans Hitprick'.[37] At the same time a small number of works also began to appear, such as *Questions worthy to be consulted*, which were seditious in the sense that they claimed to detect corruption in high places, and normally took refuge in complete anonymity.[38] During these years London was a major city of refuge for Protestants fleeing from the Counter-Reformation, and a considerable number of Dutch, German and French stationers joined the influx. Of these a handful were given privileged status, and operated as printers on a considerable scale, basing themselves in the liberties attached to their churches. Stephen Mierdman, Walter Lynne and Thomas Gualthier were the most important, Lynne and Gualthier both also being patentees. Mierdman was allowed to employ a number of his fellow countrymen, and some of the more radical English printers were also hospitable, notably John Day and Hugh Singleton, so that by the end of 1549 over sixty foreigners were working in the London book trade.[39]

By 1550 the euphoria was passing. Traditional hostilities began to reappear, and the number of foreign workers fell to fifty-three. In 1552 the number of titles issued was back to the 1547 level, at 105, and many of the newly established presses were in difficulties. The council, under the tougher hand of the Duke of Northumberland and partly disillusioned with the results of leniency, clamped down severely on critics of the regime, whether secular or religious. As before, the printers tended not to suffer unduly. John Lowton, who published a ballad against Northumberland in 1552, was pilloried, but his printer, William Martin, was merely bound in recognisance to surrender all the copies in his possession.[40] It was mainly the younger and struggling printers who took this sort of risk, but most of the criticism was verbal and did not touch the stationers at all. The Catholics did not give up, but their effort was small-scale. Richard Smith and Maurice Chauncey, an ex-Carthusian, were among those who fled abroad, and Chauncey published an *Historia Aliquot Martyrum* in defence of More and Fisher, which was smuggled in.[41] One established London stationer, Robert Caly, also preferred exile to Protestantism, and settled at Rouen, where he printed a number of books including Gardiner's *An explication and assertion of the true catholique faith*, and Thomas Martin's tract against the marriage of priests.[42]

The smuggling operation from Rouen was broken up by the government in March 1551 with the arrest of William Seth, a servant of Edmund Bonner's, who was a key agent and whose testimony provides the same kind of insight into the operation as that of Necton twenty years earlier.[43] There seems to have been a considerable amount of Catholic material circulating in manuscript, such as the poems of Miles Huggarde, but whether this remained unprinted from choice, or because no craftsman of suitable sympathies could be induced to handle it, must remain uncertain.

The abrupt change of confessional domination which occurred with the accession of Mary in the summer of 1553 thus had a much more dramatic impact on the printing trade than the more gradual developments of 1547 – and in the opposite direction. Most of the foreign Protestant refugees departed during the autumn, and the remainder were expelled in February 1554.[44] Stephen Mierdman printed his last book in London in August 1553, before retiring to Emden. Printing activity suddenly contracted, and a number of presses, such as that of John Oswen at Ipswich, went out of business, although whether for lack of sympathy with the regime or lack of publishable material is not clear. The first year of Mary's reign saw about seventy new titles in all, roughly comparable to the latter years of Henry VIII, and well below any year of the previous reign. It is not my intention to enter into another discussion of the propaganda battles of the reign, but the queen's lack of energetic press patronage is notorious, and fewer than a hundred works of Catholic propaganda and polemic were issued in the five years.[45] Sixty-six of these came from just two presses: that of Robert Caly, whom we have already noticed as a Catholic zealot, and that of John Cawood, the Queen's Printer. Twelve other presses contributed between one and five titles each, so at least half the printers working in the city either eschewed controversy altogether or worked surreptitiously for the other side – a picture entirely consistent with the pattern we have already established for the previous period. As might be expected, most of the Protestant response, totalling some 114 titles, was produced on the continent and smuggled into England in ways graphically described by John Foxe, but not basically different from the methods used in earlier years. The main centres were Emden, where Egidius Van der Erve, sometime deacon to John a Lasco's London congregation, contributed 18 titles;[46] and Wesel, where Lambrecht and de Zuttere between them produced no less than 32 works. Several presses in Strasburg and Geneva contributed smaller numbers, bringing the total to about 70. Although many of these bore false, and even taunting, colophons, such as 'Rome, before the castle of St. Angelo', they were produced openly in cities sympathetic to the Reformation, and did not become clandestine until they entered England. There they encountered censorship of almost Henrician severity. In spite of the restoration of the Roman jurisdication in January 1555, control of the press and of book distribution remained primarily in the hands of the council, and after proclamations of August 1553 and March 1554 against spreaders of heresy and sedition, the law was twice extended. In January 1555 the law was extended by statute, so that slandering the king or queen became a felony, and the penalty a rare reintroduction of mutilation.[47] Another statute of the same session made it treason to preach or write against King Philip's title. At the same time the medieval heresy laws were revived, and in June 1555 a new index of prohibited books was promulgated.[48]

Once again, however, these severe measures seem to have had little impact on the printers. In March 1556 William Rydall, William Copland, Richard Lant and Owen ap Rogers were all summoned before the council, and bound in recognisances to deliver to John Cawood all the copies of certain books which they had printed 'to be by him destroyed'.[49] One of these books was Cranmer's recantation, which the government found embarrassing because of its Spanish endorsement; the others are not identified. The following year Cawood himself was in trouble, when the council ordered a search of his shop and house for 'unlawful writings', and in July 1558 the premises of John Kingston and Thomas Marshe were similarly searched. In this last case the Lord Mayor's officers were specifically instructed to seek for 'all such bookes corruptly sett forthe under the name of the Busshup of Lyncolne as all others as shall impugne the Catholyke Faith . . .',[50] but either they found nothing or their discoveries were of no significance, for no more is heard of the matter. Lant and Rydall, as well as Cawood, are generally reckoned to have been Catholic printers who supported the regime, and it does not appear that any of these 'detections' touched upon the main trade in illicit publications. The government's one major success in this direction was the arrest of John Day in October 1554, along with 'an odur prynter', who may have been Hugh Singleton.[51] Day was a young man, and a committed Protestant, who had already had some experience of surreptitious printing. In the latter part of 1553 and the first half of 1554 he seems to have been responsible for fifteen titles, bearing the names of 'Nicholas Dorcaster' and 'Michael Wood, Rouen'.[52] These included such important pieces as the Protestant edition of Gardiner's *De Vera Obedientia Oratio* (which the Lord Chancellor found particularly embarrassing), and *The humble and unfained confession of the beleefe of certain poore banished men*. Where these works were printed is something of a mystery. Day had a press in London, but his arrest also coincided with a report from the Imperial ambassador, Simon Renard that 'The man who used to compose and have printed, in an Imperial town near Brabant, certain slanderous books, has been found out and caught . . .', and he was caught in Norfolk, which suggests travel to the Low Countries. Fifteen titles in a little over twelve months probably means that he was conducting two operations, and it may well be that 'Dorcaster' was produced in London, and 'Wood' in Brabant – but that is mere conjecture.[53] The sequel to Day's arrest is instructive. He was not indicted for any offence, and the fact that he was imprisoned with John Rogers suggests that it may have been the intention to charge him with heresy. But in the early part of 1555 he escaped abroad,[54] and disappeared from view until 1557, when he was back in London as a legitimate printer and a recognised member of the Stationers' Company! He must have made some kind of submission, but was subsequently too valuable a protagonist of the Reformation for this to have been cast in his teeth.[55] Hugh Singleton also escaped abroad, and unlike Day became actively involved in the exiles' propaganda campaign. He operated in Basle, Strasburg and Wesel, and did not return to England until after Elizabeth's accession.[56]

The authorities enjoyed a few other small successes. The group responsible for one version of John Bradford's *Letter* was apprehended in March 1557, and a complex attempt to publish English propaganda in Danzig was frustrated.[57] However, the punishments, where they are recorded at all, were trivial, and bore no relation to the penalties inflicted on those convicted of heresy or treason. In spite of their assiduous efforts, including royal and legatine commissions, Mary's councillors seem to have persisted with the traditional view that printers were little more than neutral agents, a position which the whole experience of Edward's reign should have undermined. It also seems clear that Protestant polemic continued to be produced in London on a small scale after Day's arrest, perhaps as many as twenty titles between late 1554 and late 1558. Whether a genuine 'secret press' was responsible for any part of this output is uncertain. More likely, groups of workers collaborated, 'borrowing' type and presses from the established printers, with or without their connivance.[58] The direct involvement of members of the Stationers' Company cannot be proved, and was never subsequently claimed, when it would have been safe and prestigious to have done so.

In many respects these were lean years for the printing trade. Only about half as many stationers were actively involved in book production under Mary as had been similarly involved under Edward (41 as against 80). Grafton, Whitchurch, Wolfe, Humphrey Powell and Thomas Gualthier all ceased printing; just about everyone was left with stocks of unsaleable Protestant literature; and much of the Catholic liturgical printing that could have provided valuable new business was done instead in Paris.[59] On the other hand there was no persecution. Even Grafton, who lost his patent and was imprisoned at the beginning of the reign, was not subsequently troubled, and was Master of the Grocers' Company in 1555–6. Also, the Stationers' Company took a major step forward with the grant of a royal charter in 1557. Paradoxically, this grant probably owed more to the momentum developed in the reign of Edward VI than it did to any policy of Mary's. It had been mooted in 1551, and had been signalled in 1554 by the grant of St Peter's church as the company's new hall. By 1555 it was already established practice for every printer to present his 'copye' to the wardens before issuing a new book, and John Wallye was fined twenty shillings in July of that year for failing to present A breefe Cronacle 'contrary to our ordenances.'[60] A few years later a standard fee was charged for such registration – usually 4d. for a ballad and 8d. for a more substantial work – and in 1565 Alexander Lacey was fined 12d. for printing 'ballettes that was other mens copyes'.[61] The point of this registration was not to assist government censorship (although it might have that effect), but to protect the business interests of members against piracy. This kind of sharp practice was one of the less beneficial effects of the boom under Edward VI, which had not been an unmixed blessing to the company, as Christopher Barker testified many years later:

> In the time of king Henry the eighte there were but fewe printers, and those of good credit and competent wealth, at whiche time and before there was another sort of man . . . called Stationers; which have, and still partlye to this daye do use to buy their bookes in grosse of the said printers, and bind them uppe and sell them in theyr shoppes . . . .. In King Edward his dayes Printers and printing began greatly to increase; but the provision of letter and many other things belonging to printing was so exceedingly chargeable that most of these Prynters were dryven, through necessity, to compound before with the booksellers at so lowe a value as the prynters themselves were moste tymes small gainers and often losers . . . .[62]

Competitive conditions had, as we have seen, led some printers to take risks with censorship; apparently it led others to take liberties with other men's work. The incorporation of the Stationers did not bring about any quick or major changes in their practice. The wardens had exercised quality control before, and the company had carried out collections for city purposes, as when 92 members contributed to the Mayor's Bridewell appeal in 1556.[63] But the 97 men who were listed in the charter of 1557 clearly believed that it was worthwhile to spend several pounds upon the costs, and upon the grant of arms that accompanied it, finally consolidating the control over London printing which they had enjoyed in practice since 1534. Incorporation also had the subsequent effect of preventing the reopening of provincial presses, except by special royal privilege. In fact there were no such presses in 1557, the last, that of Edward Mychell at Canterbury, having failed in the previous year, and the concentration of legitimate printing in one place, under the control of one answerable authority, must have been in the minds of those who granted the charter.

One of the major lessons of Mary's short reign was the effectiveness of clandestine printing in undermining the morale and popularity of a regime which was made vulnerable by its own mistakes, and which failed to seize and hold the initiative in propaganda. Mary's defenders bitterly deplored the 'threehalfpenny books which steal out of Germany, replete with treasons . . . as with other abominable lies . . .', but they recognised their power, and feared the kind of mocking wit which ascribed *A supplicacyon to the Queenes Maiestie* to the press of John Cawood.[64] The impact of such propaganda may have been limited, but the minority it influenced was of critical importance. When the confessional roundabout turned another full circle in 1558–9, it remained to be seen whether the English Catholics could profit from these lessons, and turn the same devices to their own ends.

At first there was little sign of this happening. Although Protestant tracts and ballads began to appear in London within a few days of Elizabeth's accession, the Catholic response was hesitant and muted. Robert Caly gave up printing, and several Edwardian practitioners returned to work, but there was nothing like the rapid expansion of business that had occurred in 1547.[65] Both sides were cautious after the rapid fluctuations of the previous decade, and although the religious settlement of 1559 was clearly Protestant, enforcement was less energetically pursued than under either of the previous regimes. The government moved promptly to impose its control, but made no startling innovations. The Royal Injunctions of 1559 made comprehensive provision for licensing, as we have seen.[66] Overall supervision was placed in the hands of the newly established Ecclesiastical Commission, 'to which her Majesty straightly commandeth all manner her subjects, and especially the Wardens and Company of Stationers, to be obedient'.[67] Thereafter, the role of the company and its Court of Assistants, steadily increased; and although Edward Arber was right in maintaining that the company was not, and never became, a government agency, nevertheless co-operation with the Ecclesiastical Commission was close.[68] In 1566 a council decree laying down penalties for unlicensed printing included exclusion from the trade, as well as fines and imprisonment.[69] The company organised weekly searches, and its court destroyed illicit books, defaced illegal type, and fined and excluded offenders. By 1582 it was complaining of the charges it had to bear in executing warrants of search and suppression against 'popish books' on behalf of the commission.[70] In 1586 a decree in Star Chamber brought the whole licensing system back under the control of the Archbishop of Canterbury and the Bishop of London. Thereafter, royal licences appeared regularly alongside the company's own licences in the Stationers' Register, and the appointment of master printers was tightly controlled by the Court of High Commission.[71] The efficiency and stringency of censorship thus steadily increased during Elizabeth's long reign, and the developing role of the Stationers' Company largely explains the different pattern that illicit printing began to follow. The surreptitious use of established London presses for the production of dissident literature virtually ceased. An outstanding but isolated example was the publication of John Stubbes' *The discoverie of a gaping gulf* by Hugh Singleton in 1579.[72] Stubbes lost his right hand, under the penalties of the Marian statute of 1555, but Singleton was exonerated by the court after indictment and trial. More typical was the activity of the Catholic entrepreneur, William Carter, a former apprentice of John Cawood, and officially a bookbinder. Carter was regularly in trouble for distributing 'lewd pamphlettes', and had served several brief spells in prison before the pursuivants raided his house in Hart Street in 1579. There they found a secret press, which had already produced about a dozen Catholic devotional works bearing continental colophons, and a stock of François de Belleforest's *L'Innocence de Marie, royne d'Ecosse*, which Carter was clearly intending to sell.[73] He was tried by High Commission, and imprisoned again. After his release the following year, with incredible foolishness he acquired fresh type and started printing again – in the same place. Inevitably, the pursuivants called again, and this time they found Gregory Martin's *Treatise of Schisme*, which Carter was in the process of printing. Carter was sent to the Tower, tortured, and eventually executed for high treason on 11 January 1583.[74]

The record of secret Catholic printing in England was not distinguished. Richard Rowlande sought to capitalise on the execution of Edmund Campion by publishing *A true reporte of the death and martydome of M. Campion* from a press in Smithfield early in 1582, but by 14 April William Fleetwood, the Recorder of London was able to report: '. . . I pursued the matter so nere that I founde the presse, the letters the figures and a number of bookes.'[75] Rowlande made good his escape, and subsequently published two books in Paris,[76] but the Smithfield venture had been brought to a speedy end. Robert Parsons did rather better. With the collaboration of Francis Browne, the brother of Viscount Montague, he set up a press at Browne's house in Greenstreet, East Ham. There Stephen Brinkley succeeded in producing six books bearing Louvain imprints, before he was arrested and the press broken up.[77] Unlike Carter, however, Brinkley was soon released, and within months was collaborating with Parsons on a fresh venture, this time at Stonor Park, about 20 miles from London. Two books were printed at Stonor Park before that press, too, was detected and seized by Sir Henry Neville on 8 August 1581.[78] As we have already seen, the itinerant Welsh press of Roger Thackwell was detected and seized, more by luck than judgement, in 1587, and that put an end, for the time being, to the Catholic secret presses. Of course the great majority of English Catholic works were printed abroad, in Paris, Louvain, Douai and many other places. One man, John

Fowler, was responsible for over 30 titles at Louvain between 1565 and 1579, and by the end of James I's reign the total number of titles had risen to about 430.[79] Like the Protestant polemic of any earlier period, these works were sold to the faithful at good market prices; a Douai Bible was retailing for 40s. by 1625.[80] It is not surprising that the government was constantly exercised, and felt that it was fighting a losing battle against the smugglers and their agents. However, against the secret presses and clandestine printing within England the Elizabethan council did much better than its predecessors, partly because of its superior techniques for controlling the trade, and partly because of its success in stimulating a general climate of Protestant nationalism.

But there was no help to be gained from the latter sentiment against attacks from the theological left. Ironically, that same moderation which helped to swing the conformist majority behind the government also alienated some of those earnest spirits whose predecessors had been such a thorn in the flesh of Henry VIII and Mary. Although puritan dissatisfaction began early in the reign, most of its literary expressions refrained from overt attacks upon the government, and were legitimately published by a number of sympathetic stationers. However, in 1572 appeared *An Admonition to the Parliament*, which its authors, John Field and Thomas Wilcox, knew better than to entrust to an established printer. John Strowd, who undertook to produce it, was a dedicated amateur, a Somerset clergyman who had been deprived for nonconformity in 1568. He produced two editions of the *Admonition* at a secret press in Hampstead, and Lord Burleigh suspected that the Stationers were not doing all in their power to find him.[81] He was probably wrong, for the company detected and dismantled the press by August 1573, and Strowd was convented before the High Commission.[82] The experience did not chasten him, and he seems to have resumed secret printing, either in Kent or in Northamptonshire, by 1574, when he issued two editions of a *Replye to an answer made to Dr. Whitgift*. What happened to him, or his press, thereafter is not clear; he reappeared briefly in 1586 with one title, but never again stimulated sufficient indignation to be actively pursued. In fact the puritans were able, as the Catholics were not, to publish some of their controversial work surreptitiously through established presses, and this is probably what happened with the anonymous *Briefe and plain Declaration* of 1584, which triggered off a considerable controversy, but could hardly have been described as seditious.[83] Even the notorious Marprelate tracts were able to attract the services of a legitimate printer, albeit one in deep disfavour with both the government and the company. Robert Waldegrave had established his press in the Strand in 1578, and over the following decade published seventy titles, the vast majority of which might be described as 'acceptable puritan'. However, in 1584 he had ventured to print *A dialogue concerning the strife of our Church*, and the High Commission ordered the Stationers' Company to act. Waldegrave spent five months in the White Lion prison in Southwark.[84] After his release, with more devotion than discretion, he returned to the charge, printing (without licence) four treatises by John Udall. On 13 May 1588 his premises were again raided by the company's officers, his stock burned and his type defaced.[85] Waldegrave himself escaped into hiding in East Mosely, where he set up a secret press and began his association with John Penry, three of whose tracts he printed. It was from here that the first of the Marprelate letters was issued in

October 1588, with the ribald and typical colophon 'Printed overseas in Europe, within two furlongs of a bouncing priest.'[86] However, the pursuivants were aware of Waldegrave's activity, if not of his whereabouts, and the puritan establishment looked upon Marprelate with disfavour. He and his press became fugitive. The second tract was printed at the home of Sir Richard Knightley in Northamptonshire, and the third in Coventry. By this time Waldegrave had had enough, and early in 1589, deeply concerned about the radical slope upon which he found himself, he left Coventry and departed overseas.[87] Events quickly demonstrated his wisdom. Two further tracts were produced by John Hodgkins, Arthur Tomlyn and Valentine Symmes at Walston Priory, but shortly after, in the course of another 'flit', they were arrested at Warrington. This time the three printers were all put to the torture in the Tower, and although Symmes and Tomlyn were eventually released in 1590, Hodgkin was executed for felony.[88] The campaign against radical protestantism was to continue for some time, but after this grim example – the only execution of a clandestine printer – secret presses did not feature in the battle.

By 1590 the English government had a stronger grip on the domestic printing industry than any other European monarchy save that of Spain. Every court and jurisdiction played its part. Star Chamber dealt with patent and privilege cases, High Commission with ecclesiastical misdemeanours, and the common law courts with felony and treason. Sometimes the council acted directly, as it did in 1570 to suppress William Elderton's ballad *Dr. Storys Stumbling into England*, sometimes cases were heard in the assizes.[89] The main reason for this success was the co-operation of the London Stationers' Company, and the monopolistic control which that company was granted in return. Although there were occasions of friction, and the company always enjoyed normal independence, the period as a whole saw the general working out of a relationship of mutual advantage between the government and the London Stationers; a relationship which saw the gradual extinction of foreign control by 1534, and of independent provincial presses by 1557. By 1590 it was both very difficult and very dangerous to print in defiance of this formidable combination. Publishing abroad was a different matter, of course, and there the Stationers could offer little help, since such products seldom appeared in ordinary bookshops. Significantly, the period ended, as it began, with government attention focused on the apparently intractable problem of illicit imports.

Notes

1. A.F. Allison, 'Biographical Studies, 1534–1829', *Recusant History*, II (3), 1954, 38. For works by Gruffydd Robert, see A.F. Allison and D.M. Rogers, *A Catalogue of Catholic Books in English Printed Abroad or Secretly in England, 1558–1640*, London, 1964, nos. 726–9. Geraint Gruffydd, 'Gwas Ddirgel yr Ogof yn Rhiwledyn', *Journal of the Welsh Bibliographical Society*, IX (i), 1958, 1–24.
2. W.J.B. Crotch (ed.) *The Prologues and Epilogues of William Caxton*, Early English Text Society, CLXXVI, 1928, 7.
3. For a fuller consideration of press control in England under the Tudors, see F.S. Siebert, *Freedom of the Press in England, 1476–1776* (Urbana, Ill., 1952); also D.M. Loades, 'The Press under the Early Tudors', *Transactions of the Cambridge*

Bibliographical Society, IV (i) 1964, 29–51.

4. D. Wilkins, *Concilia Magnae Britanniae et Hiberniae*, London, 1737, III, p. 317; statute 2 Henry V, 1, c.7.

5. D.M. Loades, 'The Theory and Practice of Censorship in Sixteenth Century England', *Transactions of the Royal Historical Society*, 5 series, XXIV, 1974, 143. [See p. 96]

6. William Collingbourne. Edward Hall, *Chronicle*, London, 1809, p. 398. As Charles Ross has pointed out, there was more to Collingbourne's offence than the lampoon. Ross, *Richard III*, London, 1981, p. xxxiii.

7. Cyprian Blagden, *The Stationers' Company: a History 1403–1959*, London, 1960.

8. Statute I Richard III, c.9; statute 25 Henry VIII, c.15.

9. J. Strype, *Ecclesiastical Memorials*, Oxford, 1822, I, pt. i, 56–7; I, pt. ii, 21.

10. P. Took, 'Government and the Printing Trade, 1540–1560', Ph.D, London, 1978, 67.

11. Strype, *Eccl. Mem.*, I, pt. i, 113–24.

12. Ibid., 487–93.

13. *Den wirdigen henen Burgemeysteren der Stat Coelln*, London, 1526.

14. Loades, 'Press under the Early Tudors', 32. Wilkins, *Concilia*, III, p. 705.

15. A.W. Pollard and G.W. Redgrave (eds) *A Short Title Catalogue of Books Printed in England, Scotland and Ireland . . . 1475–1640* [STC]. Second edn, revised by W.A. Jackson, F.S. Ferguson and K.F. Pantzer, II (I-Z) London, 1976, 24438.

16. Ibid., 24447, 24454.

17. John Foxe, *Actes and Monuments*, ed. Josiah Pratt, London, 1853–70, IV, p. 652.

18. *A mysterye of inyquyte*, Antwerp, 1545, p. 87 (STC 1303).

19. P.L. Hughes and J.F. Larkin, *Tudor Royal Proclamations*, New Haven, Conn, and London, 1964, I, pp. 181–6. Hughes and Larkin ascribe this proclamation to 1529, but see G.R. Elton, *Policy and Police*, Cambridge, 1972, p. 218.

20. Hughes and Larkin, *Tudor Royal Proclamations*, I, pp. 193–7.

21. Took, 'Government and the Printing Trade', 68. On 1 January 1536, after his execution, all Fisher's writings and sermons were banned by proclamation.

22. Foxe, *Actes*, V, p. 569; Took, 'Government and the Printing Trade', 99–100. Gough spent a brief period in the Fleet, but Berthelet seems merely to have neglected the formality of an episcopal licence. According to Took (98) John Rastell was also active in the Protestant interest at this date, and helped Tyndale with his *Wicked Mammon* and *Obedience*, which subsequently appeared in Antwerp, but this hypothesis does not seem to be established, and in view of Rastell's close connection with More at that date, does not seem very likely. But see J.L. Douthit-Weir, 'Tyndale's *The Obedience of a Christian man*', *Library*, 5 series, XXX, 1975, 95–107, on this point.

23. E.J. Devereux, 'Elizabeth Barton and Tudor Censorship', *Bulletin of the John Rylands Library*, XLIX (i), 1966, 91.

24. Grafton put £500 of his own into the Matthew Bible, published in 1537. Cromwell at first seems to have intended to place the Great Bible with Francis Regnault of Paris, but when the project ran into trouble with the French Inquisition, shifted the work to Grafton, Whitchurch and Mayler, Took, 'Government and the Printing Trade', 7, 107, 183.

25. H.J. Byrom, 'John Wayland, Printer, Scrivener and Litigant', *The Library*, 4 series, XI, 1931, 312.

26. Hughes and Larkin, *Tudor Royal Proclamations*, I, p. 235.

27. Ibid., pp. 270–6.

28. Statute 34/35 Henry VIII, c.1.

29. *Letters and Papers, Foreign and Domestic, of the Reign of Henry VIII*, ed. J.S. Brewer et al., London, 1862–1910, XVI, no. 422; *Acts of the Privy Council*, ed. J.R. Dasent, London, 1890–1964, I, 107, 117.

30. Took, 'Government and the Printing Trade', 119. Sir Peter Carew, a member of the King's Privy Chamber, was in trouble in 1545 for being caught in possession of a lampoon against Gardiner. He was a well-known supporter of the reforming party. PRO SP 1/212 f.45.
31. Took, 'Government and the Printing Trade', 186.
32. *Greyfriars Chronicle*, ed. J.G. Nichols, Camden Society, LIII, 1852, p. 48. Foxe, *Actes*, V., App. XIII.
33. Took, 'Government and the Printing Trade', 143.
34. H.S. Bennet, *English Books and Readers, 1475–1557*, Cambridge, 1952; Loades, 'Press under the Early Tudors'. Both Somerset and Cranmer actively, but cautiously, encouraged the Protestant press.
35. J.N. King, 'Freedom of the Press, Protestant Propaganda, and Protector Somerset', *Huntington Library Quarterly*, XL, 1976, 1–10, has slightly different figures, averaging 131 over the three years. These figures are based on Took, 'Government and the Printing Trade', 147.
36. Strype, *Eccl. Mem.*, II, pt. i, 61–3; Foxe, *Actes*.
37. STC 17630; STC 6800.
38. STC 20560.7.
39. Took, 'Government and the Printing Trade', 147, 185.
40. *Acts of the Privy Council*, iv, 69.
41. Mainz, 1550; Strype, *Eccl. Mem.*, II, i, 61–3.
42. STC 11592.
43. Hatfield MSS 346 and 347, reported in the *Calendar of the Hatfield MSS*, Historical Manuscripts Commission, London, 1883, I, 83–4. Loades, 'Press under the Early Tudors'.
44. Hughes and Larkin, *Tudor Royal Proclamations*, II, pp. 31–3. [but see also Andrew Pettegree, *Foreign Protestant Congregations in Sixteenth Century London*, Oxford, 1986.]
45. E.J. Baskerville, *A Chronological Bibliography of Propaganda and Polemic Published in English between . . . 1553 and 1558*, American Philosophical Society, Philadelphia, 1979, p. 7.
46. Ibid., p. 8. F.S. Isaac, *English Printers' Type of the Sixteenth Century*, Oxford, 1936, p. 30.
47. Statute 1 & 2 Philip and Mary, c.3.
48. Statute 1 & 2 Philip and Mary, c.10. Hughes and Larkin, *Tudor Royal Proclamations*, II, pp. 57–60.
49. *Acts of the Privy Council*, V, 247–9.
50. D.M. Loades, *The Reign of Mary Tudor*, London, 1979, p. 334. *Acts of the Privy Council*. VI, 346.
51. *Diary of Henry Machyn 1550–1563* ed. J.G. Nichols, Camden Society, XLII, 1848, p. 72. Singleton is known to have been imprisoned at about this time, but Anthony Skoloker has also been suggested: C.H. Garrett, *The Marian Exiles*, Cambridge, 1938, p. 289, Took, 'Government and the Printing Trade', 229.
52. Both 'Dorcaster' and 'Wood' have been identified with Day on typographical evidence; Isaac, *English Printers' Types*, p. 47; L.P. Fairfield, 'The Mysterious Press of Michael Wood 1553-1554', *Library*, 5 series, XXVII, 1972, 221–32.
53. It has also been suggested that the man referred to by Renard was not Day, or Singleton, or Skoloker, but William Cooke, Sir Anthony's son. Took, 'Government and the Printing Trade', 231. According to this view, Sir Anthony was the 'mastermind' behind the exile propaganda at this point, and Day was merely returning from a visit to his home town of Dunwich. The evidence is not sufficient for a firm conclusion. [See also below p. 132]
54. Or was released quietly, which is perhaps more likely.

55. It is not certain that he was actually printing again under Mary, but he was certainly in business as a stationer, although probably in a small way. E. Arber, *A Transcript of the Registers of the Stationers' Company, 1554–1640*, London, 1875–94, I, p. 10.

56. Garrett, *Marian Exiles*, p. 289.

57. D.M. Loades, 'The Authorship and Publication of *The copye of a letter sent by John Bradforthe . . .*', TCBS (*Transactions of the Cambridge Bibliographical Society*), III (ii), 1960; [see above, p. 91] 160. Magistrates of Danzig to Queen Mary, 17 April 1554, *Calendar of State Papers, Foreign*, II, 105.

58. Baskerville, *Chronological Bibliography, passim.* Loades, 'The authorship . . .'.

59. E.g. STC 15843–7. The French were believed to have more expertise in this field. Took, 'Government and the Printing Trade', 224.

60. Arber, *Transcript*, I, p. 7. 21 July 1555.

61. Ibid., pp. 84–6; 121b.

62. Ibid., I, p. xx. Testimony of 1582.

63. Ibid., pp. 7–8.

64. STC 17562. Miles Huggarde, *The Displayng of the Protestantes*, London, 1556, p. 119. STC 13557.

65. H.S. Bennett, *English Books and Readers, 1558–1603*, Cambridge, 1965.

66. W.H. Frere and W.M. Kennedy, *Visitation Articles and Injunctions*, London, 1910, III, p. 25. See above, p. 105

67. Ibid.

68. Arber, *Transcript*, I, *passim*.

69. J. Strype, *The Life and Acts of Matthew Parker*, Oxford, 1821, I, pp. 442–3.

70. British Library, Lansdowne MS 48/83, f.195. W.W. Greg, *A Companion to Arber*, Oxford, 1967, p. 91.

71. Star Chamber decree concerning printers, 1586. J. Strype, *The Life and Acts of John Whitgift*, Oxford, 1822, I, pp. 423–4, II, pp. 160–5.

72. STC 23400. Leona Rostenberg, *The Minority Press and the English Crown, 1558–1642*, Nieuwkoop, 1971, p. 82.

73. A.C. Southern, *Elizabethan Recusant Prose, 1559–1582*, London, 1950, pp. 351, 409. Rostenberg, *Minority Press*, pp. 21–2.

74. Rostenberg, *Minority Press*. John Bridgewater, *Concertatio ecclesiae Catholicae in Anglia*, Treves, 1584, p. 127.

75. P.R. Harris, 'William Fleetwood, Recorder of the City, and Catholicism in Elizabethan England', *Recusant History*, VII (iii), London, 1963, 114.

76. Rowlande is much better known under his subsequently adopted name of Richard Verstegan; see A.G.R. Petti, *The Letters and Despatches of Richard Verstegan (c. 1550–1640)*, Catholic Record Society, London, 1959). LII; and 'A Bibliography of the Writings of Richard Verstegan', *Recusant History*, VII (ii), 1963.

77. *The Memoirs of Father Robert Parsons*, ed. J.H. Pollen, Catholic Record Society's Miscellany, London, 1905, II, p. 290. Rostenberg, *Minority Press*, 23–4.

78. Southern, *Recusant Prose*, p. 357 ff.

79. Allison and Rogers, *A Catalogue of Catholic Books*.

80. Rostenberg, *Minority Press*, pp. 205–6. The prices charged for recusant works were far higher than those laid down by the Stationers' Company in 1598 for similar legitimate books, but of course the costs of smuggling had to be met as well.

81. P. Collinson, *The Elizabethan Puritan Movement*, London, 1967, pp. 139, 174. Arber, *Transcript*, I, pp. 466–7.

82. Rostenberg, *Minority Press*, p. 173.

83. Attributed to William Fulke. STC 10395.

84. R.B. McKerrow, *A Dictionary of Printers and Booksellers in England, Scotland and Ireland . . . 1557–1640*, London, 1910, p. 277 ff.

85. Arber, *Transcript*, II, p. 816.

86. STC 17453 William Pierce, *An Historical Introduction to the Marprelate Tracts*, London, 1909, pp. 152, 315.

87. Rostenberg, *Minority Press*, p. 179.

88. The nature of the charge is not clear, but John Penry was to be similarly executed in 1593, and on that occasion the indictment was based, not upon Penry's part in the Marprelate project, but upon an open letter to the queen. Public Record Office [PRO] KB27/1325 r. Rex 3.

89. PRO SP12/170/48 (the case of Robert Sutton in the Norfolk assizes of 1584). Loades, 'Theory and Practice of Censorship', [see p. 106]

10 Books and the English Reformation prior to 1558

The use of printing for purposes of religious polemic was a German innovation. Only after 1520, and the first reports of Lutheran influence in England, did concern begin to be expressed about the influence of the press. Nevertheless, the association between books and heresy was over a century old by then, and English bishops had long been accustomed to confronting their subversive influence. The Lollards had been great writers, and great readers. In 1414, according to the indictment later preferred against the offenders, 'plures libros Anglicos' had been seized in Colchester, where they had been read 'both by day and (night), secretly and openly, sometimes in company, and sometimes individually'.[1] Over 230 MSS of the Lollard Bible are known and about 30 versions of the 'sermon cycle'. Contemporary evidence also suggests that large quantities of ephemera were produced, usually referred to as *schedulae*, and *quaterni*, although these now survive only in occasional fragments.[2] The manner and extent of the interaction between existing Lollard ideas and the new theology being imported from the continent in the 1520s are matters of controversy among historians of the English Reformation. It has, however, been established that a number of Lollard tracts, books and verses were printed in whole or in part by Protestant editors and publishers. For example *The Lantern of Lyght*, issued in London by Robert Redman, probably in 1535, also survives in two pre-Reformation MSS.[3] Similarly *The examinacion of Master William Thorpe* (Antwerp, 1530) was derived directly from a fifteenth-century source. At least ten other examples have been identified.[4] There seem to have been two main reasons for this. One was that their polemical armoury could be added to with very little effort, given the congruity of the ideas. The other was that the antiquity of the works themselves served a useful purpose. As the author of *A proper dyaloge betwene a gentillman and an husbandman* put it,

For here agaynst the clergye can not bercke
Sayenge as they do / thys is a newe werke
Of heretykes contryved lately.
And by this treatyse it apperyth playne
That before oure dayes men dyd compleyne
Agaynst clerckes ambycyon so stately.[5]

Not only could such arguments be used to support the Protestant historiography of the two churches, they also provided a partial answer to the Catholic gibe 'where was your church before Luther?'.

There was another continuity in the English situation which could make the voices of the early fifteenth century speak directly to the audience of the 1530s, and that was the tendency to look to the royal authority for redress of religious grievances. The author of A compendious olde treatyse, arguing for the vernacular Bible, probably in the 1430s, had written

> And therefore it were good to the Kyng and to the other lordes to make some remedy agaynst this constitucyon of Antechrist that sayethe it is unlawfull to us englyshe men to have in englyshe goddes lawe . . .[6]

A hundred years later, when the work was printed by Johannes Hoochstraten of Antwerp, it was one of a spate of books making the same point.[7] By 1530 it was generally recognised that the press had opened up formidable new opportunities to proselytisers of all kinds, and that those who opposed the traditional order were making the most frequent and effective use of its power. The anonymous Lollard who had originally written the treatyse had been over-optimistic in saying '. . . it lyeth never in Antichristes power to destroye all englyshe books/ for as fast as he brennethe/ other men shall drawe . . .'

John Foxe, writing in 1563, recognised the relative failure of the Lollards in this respect, despite the goodness of their cause, and contrasted this with the fortunes of the Protestants of his own day, ascribing the reason to the fact that 'God hath opened the press to preach, whose mouth the Pope is never able to stop with all the puissance of his triple crown . . .'.[8] In 1408 the Convocation of Canterbury had prohibited the reproduction of English translations of the scriptures, and in 1414 parliament had confirmed the legal right of ecclesiastical officials to proceed against the makers and writers of heretical books.[9] These simple measures had not prevented the production and circulation of Lollard material, but they had kept the situation under control. It was therefore with an initial sense of false security that Wolsey and his colleagues moved against the first Lutheran writings to come to their attention.

The day book of the Oxford bookseller John Dorne gives some indication of the identity of these works, which before the end of 1520 included Operationes . . . in Psalmos and De captivitate Babylonica.[10] In Cambridge a lively discussion of Luther's protest had been going on as early as 1518, apparently with reference to his reply to Prierias and the Resolutiones Disputationum. The market at this stage was primarily academic, and interest seems to have sprung from existing concerns over ecclesiastical abuses, and from the influence of Colet and Erasmus. There is no suggestion that theological similarities between Luther and the existing Lollard tradition were a factor. The identifiable books were all in Latin, and were part of the common academic currency in Western Europe. However by 1521 the impact of the Lutheran controversy in Germany, and its rapid spread into the vernacular, were well known and the ecclesiastical authorities in England were alerted. On 14 May Cardinal Wolsey issued a legatine commission, directed to all the English and Welsh bishops, and commanded to be read in every church at the time of mass. This warned its hearers against '. . . many and diverse pestiferous and pernicious propositions and errors of Martin Luther, setting forth both Greek and Bohemian heresies'.[11] All writings containing such errors (which were promulgated in a separate schedule) were to be surrendered to the bishop or his commissary within fifteen days. This was effective enough to enable the cardinal to stage a number of book burnings later in the year, but seems to have done nothing to check the stream of imports. In spite of the reference to 'Bohemian', that is Lollard heresy in the commission, Wolsey was probably more concerned to do his duty in enforcing the papal prohibition within his jurisdiction than to confront an urgent English problem. The controversy was almost exclusively clerical, and there is no indication that any Englishman had yet written on the Lutheran side, either in Latin or in English. Such English involvement as has left any record was, prior to 1525, entirely on the Catholic side.

In 1521 Richard Pynson published the king's *Assertio Septem Sacramentorum*, and in the same year Wynkyn de Worde printed the sermon that John Fisher had preached at the Paul's Cross book burning.[12] 1522 saw a second edition of the *Assertio*, and in 1523 Pynson also published *De Libero arbitrio versus Melanchthonem* by Alphonsus de Villa Sancta. John Fisher's *Assertionis Lutheranae Confutatio*, which appeared in the same year, was issued from the press of P. Quentell in Cologne, presumably because Fisher rightly saw Germany as the centre of the storm, and still regarded the English problem as marginal.[13]

The evidence for early Lutheran writing in England is slight and circumstantial. In 1524 Cuthbert Tunstall, the Bishop of London, was sufficiently concerned to summon the printers and booksellers of the city to meet him. Having warned them afresh of the consequences of handling heretical books, he then proceeded to issue the first licensing order. No book was to be imported without episcopal permission, and no new work was to be published without the consent of a board of censors consisting of himself, Fisher, Wolsey and the Archbishop of Canterbury.[14] Perhaps this latter regulation was occasioned by the appearance of some item, now lost, which was never specifically identified. More likely it was purely a precaution.

In 1526 and 1527 the English printers John Gough, Thomas Berthelet and Robert Redman were briefly in trouble for publishing without episcopal licences, but their offences seem to have been purely technical. The foreign printers, such as Pynson and de Worde, who dominated London publishing at this time, were heavily dependent on royal and ecclesiastical favour to protect them from the jealous hostility of the London Stationers, and were in no mood, or position, to take risks.[15] Controversial lines were not clearly drawn in the 1520s, and it is possible that such books as Erasmus's *Sermon of the exedynge great mercy of god* (Berthelet, 1526)[16] were regarded with suspicion, but no explicitly heretical work can be attributed to an English press until the troubled years of the following decade.

Protestant printing in English and for the English market began in 1525, when the first version of Tyndale's translation of the New Testament was attempted in Cologne. In 1526 the better known, and complete edition of P. Schoeffer of Worms followed, and it was this version which soon began to appear in large numbers on the London market. Tunstall responded quickly, and his alarm can be clearly detected in the language of his proclamation of 23 October:

> . . . many children of iniquity, maintainers of Luther's sect, blinded through extreme
> wickedness and wandering from the way of truth and the catholic faith, craftily have
> translated the new testament into our English tongue, intermeddling therewith many
> heretical articles and erroneous opinions . . .[17]

All copies were to be surrendered to the archdeacons within thirty days. Ten
further editions followed over the next decade, mostly from the Antwerp presses
of De Keyser, Cock and Hoochstraten.[18] These editions probably numbered
about 1500 copies each, and the English authorities felt deluged. Tunstall
succeeded in seizing some, and arrested one or two of the agents, but was unable
or unwilling to exact severe penalties.[19] Even when Sir Thomas More mobilised
the royal authority in support of the bishops in 1530, and two of the colporteurs
were executed, the traffic continued to grow and diversify. Tyndale followed up
his translations with A compendious introduccion . . . to the pistle off Paul to the
Romayns (Schoeffer, 1526); The parable of the wicked mammon (Hoochstraten?
Antwerp? 1528); The obedience of a christen man (ditto); and The practyse of
prelates (Hoochstraten, 1530).[20] In his wake, a number of other Englishmen also
began to publish translations or original works of controversy – George Joye,
John Frith, William Barlow, Simon Fish and William Roy. The majority of
these were also published in Antwerp, which was clearly the main centre,
although Barlow's Rede me and be nott wrothe came from the press of J. Schott
of Strasburg.[21] The importance of Antwerp was partly determined by geographic
convenience, and partly by the sympathetic presence of the Merchant
Adventurers' headquarters, which provided a periodic refuge and a regular
means of access to the trading community. Despite the risks involved, the illicit
book trade afforded a healthy profit. Robert Necton, who was arrested in 1530,
confessed to buying English books in the Low Countries for an average of 13d. a
volume, and selling them all over the south of England at 2s.4d. or 2s.8d.
each.[22] The demand was strong, and since the purchasers also ran considerable
risks it must be presumed that they paid serious attention to what they read. The
authorities had good reason to be concerned, because the actual possessors of the
forbidden books represented only the tip of the iceberg. As with the earlier
Lollard MSS, they were passed from hand to hand, and read aloud in company,
so that large numbers of the illiterate came within reach of their message. Once
Protestant polemic moved from Latin to the vernacular, the whole community
was potentially open to its influence.[23]

By 1532, when Thomas More resigned the chancellorship and the climate in
England began to change, some twenty-seven or twenty-eight English Protestant
books had been printed on the continent, eight of them translations of
scriptures. Henry VIII's growing dispute with the papacy over his marriage did
not make it safe to publish heretical works in England, and did not affect the
king's formal hostility to Lutheranism, but it did reduce pressure on the book
trade and complicate the role of the royal authority in censorship. In 1530 the
Crown had effectively taken over control of printing and distribution from the
church, issuing its own index and placing supervision in the hands of the
council.[24] By 1532 it was clear that this control was going to be used for political
rather than doctrinal purposes, and that the king's attitude towards vernacular
scripture in particular was becoming ambivalent. The appearance of John

Fisher's *De Causa Matrimonii serenissimi Regis Angliae* in Alcalá in 1530 was sufficient indication of the dangerous cross-currents ahead. During the years of Thomas Cromwell's ascendancy, between 1532 and 1540, nineteen translations of portions of scripture into English were printed on the continent, mostly in Antwerp or Paris, but only fouteen other books with Protestant implications. Of the latter, five were editions of two works by Girolamo Savonarola, the fifteenth-century Florentine reformer, *An exposition after the maner of contemplacyon* (Antwerp, Ruremond and Rouen, Le Roux) and *An exposicyon upon the li psalme* (Le Roux and Paris, Reynault).[25] The fates of William Tyndale on the one hand and Sir Thomas More on the other indicate the strict and idiosyncratic path of orthodoxy to which the King of England expected authors to adhere during this period.

After the passage of the Act of Six Articles in 1539, and Cromwell's fall in the following year, the situation of the late 1520s briefly returned. John Bale, John Hooper, Miles Coverdale and a number of others who had enjoyed the patronage, protection or indulgence of the Lord Privy Seal withdrew to the continent, and the scale of exile publishing again increased.[26] The pattern however was different in a number of respects. Vernacular scripture, which had been the main issue in the earlier period, was no longer contentious because the reaction in England did not extend to the withdrawal of the Great Bible. Nor did old Lollard works any longer feature. Straightforward polemic was much more in evidence; works such as John Bale's *The image of bothe churches after the revelacion of saynt Johan the evangelyst* (Antwerp, Mierdman? 1545?), Henry Brinkelow's *The Complaynt of Roderyke Mors* (Strasburg, W. Kopfel, 1542?) or William Turner's *Huntyng and fyndyng out of the romishe fox* (Bonn, L. Mylius, 1543)[27] The influence of Switzerland and of Swiss theology was also apparent for the first time. Antwerp was no longer secure, and Lutheran territories less welcoming, so the English exiles went instead to Martin Bucer's Strasburg or Heinrich Bullinger's Zurich. Bibliander's *Godly consultation* was translated into English in 1542 (Antwerp, M. Crom), Bullinger's *The christen state of matrimonye* in 1541 (same) and *The reckening and declaration of the faith of Zwingly* in 1543 (Antwerp, Ruremond).[28] Justus Jonas and Melanchthon also attracted translators, but these were the years in which the Swiss connection, which was to dominate English theology after 1547, became firmly established.[29] Over forty English titles were published abroad between 1540 and 1547, and less than a quarter of those were bibles or parts of bibles. In spite of its general lack of attractiveness to religious exiles, Antwerp was still very much the main publishing centre, twenty-eight English titles coming from its presses during these years. Strasburg, Wesel, Bonn and Zurich produced the remainder.

The years immediately after Henry VIII's death saw dramatic developments in domestic publishing, as we shall see, but the position and attitude of the exiles changed more slowly. John Hooper, for example, remained in Zurich until 1549, producing three works from the press of Anton Fries – *An answer unto my lord of Wynchesters booke* (1547), *A Declaration of Christe and of his offyce* (1547) and *A declaration of the ten holy commandmentes* (1549).[30] John Bale published two books in Wesel with Van der Straten, and one in Antwerp with Mierdman, before returning in 1548. No more than eleven or twelve English Protestant works were published abroad during Edward VI's six-year reign, plus six new testaments and an edition of the Matthew Bible from Froschauer of Zurich in 1550.[31] By that time the traffic was moving the other way, with Martin Bucer, Peter Martyr and a substantial number of other continental Protestants seeking refuge in England. By 1550 even those Englishmen who had been most thoroughly imbued with the radical theology of Zurich and Geneva felt that it was safe – and indeed necessary – to go home, and for a short period exile publishing ceased altogether. At this time also Stephen Mierdman, who had already handled a number of English books in Antwerp, was able to set up business in London. Walter Lynne, Thomas Gualthier, Egidius van der Erve and over fifty other foreign printers, stationers and booksellers followed suit, and for a short time the exclusiveness of the London companies was overcome.[32]

However, the days of Josias were short, and by the end of 1553 most of these expatriates had returned from whence they came, spurred on by Queen Mary's council, and the return of the mass to English churches. Over the next five years, English Protestant exiles returned to Germany, Switzerland and the Rhineland in unprecedented numbers – almost 800 have been counted.[33] Of these only a handful became involved in the process of religious polemic, but their impact was out of all proportion to their number. Some seventy works of polemical or pastoral nature were printed abroad during the five years of Mary's reign, and smuggled into England – a source of constant anxiety and unceasing effort on the part of the council.[34] To what extent this was an organised campaign, and to what extent the result of the uncoordinated zeal of groups and individuals remains uncertain. Fifty years ago Christina Garrett argued that a 'committee of sustainers' in England provided the financial backing, and a 'master mind', whom she tentatively identified as Sir John Cheke, organised the actual publication.[35] Close examination has undermined much of this hypothesis, but recently (in an unpublished thesis) Patricia Took has revived the idea, suggesting that there were actually several groups operating at different times.[36] The first, consisting of John Day, Hugh Singleton and Anthony Skoloker, all established London printers, produced about twenty-six books over the first fifteen months of the reign until broken up by the arrest of Day and (probably) Singleton in October 1554. According to his theory Day and Singleton produced the fifteen titles bearing the imprint 'Michael Wood, Rouen', and Skoloker those bearing the imprint 'Nicholas Dorcaster'. 'Wood' may have been produced in the Low Countries, or at a secret press in London or East Anglia; 'Dorcaster' most likely in Antwerp. The responsibility of Day for the 'Michael Wood' titles seems to be reasonably well established, but the evidence for the remainder of this thesis is largely circumstantial.[37] What is clear is that over twenty books of non-violent, and largely non-political, Protestant exhortation had been released on to the London market by the summer of 1554. Typical of these works was A dialogue or familiar talke betweene two neighbours concernyng the chyefest ceremonyes set uppe agayne (Wood, Feb. 1554)[38] William Cooke, son of the prominent exile Sir Anthony, and brother-in-law of Sir William Cecil was, according to John Foxe, arrested in 1554 for being involved with Day in the publication of the 1553 edition of Stephen Gardiner's De Vera Obedientia Oratio.[39] This suggests that the Cooke household may have been behind 'Michael Wood', either as patrons or directors, but the evidence will not sustain a firmer conclusion. Day and Singleton both fled to the continent in the early part of 1555, and the second phase of the exile campaign began. In this phase neither Day nor (apparently) Skoloker played any part, but Singleton went to Wesel, and in collaboration with Johan Lambrecht published fourteen titles before returning to England on the accession of Elizabeth.[40] The other main centre of exile printing was the conveniently placed town of Emden, where the press of Van der Erve, the one time deacon of John a Lasco's London congregation, published sixteen titles in 1555 and 1556. Strasburg, Zurich, and later Geneva also saw the production of exile literature, but on a smaller scale.

Whether any single mind controlled this activity is uncertain. John Bale was certainly an active author, editor and translator, as well as a tireless controversialist.[41] He travelled widely, and may well have been responsible for a number of anonymous tracts, but only *The vocacyon . . . to the bishoprick of Ossorie in Irelande* (Wesel, Lambrecht? 1553) appeared over his own name.[42] Another possible candidate is John Ponet, the Edwardian Bishop of Winchester. He was the highest-ranking ecclesiastical exile, and helped to steer the propaganda campaign on to a more political course with his *Shorte treatise of politike power* (Strasburg, W. Kopfel, 1556).[43] He published two other controversial works in Strasburg, but his influence in other centres can only be conjectured. Straightforward religious polemic continued to be the staple diet of the exile propagandists, well aware of the extreme pressure that the English government was bringing to bear on dissidents after March 1555, and of the need to stiffen their perseverance in the faith. Two works by Thomas Becon, under the pseudonym 'Gracious Menewe' were typical of this genre, *A confutacion of that Popishe and Antichristian doctryne whiche mainteineth . . . the sacrament under one kind* (Wesel? Singleton? 1555) and *A plaine subversyon of or turnyng up syde down of all the Arguments that the Popecatholykes can make for the maintenaunce of auricular confession* (ditto).[44] However, after the arrival of Philip in England in July 1554, the revival of papal jurisdiction in December, and the beginning of active persecution in March 1555, exile propaganda began to acquire a more political edge. One new development was the direct celebration of the recent martyrs, works such as *Certein godly learned and comfortable conferences betwene the two Reverende Fathers and the holy martyrs of Christe D. Nicholas Ridley . . . and M. Hughe Latimer* (Emden? Van der Erve? 1556) and *A Godly Medytacyon Composed by . . . J(ohn) B(radford) Precher who lately was burnte at Smytfelde . . .* (1555).[45] A second development consisted of challenging the legitimacy of the queen's government on religious grounds. This was done most notably in books such as Christopher Goodman's *How superior powers oght to be obeyd* (Geneva, J. Crispin, 1558) and John Knox's *First Blast of the Trumpet against the Monstrous Regiment of Women* (Geneva, J. Poullain, 1558).[46] This would have been deeply repugnant to the earlier generation of Protestant leaders, such as Cranmer, and was symptomatic of the extent to which continental, and particularly Calvinist, influences were beginning to transform English thinking. This was a transformation cut short by Elizabeth's accession, but with considerable long-term importance in English puritanism. Some of the exile products, such as *A Warning for England* (Emden? Van der Erve? 1555) or Bartholomew Traheron's 1558 tract with the same title, were so frankly political as scarcely to warrant consideration in this context.[47] Nevertheless, the most influential product of the exile press was not political at all, and harkened back to the days of Tyndale's New Testament. This was the Geneva Bible, set up by Sir Thomas Bodley, and prepared by William Whittingham and Anthony Gilby. By the accidents of fortune, it was not published until after Elizabeth was on the throne, but no discussion of the exile would be complete without reference to it.

The distribution of exile writings in England appears to have been a sophisticated and successful operation, but many things about it are unclear. Foxe is our main source of information, and he was mainly concerned to record the things that went wrong, as when about sixty Londoners were arrested in October 1554 for 'having and selling certain books which were sent into England by the preachers that fled to Germany and other parts . . .'.[48] The imprisonment of William Seres for unspecified offences, and his connections with Cecil, may point to another part of the machinery which the authorities succeeded in dismantling, but the books kept on coming. In December 1555 Giovanni Michieli, the Venetian ambassador reported that 'of late a great quantity of books printed in English have been distributed clandestinely throughout London, concerning the king individually and his mode of government . . .'.[49] The Marian council was no more successful than its predecessors had been in checking the illicit import of forbidden books, which continued to be one of the most important features of the English Reformation.

Because of the distinctive manner in which the Reformation developed in England, there was also an intermittent but at times substantial traffic in Catholic literature printed abroad. The largest and most straightforward part of this traffic was not controversial, but arose from the limitations of skill and resources within the home-based industry. Most kinds of service book could be produced more cheaply and efficiently in Antwerp or Paris than in London, and before 1534 the vast majority were imported – 47 different editions of the Sarum Breviary (as against 4), and 54 editions of the Sarum Missal (as against 6).[50] Only primers were printed in England in any quantity – 37 editions as against 52 imported. However in 1534 the statute which finally withdrew the special privileges of the foreign printers in London also placed considerable restrictions on the importation of books.[51] The reason offered for both actions was the same – that the skills of the English printers themselves were now adequate to meet all demands. Between 1534 and 1553 no breviaries or missals were imported, but this change probably owed as much to the changing religious climate as it did to the enforcement of the Act. Three breviaries and no missals were produced in England during the same period. Primers were less affected by the 'King's proceedings', and are probably a better measure of the Act's effectiveness. Over the same nineteen years 65 primers were printed in England, and 21 imported.[52] After the systematic destruction of such service books during the reign of Edward VI, the restocking required by Mary's council resulted in a sharp upturn of demand, and at first the London Stationers do not seem to have been concerned to enforce the 1534 Act. Of the eight breviaries produced between 1553 and 1558, two were printed in London and six imported; for missals the comparable figures are two and three; while no fewer than twenty-four primers were issued in England, and ten imported. It was not until 1557 that a test case was brought against a London stationer for having imported 178 bound service books from Rouen, in contravention of the statute;[53] and shortly thereafter the outbreak of war with France finally brought that lucrative trade to an end.

Catholic controversial literature was much less significant in quantity, although the individual items were often important. Henry VIII's divorce was the first incident to drive dissident authors overseas. Apart from Fisher's tract which we have already noticed, in 1532 Thomas Abell resorted to De Keyser's press in Antwerp to print *An answere. That by no maner of lawe maye it be lawfull for King Henry the ayght to be divorsid*,[54] while Reginald Pole's celebrated *Pro ecclesiasticae unitatis defensione* was published in Rome in 1536. Of these only Abell's could possibly be described as popular polemic, and those Catholic authors who later endeavoured to oppose the Edwardian settlement by similar means retained the same scholarly and somewhat limited appeal. Richard Smith, Maurice Chauncey (an ex-Carthusian), William Rastell, and the printer Robert Caly were among those who fled abroad to escape the Prayer Book. Caly printed a small number of books in Rouen, including Stephen Gardiner's *An explication and assertion of the true catholique fayth* and Smith's tract against the marriage of priests. Chauncey went as far as Mainz to find a printer for his *Historia Aliquot Martyrum* (1550) in defence of the Carthusians, More and Fisher;[55] but the efforts of these exiles can only be described as fragmentary and muted by comparison with those of the Protestants who were to follow them across the Channel in the next reign. It was not to be until the reign of Elizabeth that an effective Catholic press in exile began to develop. The adherents of the traditional faith did not adapt easily to the roles of opposition and evangelism.

The earliest involvement of the London Stationers with heretical printing is, as we have seen, very hard to trace. Apart from Tunstall's warning of 1524, there is no suggestion of their participation before the arrival of the first Tyndale New Testaments. In 1527, however, Robert Wyer appeared before the Vicar-General, charged with publishing a work entitled *Symbolum Apostolicum*, which was said to contain many errors, and to have been printed without licence.[56] At the same time, when Tyndale himself was in London, he seems to have had secret discussions with John Rastell for the printing of his *Wicked Mammon* and *Obedience of a Christen man*, discussions which were abandoned owing to the vigilence of the ecclesiastical authorities, and the work transferred to Antwerp.[57] Over the next five years, while the defence of traditional orthodoxy was still unambiguous, no offensive works found their way into print in England, although Thomas Berthelet's two editions of Colet's famous sermon of 1511 (1530 and 1531) must have been sailing fairly close to the wind.[58] The two royal proclamations of 1529 and 1530 were accompanied by schedules of forbidden books, all of which appear to have been either Lollard MSS or works printed abroad.[59] But by the end of 1532 the situation had changed sufficiently for Robert Redman to publish *The Lanterne of Lyght*, a well-known Lollard work, bearing his own colophon.[60] Redman, Rastell and Stephen Gough were all strong Protestant sympathisers, and under the patronage and protection of Thomas Cromwell issued a number of reforming works until 1539. In 1536, for example, Redman published Richard Taverner's translation of *The confessyon of the fayth of the Germaynes. To whiche is added the apologie of Melanchthon*.[61] Books by Robert Barnes, Thomas Becon and Johann Bugenhagen were also published in London during the same period, and the changing official attitude towards vernacular scripture can be seen in the appearance of *Hereafter folowe x certayne places of scrypture* (Wyer, 1533) and *A concordance of the New Testament* (T. Gybson, 1535).[62] Convocation had in 1534 asked the king to approve a translation for general use, and although he did not actually do so until 1537, John Nicholson of Southwark had by then published three editions of Coverdale's version without hindrance.[63] The main driving force behind this campaign was probably Thomas Cranmer, the Archbishop of Canterbury, but it was also consistent with Thomas Cromwell's plans for the promotion of the religious settlement which he had helped to engineer. Although Henry VIII never relaxed his hostility to sacramental heresy, he was prepared to accept a wide range of reforming measures. The monasteries were dissolved, many saints' days abrogated, and pilgrimage shrines destroyed. *The institution of a christen man*, published by Thomas Berthelet in 1537, and usually known as the Bishops' Book, marked the most advanced point in the Henrician Reformation.[64] By the following year clerical alarm and the king's own uncertainty had checked the reforming initiative. A proclamation of 16 November 1538 clearly reflected the tensions within the English church. Existing licensing regulations in respect of imported or home-produced books were repeated:

> . . . that no person or persons in this realm shall from henceforth print any book in the English tongue, unless upon examination made by some of his grace's Privy Council, or other such as his highness shall appoint, they shall have licence so to do . . .

Books 'of divine Scripture in the English tongue with any annotations in the margin, or any prologue or additions . . .' were to be treated in the same way.[65] Plain translations were not affected, nor works written in the learned tongue. Anabaptists and Sacramentaries were fiercely condemned, and the canon law on clerical marriage upheld. On the other hand the cult of Thomas Becket was denounced, and the use of traditional ceremonies restricted to those 'yet not abrogated by the King's authority'.[66] No fewer than fourteen editions of the English Bible were printed between 1535 and 1541, together with several New Testaments, three versions of the Psalms and two of the Proverbs. Despite the apparently draconian regulations in force from 1530, such overtly Protestant tracts as George Joye's *Compendyouse somme of the very christen relygyon*, or the same author's *An apologye made to satisfye . . . W. Tindale* (both J. Byddell, 1535) were allowed to circulate freely.[67]

Thomas Cromwell's propaganda campaign on behalf of the royal supremacy, which produced a number of works like Thomas Starkey's *Exhortation to the people* (T. Berthelet, 1536) and Stephen Gardiner's *De Vera Obedientia oratio* (Berthelet, 1535),[68] is a well-known phenomenon which falls outside the scope of this discussion, but should be noticed in passing because of the peculiarly political nature of the religious changes that took place during his ascendancy. With his fall in 1540, effective censorship returned. Although new patents were issued to Cromwell's protégés Grafton, Whitchurch and Mayler, and the Great Bible continued in authorised use, no fresh editions were printed between 1541 and 1547. In the former year Richard Grafton was imprisoned for daring to print so sensitive a work as Melanchthon's tract against the Act of Six Articles, and eight other printers were interrogated by the council and placed under recognisances in 1543.[69] This flurry of activity was partly the result of Gardiner's ascendancy in the council, and partly of a rapid upsurge in the output of controversial ephemera. These constituted a new phenomenon in English printing, akin to the German *Flügschriften* of the 1520s. Very few now survive, but they appear to have consisted mostly of scurrilous attacks on the mass or the clergy, lampoons against Gardiner, attacks on Cromwell's memory, and defences of him.[70] Some were hand-written, but most took the form of printed broadsheets and ballads. The appetite of the Londoners for such entertainment was immense, and the temptation irresistible to young printers squeezed by the patent monopolies. At a more serious level the conservative supremacy was seriously undermined by the fall of Catherine Howard in 1543, and by the failure of Gardiner's attempts to destroy Cranmer's influence with the king. There was no dramatic increase in Protestant publishing as the king's life drew to a close, but Richard Grafton was able to print *Praiers of the holi fathers*, in 1544 and John Herford (rather more surprisingly) George Joye's *The refutation of the byshop of Winchesters derk declaration* in 1546.[71] At the end of the reign both sides were falling foul of official policy. John Bale complained bitterly of the popularity of the *Genealogy of Heresy*, and of Eck's *Enchiridion*, which he denounced as 'popish', but his own *Actes of the Englysh votaryes* (Antwerp, Mierdman, 1546) was equally unacceptable to authority.[72] Apart from Cromwell's propaganda, the wishes of the government were represented by the Great Bible, by the patents for primers and service books, which endeavoured to bring the whole of that large market under stricter control, and by the *Articles* and *Injunctions* which came from the press of Thomas Berthelet in numerous editions between 1536 and 1538.[73]

Between 1547 and 1549 the whole situation was transformed by the decision of the minority government of Edward VI, led by the Duke of Somerset, to implement a moderate but fully Protestant ecclesiastical settlement. At the official level this meant the disappearance of missals and breviaries of the Sarum rite, of primers, manuals and processionals. In their place came the reformed *Order of Communion* (1548) and the Prayer Books of 1549 and 1552. New ABCs for children '. . . set forthe by the kinges majestie' replaced the old primers, and there was a fresh spate of bible publishing – 15 full editions in five years, plus innumerable selections of one kind or another. This official programme had behind it an evangelical thrust and sense of purpose which had perforce been lacking from the more equivocal policy of the previous reign, and the terms of the printers' patents reflect that thrust, referring to the 'overcoming of superstition and idolatrye'.[74] At least 20,000 prayer books were issued, and imposed on parishes all over the country, while strenuous efforts were made to collect and destroy the earlier liturgies. At the same time the complex restraints under which the printing industry had theoretically been working were swept away. Whether this was done on the idealistic principle that the truth will prevail if it is set free, or from a shrewd judgement that the vast majority of stationers favoured the Reformation, was never made clear. The consequences, however, were immediate and obvious. Explicit works of Protestant theology, such as Henrich Bullinger's *Two Epystles* (R. Stoughton, 1548) or Calvin's *A faythful and most godly treatyse* (N. Hill, 1548), began to appear in ever-increasing numbers,[75] and there was a major explosion of pastoral and polemical treatises. The total number of titles issued went up from about 100 in 1547 to 225 in 1549, and the number of presses from 25 to 39.[76] The enthusiasm of some of the more radical printers, such as John Day and William Seres, began to outrun the government programme, and scurrilous pieces like *The upcheringe of the mass* and *A dyalogue betwene a gentylman and a preest* were published with the bogus colophus of 'H. Lufte, Wittenburg' or 'Hans Hitprick'.[77] As we have seen, foreign printers also began to return to the London scene in numbers, and the refugee congregations were supplied with copies of the Prayer Book translated into their own languages, although it is unlikely that they made much use of them. By 1550 the peak of this euphoria was passed. The council began to reimpose restrictions with an air of disillusionment:

> '. . . having caused God's word to be truly and sincerely taught and preached, and a godly order for the administration of the sacraments' the young king was declared to be '. . . most sorry, and earnestly from bottom of his heart doth lament . . . to hear and see many of his subjects to abuse daily by their vicious living and corrupt conversations that most precious jewel the word of God . . .'[78]

By 1552 the number of titles issued was back to its 1547 level, at 105, and the foreign workers had begun to drift away again. The Duke of Northumberland, like Cromwell before him, was particularly concerned to suppress criticism of the government, and treated authors much more severely than printers, when both were caught. In 1552 John Lowton the author of 'a seditious ballet' was pilloried, while the printer, William Martin, merely had his stock confiscated.[79] All governments within the period seem to have shared the view that printers were men of commerce rather than propagandists, and to have treated them as accessories rather than principals. In the light of what we now know about some of their views and activities, we may well conclude that such a view was disingenuous.

With the accession of Mary the Protestant press in England was driven underground. In spite of the conciliatory tone of the queen's first proclamation on religious policy, the last works of Protestant exhortation to be openly published in London were John Bradford's *Sermon of Repentaunce* and *Godlye treatyse of prayer* issued by Stephen Mierdman early in August 1553.[80] Mierdman soon afterwards departed, and although it now appears that far more foreign Protestants remained in London than was once thought,[81] there is no evidence to suggest that any of them were involved in clandestine printing. It seems likely that John Day, operating as 'Michael Wood', was the only substantial publisher of underground Protestant literature, until his arrest in October 1554. Thereafter nothing of any substance can be ascribed with certainty to an English press, although the constant anxiety of the authorities and the frequent references to 'light and seditious' ballads and broadsheets suggests that the Edwardian tradition was to some extent being maintained.[82] Mary's council, like that of Henry VIII between 1525 and 1532, controlled home-produced heresy with some success, but totally failed to stem the flood from abroad. Mary was the more unfortunate in that the opposition with which she had to deal was larger in scale, better organised, and eventually much more political. After 1532 Thomas Cromwell had brought the situation under control by seizing the political initiative. It could be argued that Mary did not have the time in which to do that, but such an interpretation is hard to sustain in the light of the Edwardian achievement, based on an equally short reign. Mary believed that she had restored normality, and as one scholar has recently put it, left 'market forces' to refurbish and revitalise the Catholic church.[83] Almost nothing of the copious literature of the developing Counter-Reformation was translated into English or adapted for English use. In spite of the return to papal allegiance and the leadership of Cardinal Reginald Pole, the Marian church remained curiously isolated, and fought its war without the aid of its most obvious allies. Its Protestant opponents did not make the same mistake.

The production of orthodox and traditional religious literature in England began almost as soon as the first printing press was set up in 1477, and had a significant history before the Reformation controversies began. Some of this output was learned, like the *De septem sacramentis* of Gulielmus Parisiensis (R. Pynson, 1516), but most was geared to popular piety – a translation of Bonaventura's *Speculum vitae Christi* (Caxton, 1484) which went through eight further editions by 1530, or *A lytyll treatyse called ars moriendi* (Caxton, 1491) which was reprinted in 1492, 1495, 1497, 1506 and 1532.[84] John Mirk's *Liber Festivalis*, a handy guide for clergy which was first issued by Caxton in 1483, went through twenty-three further editions thereafter, finishing in 1532. The ending of these popular sequences is at least as significant as their existence. The *Legenda aurea* of Jacques de Voraigne went through eleven editions, the last being in 1527.[85] Individual lives of the saints, reasonably popular until the 1520s, peter out after the *Lyfe of saynt Edwarde confessour* (De Worde, 1533). Only *The wais of god . . . unto Elizabeth* (R. Caly) briefly revived the genre in 1557.[86] Initial response to the Lutheran challenge was, as we have seen, very limited, and mostly the work of the king himself. There were two editions of the *Assertio*, and no fewer than six of the *Literarum . . . ad quondam epistolam* M. *Lutheri* (R. Pynson, 1526) including two in English.[87] Eck's *Enchiridion . . . adversus Lutheranos* came from the press of H. Pepwell in 1531,[88] but thereafter official policy did its best to impose silence on both sides while Henry established his new, and distinctive, position. In this connection the growing popularity of Erasmus must be seen as significant. The *Christiani hominis institutum* (De Worde, 1520) appeared in four editions altogether, the last being in 1556. *De misericorde domini* (Berthelet, 1526?), was reissued in 1531, 1533 and 1546; while the *Enchirdion militis christiani* (J. Bydell, 1533) was reprinted eight times at regular intervals until 1552, without regard to the twists and turns of ecclesiastical policy.[89] Richard Whitford, the monk of Syon, had a more limited appeal, but he is particularly interesting in that he represents most aptly the positive theological and pastoral aspects of the precarious Henrician compromise. Although strictly orthodox, he eschewed controversy and became the character-istic voice of the English church during the troubled 1530s. His *Werke of preparacion unto communion* was printed twice by Robert Redman (whose links with the reformers we have already noticed), in 1531 and 1537, and once by John Waylande, also in 1537.[90] *The pomander of prayer* went through four editions between 1528 and 1532; and the most popular of all, *A werke for householders*, appeared seven times between 1530 and 1537.[91] Whitford, like Erasmus, placed great emphasis on simple and practical piety, particularly of a domestic nature, and relatively little on the sacraments, or on the traditional rites and practices of the church. Another author whose works were consistently popular was the conformist Bishop of Lincoln, John Longland. In the eleven years from 1527 to 1538 he published five commentaries on the psalms, a similar number of sermons 'spoken before the king', and an edition of *The paternoster, ye creed and the commaundmentes*, which was reprinted seven times.[92] Sir Thomas More, who enjoyed similar popularity while he was in favour, disappeared abruptly from the booksellers' catalogues after 1533, to be replaced by official apologists such as Thomas Lupset, whose *Compendious . . . treatyse . . . of dyenge well*, *Exhortation to yonge men* and *Treatise of charitie* all appeared from the press of the Royal Printer Thomas Berthelet between 1533 and 1544.[93] Occasional works of more traditional piety, such as Richard Bonner's *Lytell boke that speketh of purgatorie* (R. Wyer, 1534?) continued to be issued, but the main impression is one of major change in the reading habits of the faithfull. Scripture, homiletics and private devotion had by 1540 almost entirely displaced the older style of devotional book based upon familiar rituals or the lives of the saints. How far this was a spontaneous response to changing fashions of piety, and how far the result of official pressure is very hard to say. However the reformers, Catholic as well as Protestant, had transformed religious publishing in England by the time that the Act of Six Articles appeared to throw the whole process into reverse.

In fact the appearance was temporary, and partly deceptive. The total number of books published in England collapsed from 125 in 1540 to 42 in 1541, because the reformers were briefly silenced, and there was no natural resurgence of the older piety to take their place. As the number of titles began to recover – sixty-two in 1542, eighty-eight in 1545, 105 in 1546 – the works were of the same kind as those which had filled the catalogues of the previous decade.[94] There were six editions of Queen Catherine Parr's *Prayers stirryng the mynd . . .* (T. Berthelet, 1545 etc.), two editions of Bullinger's *Christen state of matrimony* (J. Gough, 1543) and three editions of *The bokes of Solomon* (E. Whitchurche, 1545).[95] By the end of Henry VIII's reign the position had changed to such an extent that the main object of conservative polemic was the defence of the mass, an issue which had scarcely been raised before 1540. Stephen Gardiner, defeated politically by the reformers during 1546, struck back with *A declaration of such true articles . . .* (J. Herford) and *A detection of the devil's sophistrie* (Herford); while Richard Smith's *Defence of the blessed masse* (Herford) went through three editions in the same year.[96] Smith and Gardiner were thus naturally among the first to find themselves in trouble with the new government in 1547. Smith was forced to recant 'popish' doctrine at Paul's Cross in May 1547, and to burn copies of his *Defence* and *Brief treatyse settynge forth divers truthes* (T. Petit, 1547).[97] His own recantation was subsequently published by the authorities, and he continued his opposition from a safer refuge abroad.[98] Some conservative tracts were published during the period of emancipation, between 1547 and 1551, including Smith's *Of unwryten verytyes*,[99] but they were insignificant in quantity beside the reforming and radical output, and once restrictions began to be reimposed they disappeared altogether.

The restoration of Catholicism by Mary in 1553 was thus a far more traumatic experience for the printing industry than the brief reaction of 1540–2. The number of stationers working in London was halved, from eighty to forty-one, and a substantial number of presses went out of business. The number of religious works published during the first year of the reign, at about forty was similar to the equivalent figure for 1547, and well down on the boom years 1548–50.[100] More significantly, twenty of those titles came from just two presses – that of John Cawood the Queen's Printer, and that of Robert Caly, the only Catholic printer to have sought exile in the previous reign. Mary's council controlled its opponents at home with reasonable efficiency, but there are serious doubts about the effectiveness of its counter-attack. Spontaneous tracts and ballads celebrating the queen's triumph, like *A godly psalme of Marye Queene*, were numerous during the first few months,[101] and there were a few works of more substantial polemic, such as Miles Huggarde's *Treatise declaring howe Christ by perverse preachyng was banished out of this realme* (Caly, 1554) and the same author's *Assault of the sacrament of the altar* (ditto).[102] The only official guidance to appear in print was *A copie of a letter wyth articles, sente from the Queenes Majestie to the Bysshoppe of London* (Cawood, March 1554).[103] Pastoral or devotional works of the Catholic persuasion numbered fewer than half a dozen, and most of those were reissues of old material, such as Fisher's Paul's Cross sermon of 1521 or a translation of *Pro catholicae fide* by St Vincent of Lerins (Richard Tottel, June 1554).[104] A somewhat similar pattern was also followed in the peak year of 1555. The ballads and celebrations had by then disappeared, and a small number of works of political propaganda, such as Proctor's *Historie of Wyates rebellion* (Caly, Jan. 1555), appeared in their place.[105] Religious polemic was represented by two or three tracts, notably *An Exclamation upon the erronious and fantasticall spirite of heresy* (R. Lant) – one of the few pieces to pay the radical Protestants back in their own coin – and popular piety by *A plaine and godlye treatise concernynge the Masse* (J. Wayland).[106] Thirty-two Catholic works were published during the year, of which twenty-six came from Caly and Cawood. The most significant achievement, however, was undoubtedly the officially inspired *Profitable and necessarye doctryne with certayne homilies* by Edmund Bonner, the Bishop of London, which went through fifteen editions within the year.[107] This was the standard manual of orthodoxy and devotion, and the only serious attempt to explain the full doctrinal position of the church. Although the Great Bible continued in use, there were no fresh scriptural publications, and apart from primers and ABCs most of the new service books required were printed abroad. The *Homilies*, supported by some 12–15 devotional treatises and aids, absolve the Marian church from the charge of completely neglecting its pastoral responsibilities, but they fell far short of what was needed to re-establish the old faith after a period of such upheaval and change.

After 1555 the publication of all kinds of promotional literature for the Catholic faith declined – 15–20 titles for 1556, less than ten for 1557.[108] A virulent and widespread outbreak of influenza, accompanied by high mortality, may have been partly responsible for this, but if that were so it would only serve to confirm the view that private enterprise had played a larger part than the council in sustaining the higher rates of 1554 and 1555. The nature of the material published did not change greatly. Sermons by prominent divines, John Feckenham, James Brookes and Thomas Watson, remained staple fare, as did expositions of sacramental devotion, such as Watson's *Holsome and catholyke doctrine concerninge the seven sacraments* (Caly, 1558).[109] Translations and paraphrases of the Fathers of the church also feature, like *A devout prayer of S. Ambrose, very expedient for all suche as prepare themselves to saye masse* (Cawood, 1555) or *Twelve of S. Augustine's sermons* (Cawood, 1553);[110] and, of course, attacks upon Protestants. Some of these, notably Huggarde's *Displaying of the protestantes*, were witty and hard hitting; others, such as John Gwynneth's *Playne demonstration of John Frithe's lacke of witte* (Powell, 1557) somewhat obsolete in their approach.[111] What was not published is, in some respects, more significant than what was. On the one hand, the literature of the Counter-Reformation was almost totally absent, and hardly any of the effective anti-Protestant polemic produced on the continent over the previous thirty years was called into service. On the other hand, there was no attempt to go back to the popular approach of the *Golden Legend* or the *Fifteen Oes*. The restored Catholicism was also a reformed Catholicism in a distinctively English mould. Erasmus continued to be popular, with eleven editions of various of his works over the five years, and even Catherine Parr achieved a reissue in 1556 (A. Kitson).[112] There was little sign of any revival of the cult of Our Lady, and no works were specifically devoted to the merits of pilgrimages. The literature of the restored Catholic church under Mary reflects the very specific history of the English Reformation; its politics, its frequent and prolonged doctrinal ambiguities, and its detachment from the powerful, papally led initiatives of the Council of Trent. If we take the year 1558 to mark the end of the first phase of the Reformation in England, we find the paradoxical situation of a Catholic church in power, but uncertain of its orientation and not fully in tune with its majority popular support; whereas the Protestants, in exile and under persecution, are nevertheless well organised, determined, and victorious in the field of literature and published polemic.

Notes

1. Public Record Office [PRO] KB 9 204/1 nos 10–11, cited in Anne Hudson *Lollards and Their Books*, London, 1985, p. 182.
2. Schedulae were probably single sheets, like the later printed broadsheets, and none are known to survive. Quaterni were small quires of four or eight leaves. One survives intact among the Cosin MSS in Durham, and portions of others in composite MSS. Hudson, *Lollards*, pp. 183–4.
3. *A Short Title Catalogue of Books Printed in England, Scotland and Ireland, . . . and of English Books Abroad*, London, ed. A.W. Pollard and G.R. Redgrave 1926, and revised by W.A. Jackson, F.S. Ferguson and K.F. Pantzer, London, 1976–86 [STC]. 15225. Hudson, *Lollards*, p. 230.
4. STC 24045. Other examples include *Jack up Lande*, John Gough, 1536? (STC 5098) and *The dore of holy scripture*, John Gough, 1540 (STC 25587.5) Hudson, *Lollards*, pp. 230–1.
5. STC 1462.3, sig. C6v.
6. STC 302, sig. A6 and A6v.
7. E.G. *An exposition touching al the bokes of holie scripture*, R. Grafton, 1533 (STC 3033.5) and *The summe of the holye scripture*, Antwerp, 1529 (STC 3036).
8. John Foxe, *Actes and Monuments of the English Martyrs*, ed. S.R. Cattley and G. Townsend, London, 1837–41, III, p. 720.
9. D. Wilkins, *Concilia Magnae Britanniae et Hiberniae*, London, 1737, III, p. 317;

statute 2 Henry V, 1, c.7. This latter confirmed an earlier statute of 1401. Such proceedings were under the common law.

10. *The Day Book of John Dorne, Bookseller in Oxford A.D. 1520*, ed. F. Madan, Oxford, 1885.

11. J. Strype, *Ecclesiastical Memorials*, Oxford, 1822, I, pt.ii, 21. [*Eccl. Mem.*]

12. STC 13078. *The sermon of John, the bysshop of Rochester . . .* (STC 10894), which was reprinted in 1522, 1527, 1554 and 1556.

13. STC 24728. Fisher also published two further anti-Protestant works in Cologne, *Defensio Regie assertionis* (1525) and *De vertiate corporis et sanguinis Christi* (1527). W. Clebsch, *England's Earliest Protestants, 1520–1535*, Yale, 1964, pp. 14–19.

14. P. Took, 'Government and the Printing Trade, 1540–1560', Ph.D, London 1978, 67.

15. A statute of 1484 (1 Richard III c.9) had explicitly exempted printers and booksellers from the ban which prohibited other alien craftsmen from working in the city. The Stationers' Company, to which most of the English printers belonged, campaigned assiduously thereafter for the removal of that exemption. Cyprian Blagden, *The Stationers' Company; a History, 1403–1959*, London, 1960.

16. STC 10474.

17. Wilkins, *Concilia*, III, p. 705. The Cologne imprint was frustrated by the local authorities, and only a few copies of the Gospels of Matthew and Mark reached England.

18. STC 2823–2830.5. C.H. Williams, *William Tyndale*, Stanford, California, 1969.

19. Humphrey Monmouth, Tyndale's principal financial backer, was arrested and interrogated in 1528, but his influential friends in the City managed to secure his release. Van Ruremond, one of the main colporteurs, was likewise caught, but released after doing penance. Strype, *Eccl. Mem.* I, pt.i, 487–93.

20. STC 24438; 24454; 24446; 24465.

21. STC 1462.7. See also B. Cottret, 'Traducteurs et divulgateurs clandestens de la Réforme dans l'Angleterre henricienne', in *Révue d'histoire moderne et contemporaine*, XXVIII, 1981, 464–80.

22. Foxe, *Actes and Monuments*, ed. Josiah Pratt, London, 1853–70, IV, p. 652.

23. For a full consideration of this point, see Margaret Aston, *Lollards and Reformers: Images and Literacy in Late Medieval Religion*, London, 1984.

24. In May 1530 the king issued a decree in Star Chamber condemning Tyndale's New Testament, and set up a commission from the universities 'to examine certain English books commonly read among the people containing erroneous and pestiferous words, sentences and conclusion', *Letters and Papers of the Reign of Henry VIII*, London, 1862–1910, IV, 3, No. 2059. A proclamation of June 1530 effectively set up the king as the arbiter of heresy. P.L. Hughes and J.F. Larkin, *Tudor Royal Proclamations*, London, 1964, I, pp. 193–7.

25. STC 21789.5; 21789.6; 21790; 21790.5. Three editions of the *Exposition* were also printed in England.

26. For a consideration of Cromwell's role as patron and protector of radical writers and preachers during this period, see Susan Brigden, 'Thomas Cromwell and the Brethren', in *Law and Government in Tudor England: Essays Presented to Sir Geoffrey Elton*, Cambridge, 1988. On the exile of this period, see E.F.M. Hildebrandt 'English Protestant Exiles in Northern Switzerland and Strasbourg, 1539–1547', Ph.D, Durham, 1982, *passim*. [also S. Brigden, *London and the Reformation*, Oxford, 1989.]

27. STC 1296.5; 3759.5; 24353.

28. STC 3047; 4045; 26138.

29. Hildebrandt, 'English Protestant Exiles'.

30. STC 13741; 13745; 13746.

31. *STC* 2079.8.
32. Mierdman was allowed to employ a number of his fellow countrymen, and some of the English printers, particularly Day and Singleton, were hospitable to the foreign workers, thus affording them protection. Took, 'Government and the Printing Trade', 147, 185.
33. C.H. Garrett, *The Marian Exiles*, Cambridge, 1938, p. 32.
34. E. J. Baskerville, *A Chronological Bibliography of Propaganda and Polemic Published between 1553 and 1558*, American Philosophical Society, Philadelphia, 1979; J. Loach, 'Pamphlets and Politics, 1553–1558', *Bulletin of the Institute of Historical Research*, XLVIII, 1975, 31–45; Took, 'Government and the Printing Trade'.
35. Garrett, *Marian Exiles*, pp. 1–29.
36. Took, 'Government and the Printing Trade', 225–237, which also suggests that Nicholas Hill, a Dutchman by birth, may have returned to the continent and been collaborating with Van der Erve at Emden.
37. L.P. Fairfield, 'The Mysterious Press of "Michael Wood", 1553–4', *The Library*, 1972, 221–232. [See also p. 117 above, and n. 53]
38. *STC* 10383. John Knox, so fiercely polemical later in the reign, was at this stage producing such works as *A faythfull admonition* (STC 15069) and *A percel of the vi psalme expounded* (STC 15074.4).
39. Foxe, *Actes* (ed. Pratt) VIII (App.); Took, 'Government and the Printing Trade', 225.
40. Baskerville, *Chronological Bibliography*, pp. 6–10. For the arguments relating to Skoloker's involvement, see Took, 'Government and the Printing Trade', 225–6.
41. L.P. Fairfield, *John Bale*, West Lafayette, Ind., 1976; Took, 'Government and the Printing Trade', 115.
42. *STC* 1307.
43. *STC* 20178; D.H. Wollman 'The Biblical Justification for Resistance to Authority in Ponet's and Goodman's Polemics', *Sixteenth Century Journal*, XIII, 1982–3, 29–41. W.S. Hudson, *John Ponet: Advocate of Limited Monarchy*, Chicago, 1942.
44. *STC* 17821, 17822.
45. *STC* 21047.3, 3483.
46. *STC* 12020; 15070. Wollman, 'Biblical Justification'. See also J.E.A. Dawson, 'Christopher Goodman and his Place in the Development of English Protestant Thought', Ph.D, Durham, 1978.
47. *STC* 10024; *A warning to England to repente*, Wesel, P. de Zuttere? (STC 24174).
48. Foxe, *Actes* (ed. Pratt) VI, p. 561.
49. *Calendar of State Papers, Venetian*, VI, i, 269–70.
50. Took, 'Government and the Printing Trade', App. III.
51. Statute 25 Henry VIII c.15. The importation of bound books was prohibited.
52. Took, 'Government and the Printing Trade', App. III. For the comparable production of ABCs, catechisms and other elementary works, see P. Tudor 'Religious Instruction for Children and Adolescents in the Early English Reformation', *Journal of Ecclesiastical History*, XXXV, 1984, 391–413.
53. It was from the press of Robert Valentin in Rouen that the majority of English service books were imported. Between 1554 and 1557 he published 2 Manuals, 3 Missals, 9 Primers, 1 Processional and 2 Breviaries for the English market. (Took, 'Government and the Printing Trade', 256). By 1556 the demand for these works seems to have been declining, because the expected monastic revival had not materialised. For the case against Francis Sparge, see H.J. Byrom 'Some Exchequer Cases Involving Members of the Book Trade, 1534–58', *The Library*, 1936, 413.
54. *STC* 61.
55. *STC* 11592; Strype, *Eccl. Mem.* II, pt.i, 307.
56. Took, 'Government and the Printing Trade', 100.

57. Ibid., 98.
58. STC 5550; 5550.5. Colet's sermon had originally been published in Latin in 1512, so the reason for its translation and reissue at this stage must be in question. On the significance of Colet see also P. I. Kaufman 'John Colet's *Opus de Sacramentis* and Clerical Anti-clericalism', *Journal of British Studies*, XXII (i), 1982, 1–22.
59. Hughes and Larkin, *Tudor Royal Proclamations*, I, pp. 185–6, 194.
60. STC 15225. This dating follows Took, 'Government and the Printing Trade', 99. STC suggests 1535? Other Lollard works, such as *The praier and complaynte of the ploweman unto Christe* (STC 20036.5) were also printed in London before the end of 1532.
61. STC 908.
62. STC 3034.5; 3046.
63. Strype, *Eccl. Mem.*, I, i, 472; STC 2063.3, 2064, 2065.
64. Strype, *Eccl. Mem.*, I, pt.i, 485–7; STC 5163–7 (5 edns).
65. Hughes and Larkin, *Tudor Royal Proclamations*, I, pp. 270–6. For these marginalia, see also Strype, *Eccl. Mem.*, I, pt.i, 486.
66. Hughes and Larkin, *Tudor Royal Proclamations*, I, p. 273.
67. STC 14821; 14820.
68. STC 23236; 11584. Another work of equal significance was Edward Fox's *De vera differentia regiae potestatis et ecclesiasticae*, T. Berthelet, 1534 (STC 11218). See also Strype, *Eccl. Mem.*, I, pt. i, 263–71. For a recent scholarly discussion of Cromwell's propaganda campaign, see G.R. Elton, *Reform and Renewal*, Cambridge, 1973.
69. *Letters and Papers*, XVI, 422. *Acts of the Privy Council*, ed. J.R. Dasent, London, 1890–1964, I, 107, 117. The extent to which this development took reformers outside England by surprise can be judged from a letter written by John Butler to Bullinger from Basle in February 1540: 'Barnes and others are preaching the word powerfully in England. Books of every kind may safely be exposed for sale; which fact is so important to my excellent friend Froschauer that I have thought it right to make him acquainted with it.' *Original Letters Relative to the English Reformation*, ed. H. Robinson, London, 1847, II, 627.
70. Took, 'Government and the Printing Trade', 121–9.
71. STC 20200; 14828.5. The uncertainty of the period is well reflected in the words of one author, written in 1543: 'the laws concerning the wealth, governance and good order of the church, they are now firmly decreed and set forth, and tomorrow unmade and marred again. They are treated and retreated, acted and unacted . . .' *Our Saviour Christ hath not overcharged his chirche*, Antwerp, C. Ruremond (STC 14556) sig. Aiir.
72. STC 1270.
73. STC 10033–87 (nine edns). The council had great difficulty in preserving the precarious balance of enforcement at the end of Henry VIII's reign. As Cox wrote to Paget in 1546: 'Your proclamation (of 8 July) for burning books hath wrought much hurt, for in many places they have burned New Testaments, Bibles not condemend by the proclamation . . . They have burned the Kings Majesty's books concerning our religion lately set forth, and his primers . . .' (*Letters and Papers*, XXI, 2, 147). Official policy was not only frequently misunderstood, it was also widely unpopular.
74. Took, 'Government and the Printing Trade', 224. Eight patents were issued altogether, forming a coherent policy.
75. STC 4080; 4409.5.
76. Took, 'Government and the Printing Trade', 331 and App. II
77. STC 17630; 6802.5.
78. Hughes and Larkin, *Tudor Royal Proclamations*, I, p. 515.
79. *Acts of the Privy Council*, IV, 69.
80. STC 3496; 17791.

81. For a full discussion of the extent to which the 'stranger communities' remained underground in London during Mary's reign, and of the nature of the protection afforded to them, see A. Pettegree, *Foreign Protestant Communities in Sixteenth Century London*, Oxford, 1986, pp. 113–32.

82. D.M. Loades, *The Reign of Mary Tudor*, London, 1979, pp. 337–40. A study of the surviving account of one London bookseller for 1553–4 'confirms(s) the view that protestantism maintained its sway unimpeded in London early in Mary's reign'; J.N. King 'The Account Book of a Marian Bookseller, 1553–4', *British Library Journal*, XIII(i), 1987, 33–8.

83. Took, 'Government and the Printing Trade', 255. 'No attempt was made by the government of Mary to ensure that the books which it insisted on the churches possessing were in fact available.' For a different view, see Jennifer Loach 'The Marian Establishment and the Printing Press', *English Historical Review*, CI, 1986, 135–48.

84. STC 12512.5; 3259; 786–90.

85. STC 17957–75; 24873–80.5.

86. STC 7500; 7605.5.

87. STC 13084–7.

88. STC 7481.4.

89. STC 10450.2; 10474–6; 10479–86.5.

90. STC 25412–13.5.

91. STC 25421.2–25422.6; 25421.8–25.5.

92. STC 16790–3.5; 16795–7; 16820–1.7.

93. STC 16934; 16936; 16939.

94. The figures are derived from Took, 'Government and the Printing Trade', App. II.

95. STC 4818–24a; 404.5, 4047; 2754–6.

96. STC 11588, 11591; 22820–1.

97. STC 22818. Strype, *Eccl. Mem.* II, i, 61–3.

98. STC 22824.

99. STC 22823.

100. Took, 'Government and the Printing Trade', 244 and App. II. Baskerville *Chronological Bibliography*, pp. 6–9.

101. STC 1655, by T. Brownell.

102. STC 13560.5; 13556.

103. STC 9182.

104. STC 10897; 24754.

105. STC 20408; also *The copie of a letter sent into Scotlande* by John Elder, a celebration of the queen's marriage (STC 7552).

106. STC 10615; 17629.

107. This was actually two works. *The Profitable . . . doctryne* with the homilies appeared in five editions (STC 3281.5–83.7. The thirteen homilies alone in a further ten editions (STC 3285.1–5.10).

108. Baskerville, *Chronological Bibliography*, p. 7.

109. STC 25112. Loach, 'Marian Establishment' makes the valid point that the priorities of the church under Mary were different from those under Edward, and that the authorities were anxious to ensure that the laity were trained by the clergy, rather than directly by their own reading. As Gardiner put it to one Stephen Gratwick, 'we will use you as we will use the child; for if the child will hurt himself with the knife, we will keep the knife from him. So because you will damn your souls with the word, therefore you shall not have it.' Foxe, *Actes*, (ed. Pratt) VIII, p. 319. There was strong opposition to the continued use of the English Bible, but Pole had supported (vainly) vernacular scriptures at Trent, and did not change his mind.

110. STC 548.7; 923.
111. STC 13557 (R. Caly, 1556); 12560.
112. STC 4825.

Part III: The English Reformation

11 Martin Luther and the Early Stages of the English Reformation

> I entreat you, my master, not to say or write anything against charity or Godliness for the sake of Luther . . . Although I readily acknowledge with thankfulness the gifts of God in him who is now no more, yet he was not without his faults . . .

So wrote John Hooper from Zurich in June 1548 to Martin Bucer in Strasburg;[1] a cool reflection on the career of a great reformer with whom both of them had had profound disagreements, and an indication that the church order which was about to emerge in England would not follow a course acceptable to the adherents of the Confession of Augsburg. Two years later, when both correspondents were in England, although they found plenty to displease them in the state of the church, it was the strength of Catholicism and not the rival influence of the disciples of Luther that they feared.[2] Church historians are now so familiar with the idea that the theology of the Church of England (in so far as it had one) followed Swiss rather than German teachings, that they have never provided any very convincing explanation of why this should have been so. Luther's influence in England had followed very quickly upon his original protest. As early as 1518, while it was still perfectly legitimate to do so, some of his writings, probably the *Reply to Prierias* and the *Resolutiones Disputationum*, were being read and discussed in Cambridge.[3] Thomas Bilney and Robert Barnes were the early leaders of this Cambridge group, men whose interest in Luther arose from their previous concern about abuses in ecclesiastical practice and from the study of Erasmus rather than from any dissatisfaction with the doctrine of the church.[4] It appears that Bilney was the first member of this group to embrace the specifically evangelical doctrine of justification by faith alone, and according to Foxe it was he who converted Barnes and Hugh Latimer.[5] Nevertheless, it was not Bilney but Barnes who first attracted the wrath of ecclesiastical authority, for a typically boisterous performance at Christmas 1525. This sermon seems to have had nothing to do with justification, but was a mixture of anti-clerical abuse aimed ultimately at Wolsey and some very radical-sounding sentiments about the involvement of Christians in litigation.[6] With his usual bad timing, Barnes had chosen to deliver these attacks when Wolsey was particularly concerned about the spread of heretical writings, and when sensitivity to so-called Anabaptist ideas was at its height. Only a few days after Barnes' arrest, on 5 January 1526, Wolsey wrote to the Bishop of Lincoln to arrange a book-burning at which Bishop John Fisher of Rochester was to preach.[7]

Barnes recanted, and was placed under house arrest, but shortly afterwards was caught distributing copies of Tyndale's English New Testament, and was sent to Northampton to be burned as a relapsed heretic.[8] From there he escaped to Antwerp, and in 1529 made his way to Wittenberg, where he became the friend and disciple of Luther. There, in 1531, he produced the first version of his *Supplicatyon to King Henry the eyght*, the earliest unequivocally Lutheran work by an English theologian, and one which has caused Barnes to be described by some scholars as simply a translator and paraphraser of his master.[9] By the time that Barnes reached Wittenberg, the situation in England was developing rapidly. Tyndale's New Testament, imported in large numbers from 1526 onwards, undoubtedly owed something to Luther's example, but was heretical by implication rather than by explicit statement. There were also, however, direct English translations from Luther's German, notably William Roy's rendering of *Das Siebend Capitel S. Pauli zu den Chorinthern* of 1529;[10] and in 1528 another major nest of academic heterodoxy was uncovered, this time in Oxford. The offenders were, ironically, a group of Cambridge divines who had been brought in by Wolsey to staff his new foundation, Clark, Cox, Frith and Taverner, together with some followers recruited in Oxford, such as Thomas Garrett and Anthony Dalaber.[11] A search ordered by the Bishop of Lincoln uncovered 'a marvilouse sorte of bookes . . . whiche were hidd undre the earthe, and otherwise secretely conveyed from place to place'. The reading of this circle was significant, including not only Luther and Melanchthon, but also Oecolampadius, Zwingli, Bugenhagen, Bucer, Urbanus Rhegius, and several others.[12] Ten years after the first of his writings had reached England, Luther was only one of a number of heretical authors the reading of whose work was prohibited, and he enjoyed in translation nothing like the widespread popular appeal which had kept the German printing presses so busy throughout the decade. Nor had he attracted a hard core of English followers, even among those academics to whom his ideas seem to have appealed most.

With the possible exception of Robert Barnes, the English reformers of this generation, even those who visited Wittenberg, such as William Tyndale, treated Luther simply as one source of ideas among many. Most of them had begun as humanists, critical of Wolsey and interested in the Bible. They became 'Lutherans' in the sense that they embraced the essential evangelical doctrine of justification, but disagreed with Luther (and with each other) about virtually everything else. By 1531 Tyndale, under the influence of Rhineland theologians such as Oecolampadius and Bucer, was even modifying his views on justification.[13] The second edition of Barnes' *Supplication*, published after he had left Wittenberg in 1534, also showed modifications of his earlier orthodoxy.[14] The reasons for this are not particularly hard to find. Luther enjoyed no charisma in England, and the distinctive impact of his teaching was reduced, not only by the strong influence of humanists such as Erasmus and Colet, but also by the similarity of many of his views to those of Wycliffe and the Lollards. This last factor confused the issue for both sides. Cuthbert Tunstall, while Bishop of

London in the 1520s, made no distinction between Lollards and Lutherans, and was baffled to discover an obduracy among the new heretics which had been largely missing from the old.[15] At the same time, it was among existing Lollards that Robert Barnes distributed Tyndale's New Testament,[16] and familiar ideas such as the priesthood of all believers found a much readier acceptance at the popular level than unfamiliar ones such as justification by faith alone. What preserved some uniformity among the evangelical congregations in Germany was less the compulsive quality of Luther's writings than the need to preserve temporal and ecclesiastical order. The weakness of imperial and papal power enabled cities and later principalities, to go their own way, and wherever evangelical reform was accepted by authority, it had to be defined. Church ordinances began to appear as early as 1526,[17] imposing local standards of uniformity, and this process reached its culmination in 1530 with the issuing of the Confession of Augsburg.

The situation in England was radically different. Before 1530 the attitude of ecclesiastical and temporal authority alike was one of strong hostility, modified only by incompetent enforcement and the occasional intrusion of special local circumstances, such as the anti-clericalism of the City of London.[18] John Stokesley and Thomas More did not make much distinction between Lollards, followers of Luther, and the more radical followers of Bucer or Zwingli when it came to arresting and punishing heretics. Nor did the kings's 'great matter' provide much relief at first. The king is said to have received a copy of Tyndale's *Obedience of a Christian Man* from Anne Boleyn, and to have commended it warmly, but when Tyndale refused to support the king's position on the divorce he forfeited any possibility of compensating for his heresy by political usefulness.[19] Robert Barnes, on the other hand, did enter the king's service (or at least make himself useful), and his subsequent career provides a very good example of the ambivalent relationship between the Crown and the reformers which prevailed for the rest of the 1530s. Barnes was *persona grata* in Germany. As Foxe put it:

> Dr. Barnes was made strong in Christ, and got favour both with the learned in Christ and with foreign princes in Germany, and was great with Luther, Melanchthon, Pomeran, Justus Jones, Hegendorphinus, and Aepinus, and with the Duke of Saxony and the king of Denmark.[20]

He was also very loyal to Henry VIII, and at a time when the king was seeking desperately for some political leverage against Charles V and Clement VII, he represented an opportunity which was too good to be ignored. Stephen Vaughn sent Cromwell a copy of the first edition of his *Supplication* in November 1531, and in spite of its overt Protestantism, Barnes was recalled to England under safe conduct by the end of the year.[21] Sir Thomas More was incensed by the king's action, and declared '. . . but for the King's safe conduct he should have standed in peril to be burned and his books with him . . .'.[22] Unfortunately for Barnes, and also for his own future influence in England, Luther refused to support the king's divorce. Barnes returned to Germany when his safe conduct expired, but his *Supplication* continued to be printed in England with royal permission, and he continued to act intermittently as the king's commissioner in negotiations with the princes and cities of the Schmalkaldic League.[23]

Meanwhile the declaration of the royal supremacy in England left the king on an ecclesiastical tightrope. By the end of 1535 he had been excommunicated and had broken off diplomatic relations with Rome.[24] Although he could not countenance Henry's divorce, Luther could not logically object to his assuming ecclesiastical authority very similar to that which was being assumed, with his blessing, by princes and cities in Germany. However deep the theological divisions between them, Henry and the reformer were on the same side against the Pope. Luther, however, saw no reason why he should make overtures to 'Junker Harry', whose moral character and religious principles alike he despised.[25] Barnes got into increasingly deep water by trying to remain loyal to both sides, and the links between the English and German reformers, which had promised so well in the 1520s, did not really develop. Part of the trouble, of course, was the Confession of Augsburg itself, with its uncompromising doctrinal statements. Although Thomas Cromwell and Thomas Cranmer were both sympathetic to several aspects of Luther's teaching, neither could have accepted the whole package. Consequently, although reform in England developed along cognate lines – Erastian church government, vernacular scriptures, destruction of pilgrimage shrines, dissolution of religious houses – there was no move towards justification by faith alone, and no attack on the mass was countenanced. Between 1537 and 1539 the English Reformation moved as close to Lutheranism as it was going to get,[26] and it must have seemed possible that the king's paranoid hatred of Sacramentarianism, together with his greed for power and wealth and his unrelenting animosity to the papacy, would open the way for a religious settlement upon Saxon lines.

That this did not come about seems to have been due to two main factors. In 1540 the unstable Henry VIII took fright at the evident inability of the moderate reformers to control more radical preachers, particularly in London, and moved sharply against both. The executions of Thomas Cromwell and Robert Barnes in that year removed the principal advocates of both the political and the theological links with Luther. At the same time personal links began to develop with Switzerland and the Rhineland which soon eclipsed those with Wittenberg. The origins of these connections seem to lie in trade – a trade which passed through Antwerp and up the Rhine to Frankfurt, Strasburg and Basle. Strasburg was the home of Martin Bucer, and of the rival Tetrapolitan Confession of 1530. The researches of Dr Hildebrandt have revealed that, as early as 1536, Bucer was commending young Englishmen to the attention of his friend Henrich Bullinger in Zurich.[27] John Butler, Nicholas Partridge and William Woodroffe appeared in August of that year, soon to be followed by Bartholomew Traheron and others, while Rudolph Gualther, Bullinger's foster-son, made the journey in the opposite direction. These contacts quickly bore fruit and flourished, partly because of the personality of Bullinger, who was a hospitable soul and an indefatigable correspondent, partly because they were sustained by regular commercial transactions, and partly because the Englishmen undoubtedly found Zurich theology congenial. The reason for this last factor can only be inferred, but the most obvious point of disagreement between Luther and the Swiss was the nature of the eucharistic presence. It had been the former's insistence upon his own subtle and complex definition which had broken up the colloquy of Marburg in 1529 with Zwingli, and Bullinger had followed Zwingli very closely on that issue. Bucer did not fully agree with the Swiss position, and was to receive some very uncharitable criticism in that connection during the last years of his life,[28] but was much closer to Bullinger than he was to Luther. Significantly, denial of the Real Presence had been one of the most generally and strongly held convictions of the English Lollards. 'The sacrament of the altar ys but a figure or shadowe in comparison to the present body of God . . .', Thomas Fougeler had declared in 1428.[29] In 1499 two Lollard priests had declared that only 'pure bread' remained in the consecrated hosts, and that the body of Christ was ascended into heaven. In 1528 John Pykas of Essex expressed the view that 'the body of Christ was in the Word and not in the bread . . .'.[30] Numerous other examples could be, and have been, cited, but the point does not need labouring.

Lollard influence was strong in London, and although it is very elusive in the upper echelons of the City, the connection between religious dissent and the cloth trade seems reasonably well established. It was in the Merchant Adventurers' house in Antwerp that William Tyndale found refuge in 1525, and Humphrey Monmouth, a substantial member of that company, had already given him patronage and protection before that.[31] Similarly it was the Merchant Tailors who led the charge with complaints about probate and mortuary fees when *gravamina* were collected from the City MPs before the beginning of the Reformation parliament.[32] More specifically, it was to the Merchant Tailors' Company that Richard Hilles, later a busy contact man between London and Zurich, belonged after 1535. Hilles had first got into trouble as an apprentice for writing an exposition of the epistle of St James at the request of 'a good honest young man' who was exercised about the passage that declared 'how Abraham was saved by works'.[33] This sounds like a Lutheran exercise, and must have happened towards the end of his apprenticeship, since it was to Cromwell that he wrote to avert the wrath of the Bishop of London.[34] However, the Epistle of James was also a favourite Lollard text. After a discreet sojourn abroad 'about his master's business', Hilles returned and was duly admitted to his freedom; but he was a marked man, and when a group of his friends and neighbours were rounded up after the Act of Six Articles, he moved to Strasburg, where he set up in business and received a residence permit in 1541.[35] Hilles was not exactly a typical figure, but he was close to the centre of a network of business and evangelical contacts which linked the London Protestants ever more closely with Strasburg and Zurich as the 1540s advanced.

It is not surprising, therefore, that when Thomas Cranmer invited a number of leading continental theologians to come to England in 1548 and 1549 to assist in the process of establishing a godly reformation, it was the Rhinelanders and the Swiss who responded. Other circumstances also conspired to produce the same result. The Lutherans were in disarray after the defeat at Mühlberg, but they were not fugitives; moreover Philip Melanchthon was already under attack from other self-appointed custodians of Luther's pure word, and could hardly have left Germany without sacrificing the leadership which he had inherited. Martin Bucer, on the other hand, was forced to leave Strasburg after the imperial Interim, and came to England if not willingly, at least with some relief.[36] Of the other major reformers who came to England, Peter Martyr was Italian and John à Lasco a Pole, but both were far closer theologically to Bucer and Bullinger than they were to Luther. Lesser figures, often no more than students, included Martin Micronius, John Stumphius, and John and Conrad ab Ulmis. Each of these, and several others, belonged to the Zurich tradition. Wittenberg was almost, if not quite, unrepresented among those who crossed the Channel during these unsettled but promising years. Cranmer himself did not at first show any particular partiality for the Swiss. Faced with the practical problems of trying to shape a Protestant establishment for an overwhelmingly conservative country, he did not respond to their radical suggestions. The 1549 Prayer Book was a deep disappointment to them, and their criticism of the 'Lutherans' among themselves was unstinting.[37] Cranmer's position was generally misunderstood. Later, during his trial in Oxford in 1555, he was accused of having been first a Catholic, then a Lutheran, and then a Zwinglian.[38] He rejected both the latter labels, and indeed the influence of his continental contemporaries seems to have been no greater than that of the Latin and Greek Fathers, in which he was thoroughly read, and it may have been much less. He was a superb liturgist and an unremarkable theologian, but he was no mere follower of any school. Swiss influence steadily increased after 1549 for a number of reasons. They were on the spot, and they enjoyed the active support and patronage of John Dudley, Earl of Warwick and Duke of Northumberland, who assumed political power in the autumn of 1549. The second Prayer Book of 1552 and the Forty-Two Articles of 1553, while not entirely satisfactory, were much more to their taste than earlier efforts.

However, this brief formative period from 1548 to 1553 saw neither the sudden arrival nor the complete ascendancy of Zurich theology. On the critical issue of the eucharistic presence, John Frith is probably a better indicator than either Luther or Zwingli.[39] One of the first to study the works of the continental reformers in England, a translator of Luther, and an exile in Germany for a time, he had nevertheless developed by 1533 a highly distinctive sacramental theology. Horrified by the idolatry induced by transubstantiation, he nevertheless did not reject the concept out of hand, but was quite willing to entertain it as an hypothesis. As far as he was concerned, the exact nature of the presence was *adiaphora*; what made the sacrament efficacious was the faith of the recipient:

> Blessed be thou, Jesus Christ our Lord and Saviour, which of thine abundant pity considering our miserable estate, willingly tookest upon thee to have thy most innocent body broken and blood shed, to purge us and wash us which are laden with iniquitie. And to certify us thereof hast left us not only thy word which may instruct our hartes but also a visible token to certify even to our outward senses of this great benefit, that we should not doubt but that the body and fruit of thy passion are ours (through faith) as surely as the bread, which we know by our senses that we have within us . . .[40]

Frith was familiar with the eucharistic teachings of the Lollards, as well as with those of Luther and Zwingli, but the main influences upon him seem to have been the Latin fathers and Oecolampadius. Official Anglican teaching, as later set out in the words of the twenty-ninth article, did not follow Frith in his indulgent attitude towards transubstantiation, describing it as 'repugnant to the plain word of scripture', but was equally non-committal as to the positive nature of the presence, and similarly specific about the need for faith: '. . . to such as rightly, worthily and with faith receive the same, the bread which we break is a communion of the body of Christ'.[41] Significantly this formula, which could accommodate the common Lollard view, as well as the more sophisticated and distinct views of Bucer and Hooper, was unacceptable to an orthodox Lutheran, and a stumbling block in all subsequent negotiations with Lutheran states.

Like Frith, John Hooper also, I think, provides a useful illustration of the way in which Swiss doctrine on the eucharist was mediated to England. Hooper has recently been described by Dr Davis as a Lollard,[42] and the origins of his Protestantism are unknown, but he chose to go to Basle in about 1545 when his outspokenness had made life in England dangerous. There he adopted the views of Bullinger, and was certainly a Zwinglian when he returned to England in 1549. Understandably he was a great favourite with the Swiss students in England, and his views on the eucharist were entirely orthodox from their point of view, but he went out of his way to dissociate himself from the crude opinion that the sacrament was a mere sign or commemoration: 'the holy supper', he wrote, 'is a testimany of grace and a mystery of our redemption, in which God bears witness to the benefits bestowed upon us by Christ . . .'.[43] Hooper, more than Frith, or Barnes, or Cranmer, illustrates the closeness of Swiss sacramental theology to the traditional English heresy. I do not think that he was a Lollard, but the opinion is a useful corrective to the automatic assumption that he learned all his Protestantism in Zurich. He has also been described as the founder of English puritanism, but that also seems to me mistaken. He certainly helped to articulate what later became known as puritan views, but the roots of puritanism lay in Lollardy.

In short Lollardy provided the fruitful soil in which the English Reformation, in both its official and its popular forms took root. Because of the nature of that soil the Swiss and Rhineland seeds flourished, whereas those from Wittenberg, in spite of their early arrival and some promising patronage, did not. Consequently, despite bearing many superficial resemblances to the established churches of Scandinavia and north Germany, the Anglican church became the only major national church to adopt the theology of Zurich, and that in a modified and distinctive form. It is not surprising that the Lutherans were puzzled by developments in England, or that cities such as Wesel were extremely reluctant to receive the Marian exiles.[44] As Dr Kouri has recently shown, the suspicion continued after 1559, and seriously affected diplomatic relations between Elizabeth and the German princes.[45] I do not believe that labels are helpful, and it is just as mistaken to describe the English Reformation as 'Lollard' or 'Erastian' as it is to call it 'Zwinglian' or 'Lutheran'. Nevertheless, it is necessary to consider very carefully the composition of the final blend, because only by such means can we understand its own internal tensions and divisions, let alone its relationship to the other reformed churches of Western Europe.

Notes

1. *Original Letters Relative to the English Reformation*, ed. H. Robinson, Parker Society, 1847, II, 44. [OL]
2. Bucer to Brentius, 15 May 1559, *OL*, II, 542; Peter Martyr to Bullinger, 1 June 1550, *OL*, 483.

3. H.C. Porter, *Reformation and Reaction in Tudor Cambridge*, Cambridge, 1958, pp. 42–3.

4. W.A. Clebsch, *England's Earliest Protestants, 1520–1536*, Yale, 1964, pp. 42–4, 276–8.

5. John Foxe, *Actes and Monuments*, ed. Josiah Pratt, London 1853–70, V, p. 414 ff.

6. Clebsch, *Earliest Protestants*, pp. 44–5. Barnes published his own account of this sermon in A *supplicatyon made by Robert Barnes, doctoure in divinitie . . . unto kinge henrye the eyght*, Antwerp, S. Cock, 1531 (STC 1470).

7. *Letters and Papers, Foreign and Domestic, of the Reign of Henry VIII*, ed. Brewer et al., London, 1862–1910, IV, 995 (Longland's reply). H. Ellis, *Original Letters Illustrative of English History*, London, 1824, I, pp. 179–84. A.G. Chester, 'Robert Barnes and the Burning of the Books', *Huntingdon Library Quaterly*, XIV, 1951, 211–21.

8. Foxe, *Actes*, V, 419.

9. This seems to have been true of the 1531 edition of the *Supplicatyon*; however, by 1534, when he issued a second edition, Barnes had changed his mind on many points. W.J.D. Cargill Thompson, 'The Sixteenth Century Editions of "A supplicatyon . . . to Kinge Henry the Eyght" by Robert Barnes; a Footnote to the History of the Royal Supremacy', *Transactions of the Cambridge Bibliographical Society*, III, 1960, 133–42; Clebsch, *Earliest Protestants*, 59–60.

10. STC 10493.

11. Longland to Wolsey, 3 Mar. 1528; Foxe *Actes*, (ed. Pratt), V, Appendix VI.

12. Ibid.

13. Clebsch, *Earliest Protestants*, pp. 170–1.

14. STC 1471.

15. Charles Sturge, *Cuthbert Tunstall*, London, 1938, pp. 128–35.

16. J. Strype, *Ecclesiastical Memorials*, Oxford, 1822, I, pt.ii, 54–5. [*Eccl. Mem.*]

17. One of the first was Hesse; *Reformatio ecclesiorum Hasiae* (20 Oct. 1526) in B.J. Kidd, *Documents of the Continental Reformation*, Oxford, 1911, 222–30.

18. J.A.F. Thomson, *The Later Lollards, 1414–1520*, London, 1965, *passim*; S. Brigden, *London and the Reformation*, Oxford, 1989, p. 151.

19. It was generally believed on the continent that Tyndale was supporting the queen's cause, 'which it is thought all the best men in England favour', *Letters and Papers*, V, 354. C.H. Williams, *William Tyndale*, London, 1969, pp. 41–3.

20. Foxe, *Actes* (ed. Pratt), V, p. 419.

21. Preserved Smith, 'Luther and Henry VIII', *English Historical Review*, XXV, 1910, 665. *Letters and Papers*, V, 533.

22. *The Workes of Sir Thomas More, Knyght*, ed. W. Rastell, London, 1557, p. 761; Clebsch, *Earliest Protestants*, pp. 52–3.

23. Ibid., pp. 54–5; Erwin Doernberg, *Henry VIII and Luther*, London, 1961, pp. 85–6.

24. The Bull of Excommunication was dated 30 August 1535, but its execution was suspended, and the suspension was not lifted until 17 December 1538. *The History of the Reformation of the Church of England* by Gilbert Burnet, ed. Nicholas Pocock, Oxford, 1865, IV, pp. 318–31; 331–4.

25. This estrangement was complete by 1539, following several years of intermittent contact and negotiation, as is clear from certain passages in Luther's *Table Talk*; Doernberg, *Henry VIII*, p. 115.

26. W.H. Frere and W.M. Kennedy, *Visitation Articles and Injunctions*, London, 1910, II, pp. 34–43; Second Royal Injunctions of Henry VIII, 1538.

27. E.F.M. Hildebrandt, 'English Protestant Exiles in Northern Switzerland and Strasbourg, 1539–47', Ph.D, Durham, 1982, 21.

28. John Hooper to Henrich Bullinger, 26 Apr. 1549; *OL*, I, 61.

29. A. Hudson, *Lollards and their Books*, London, 1985, pp. 209–11.

30. J.F. Davis, *Heresy and Reformation in the South East of England, 1520–1559*, London, 1983, pp. 57–9.
31. J.F. Mozley,*William Tyndale*, London, 1937, p. 53; Strype, *Eccl. Mem.*, I, pt.ii, 368 ff.
32. S.E. Lehmberg, *The Reformation Parliament*, Cambridge, 1970, pp. 81–2.
33. *Letters and Papers*, VI, 39; C.M. Clode, *Early History of the Guild of Merchant Taylors*, London, 1888, II, p. 352.
34. Hildebrandt, 'English Protestant Exiles', 66.
35. Strasbourg Archives Municipales; Mandates et Reglements, 1521–43; cited ibid., 68.
36. Bucer to Albert Hardenburg, 14 Aug. 1549; *OL*, II, 538–41.
37. John Burcher to Heinrich Bullinger, 16 Oct. 1549; *OL*, II, 659.
38. 'Processus contra Cranmerum', in T. Cranmer, *Works*, ed. J.E. Cox, Parker Society, 1844–6, II, p. 541.
39. Clebsch, *Earliest Protestants*, pp. 122–7.
40. *The Whole Workes of W. Tyndall, John Frith and Doct. Barnes . . .*, London, 1573, p. 157; a prayer for use before receiving the sacrament.
41. E.C.S. Gibson, *The Thirty Nine Articles of the Church of England*, London, 1910.
42. Davis, *Heresy*, p. 109.
43. *Later Writings of Bishop Hooper*, ed. C. Nevinson, Parker Society, 1852, p. 408. On the question of Hooper's conversion, see his autobiographical letter to Bullinger of Jan. 1546; *OL*, I, 34; also Hildebrandt, 'English Protestant Exiles', 73–4.
44. C.H. Garrett, *The Marian Exiles*, Cambridge, 1938, p. 50.
45. E.I. Kouri, 'For True Faith or National Interest? Queen Elizabeth I and the Protestant Powers', in *Politics and Society in Reformation Europe*, ed. E.I. Kouri and Tom Scott, London, 1987, pp. 411–36.

12 The Collegiate Churches of County Durham at the Time of the Dissolution

When the commissioners came to investigate those foundations dissolved under the provisions of the Act of 1547, there were in County Durham six institutions which could be described as collegiate churches. Of these, four were constituted in the ordinary way with a dean and prebendaries; Darlington, Chester-le-Street, Lanchester and St Andrews, Auckland; one was a chantry college attached to Staindrop Hospital; and one (Norton, near Stockton) preserved the antique constitution of eight portionaries amongst whom the endowment was equally divided.

Darlington, Auckland and Norton were traditionally founded at the end of the eleventh century to absorb the dispossessed canons of Durham when they were expelled to make way for the conventual chapter.[1] What constitutions these churches then had is uncertain, but at the end of the twelfth century Bishop Hugh de Puiset remodelled the college at Darlington, giving it an establishment of four portionaries.[2] Bishop de Puiset, like the majority of his successors, favoured the secular colleges because they presented valuable opportunities for patronage, which could be thrown into the scale against the wealth and power of the cathedral monastery. This was particularly true of Anthony Bek, whose relations with the monastery were constantly disturbed. In 1294 Bek reconstituted Auckland college with a dean and twelve prebendaries, replacing the portionary system which had probably existed there for the best part of a century.[3] In addition he founded two new colleges: Lanchester in 1284 and Chester-le-Street in 1286. In both these cases collegiate establishments could be justified by the ample revenues and extensive natures of the parishes, but in both cases Bek was careful to present to stalls lawyers and administrators, whose service were thus rewarded and retained.[4]

In each of Bek's three foundations the cure of souls was the responsibility of the dean, who was expected to appoint chaplains to assist him, and to reside in his cure. The prebendaries were clearly not expected to reside, since in each case the status and emolument of the vicar choral who was to perform the actual duties were laid down in the statutes.[5] In the two foundations which Bek did not touch, Norton and Darlington, the cure of souls rested entirely with the vicar, whose endowment was separate from that of the portionaries. The latter performed no spiritual functions, and were not required either to reside or to provide ministers. By the end of the thirteenth century it is probable that the eight portions of Norton were already being used to support scholars at the universities, a function which they continued to perform, more or less, down to the dissolution.

At the time of the ecclesiastical taxation of 1291 each of the five colleges had a full set of incumbents,[6] which is not surprising in view of the valuable patronage which they represented. The four portionaries of Darlington each drew 25 marks for doing nothing at all; the portionaries of Norton each enjoyed an exhibition of £6; the wealthiest prebend of Lanchester was worth £16 13s.4d., and that of Chester-le-Street £20. The portionaries of Auckland divided £220 between them, and none was expected to pay his vicar more than 10 marks when the new statutes were drawn up only three years later.[7] Between 1294 and 1547 the only major constitutional change in any of these foundations was the reform of Darlington, carried out by Bishop Neville in 1439. In that year the college was reconstituted to consist of a dean and four prebendaries, on the same lines as Bek's establishements.[8] The chantry college attached to Staindrop Hospital was founded and endowed by Ralph Neville, Earl of Westmorland, in 1408, to consist of a master, six chaplains and two lay clerks. This constitution did not change until the Reformation, and the patronage remained in the hands of the earl's successors.

When we come to examine these foundations in the light of the *Valor Ecclesiasticus* and the chantry certificates of 1548, several developments at once become apparent. The most obvious is the huge financial gap which has developed between the deaneries and the remaining prebends. Auckland is the most extreme example of this. In 1291, just before the refoundation, the dean's predecessor, the vicar, had enjoyed £40 a year, and the wealthiest of the portions was £46 13s. 4d.[9] In spite of an equalisation which had been carried out by Bishop Langley in 1428, by 1535 the deanery was worth £101 and the wealthiest prebend no more than £10.[10] The same tendency can be seen in the other colleges. At Chester-le-Street in 1291 the equivalent figures were £33 and £20; by 1535 they had become £41 and £10. At Lanchester the gap between £23 6s.8d. and £16 13s.4d. had widened to that between £42 and £7 6s.8d. At Darlington in 1535 the deanery was worth £36 13s.4d., and the best prebend £5. There does not seem to be any single explanation of this. Ordinary economic vicissitudes, such as Langley corrected at Auckland, could not have produced such a consistent result. Revenues derived from tithes always showed a tendency to wither, and at first the deans, being resident, would have been in a better position to prevent such wastage. At Auckland in 1294, and at Darlington in 1439, additional prebends were created by the bishop and annexed to the deaneries for the specific purpose of increasing the revenues. It is also possible that the deans succeeded in encroaching upon other college revenues not specifically allocated to prebends, such as the tithes of Waldridge and Plawsworth, which were originally designated for the additional upkeep of the premises at Chester. By the sixteenth century the wide discrepancies which had already developed would have been perpetuated and increased by the greater care with which the more valuable revenues would have been overseen.

In 1535 the greatest effects of the price rise were still in the future, but even without making allowance for inflation it is clear that these prebends were no longer significant rewards. It appears from the chantry certificates that the provision of ministers to perform the spiritual offices of the prebendaries was effectively insisted upon,[11] and since this necessitated the payment of something like a living wage to the minister, the net revenues of all the prebends were very small, and of some nothing at all. There were ten prebends of Auckland in 1535, all occupied, and the prebendaries drew revenues varying from £3 6s.8d. to £1. At Chester the net profits ranged from £5 to 6s., and at Lanchester from £3 6s.8d. to nil. Probably the chantry certificates and the *Valor* present an idealised picture of the way in which the statutes were being observed under these unsatisfactory conditions. We know, for instance, that in 1532 the revenues of the prebendaries of Auckland were sequestered on account of their failure to repair the chancel of St Andrew's church,[12] and there were frequent complaints from the ministers in all the collegiate churches that their stipends were not paid fully, or on time. In general, it seems that by the time of the dissolution the prebends in these churches were little more than insignificant titbits given by the bishop to his chaplains and offices, or to minor royal servants. For instance Anthony Bellasis, who held prebends in both Auckland and Chester, was Thomas Cromwell's chaplain; and Lancelot Thornton and Simon Binks, prebends of Auckland and Darlington respectively, were Tunstall's own chaplains. Henry Eglionby, who became a prebendary of Auckland in 1544, was chaplain to the king. Such places could no longer be used to purchase or reward the good offices of important men, although some continued to contribute in a small way to the incomes of great ecclesiastical pluralists. William Franklin, prebendary of Auckland in 1548, was also concurrently prebendary of York, archdeacon of Durham, rector of Houghton-le-Spring, and dean of Windsor.[13] A prebend in itself was no more remunerative than a humble curacy. About half the prebendaries in 1548 are known to have had other ecclesiastical preferment, in several cases outside the diocese, and the remainder must have enjoyed additional income which cannot now be traced, since they provided ministers rather than desiring to reside.

By contrast, the deaneries were still important factors in the bishop's patronage, and significant rewards for important service. Robert Hindmer, who was Tunstall's chancellor, and had been one of the commissioners who drew up the returns for the *Valor* in 1535, held the deaneries of both Auckland and Lanchester in 1548 and drew from them a substantial proportion of his income. As a result, the deans no longer performed their original functions of residing and providing the cure of souls. Between 1532 and 1538 Cuthbert Marshall, Dean of Darlington (who was also archdeacon of Nottingham) leased the deanery to a layman, one William Wytham, a gentleman of the king's household.[14] This was not an isolated case, prebends were also occasionally leased,[15] and the consequences for the colleges could be serious. As a result of Marshall's action the buildings fell into disrepair and the salaries of the ministers were unpaid. According to the certificate of 1548 Marshall was then maintaining a minister at Darlington, and Hindmer one at Auckland and three at Lanchester. No minister is mentioned in connection with the deanery of Chester-le-Street, and it seems that there the dean, William Warren, resided in accordance with the statutes.[16]

While not being absolutely disgraceful, it is clear that the condition of these four colleges in the 1540s left a good deal to be desired. The prebends were virtually useless for the purpose for which they had been intended, and the deaneries partly supplied the need for patronage at the expense of the cures which they had been established to maintain. With the exception of Chester, the spiritual functions of the colleges were performed almost entirely by substitutes whose rate of remuneration precluded excellence and offered no encouragement to diligence. The great tithes of the parishes, which formed the endowments, were ample to pay adequate incumbents. The gross revenues of Auckland in 1548 stood at £172 1s.2d., of Darlington at £53 6s.8d., of Lanchester at £73 10s., and of Chester probably at £77 2s.8d.[17] In purely functional terms the case for reform was overwhelming, and for the dissolution of the colleges in their existing form very strong.

The cases of Norton and Staindrop were different. Staindrop was primarily a hospital for sick and elderly retainers of the earls of Westmorland, and of its gross revenues of just over £206 in 1548, only about £50 was devoted to the maintenance of the master and chaplains.[18] The vicarage of Staindrop parish, although maintained out of the revenues of the hospital and normally occupied by one of the chaplains, was not a part of the college. In so far as the chaplains of Staindrop had a cure of souls, it was confined to the inmates of the hospital, and their chief spiritual function was to maintain a chantry for the souls of their founder and his descendants. The portionaries of Norton had, as we have seen, no spiritual responsibilities, and since the use of these portions as university exhibition was purely traditional, it is very difficult to determine what constituted an abuse. Four of the eight portionaries in 1548 had held their preferments for thirteen years or more, and there is no suggestion that tenure was limited to a term of years, or conditional upon continued study.[19] It seems probable that most of the portionaries employed their preferments at the universities for part of the time, but chiefly regarded them as additional sources of income. Sometimes these portions were held by laymen, as in the case of Bernard Skelton, collated by Tunstall in 1542, and they frequently seem to have been leased to laymen.[20] Technically no doubt this was an abuse, but from an ecclesiastical point of view Norton was really nothing more than a harmless and possibly useful anomaly. At £6 a year the portions were more valuable than the net revenues of any prebend in the other colleges.

When the property of these foundations was vested in the king by the Act of 1547, a gross income of just over £610 a year was diverted to the Court of Augmentations. In addition 40 incumbents and 22 ministers or chaplains lost their preferments, and fresh arrangements had to be made for the spiritual welfare of four parishes. There seems to be no doubt that the property interest of the dispossessed weighed far more heavily in the minds of the officials responsible for the reorganisation than did the needs of the parishes. The continuance warrants issued by Mildmay and Kelway provided for a vicar in each parish, the stipend at Auckland being £20, at Chester and Darlington £16, and at Lanchester £13 6s.8d.[21] In addition, Auckland was provided with three curates, and each of the others with one, at stipends ranging from £6 13s.4d. to £8. The annual sum thus allocated to spiritual purposes was in the region of £106, less than a fifth of the income which the government had acquired. At the same time pensions were scrupulously allocated to the displaced prebendaries and ministers, in some cases up to the full amount of their previous emolument. The annual sum allocated to the pensions of deans and prebendaries was about £219, and to chaplains and ministers about £102. Thus at first some £427, over two-thirds of the income, was absorbed by pensions and stipends;[22] but of course mortality and other contingencies ensured that this was a constantly diminishing figure, and financially the government's bargain was an extremely profitable one.

With the exception of Staindrop, which yielded 34 fothers of lead and 42 ounces of plate, the colleges were not deprived of any furnishings, since these belonged to the respective parish churches. At the same time, the government hastened to scramble its eggs by leasing the rectoral tithes as quickly as possible. The revenues of Auckland deanery were leased to Sir Hugh Askew on 2 July 1548, and those of Lanchester deanery to Thomas Gerard on 16 October. The whole rectorial tithe of Norton went to one William Crofton on 26 November and some time before the end of the year the Darlington revenues were similarly leased to Thomas Windsor.[23] If Lanchester is a typical example, the government bargained well with its customers, for the net value of the deanery in 1535 had been £40, and Gerard paid £40 in rent.

In spite of the worthy sentiments expressed in the preamble of the Chantries Act, it cannot really be pretended that these parishes benefited in any way from the dissolution of the colleges. The revenues provided for the vicars under the new dispensation were adequate for the time being, but not sufficient to persuade men of energy and efficiency to reside in their cures. They were not seen to be sufficient to prevent pluralism at the very outset, since Cuthbert Marshall, the ex-dean of Darlington, was appointed both to the vicarage of Darlington and to the curacy of Chester-le-Street by the terms of the continuance warrants. At the same time, the drastic reduction in the number of assistant clergy was not adequately counterbalanced by an improvement in quality. At Darlington, in place of six ministers whose stipends varied from £2 to £4, there was one curate at £6 13s.4d. At Chester, in place of seven ministers getting between £2 and £5 there was one curate at £8, and he was presumably non-resident. At Lanchester, in place of six ministers getting between £2 and about £6, there was one curate at £8. At Auckland, where there had been no fewer than eight ministers getting £6 13s.4d. each, as well as three getting less, there were now three curates at £8. The ministers who had received only £3 or £4 a year are unlikely to have been priests, and were probably members of that extensive pre-Reformation clerical proletariat which caused so much trouble. It is unlikely that they played much part in ministering to the needs of the parish, and they probably confined themselves to the perfunctory observation of their duties in the choir. At the same time we know that some of the ministers did serve the cures of chapels within their parishes, and several probably kept small song-schools attached to the churches.[24] From the point of view of the religious life of the parishes, there was probably not very much to choose between the old dispensation and the new. What is abundantly clear is that a great opportunity for reformation and improvement had been allowed to slip, not only because of the greed of the government, but also because of its extreme sensitivity to vested interests.

Like the abbots and priors of the dissolved religious houses, the deans of the dissolved colleges did well for themselves. Robert Hindmer drew £50 a year pension from Auckland, and £20 from Lanchester, in addition to his new stipend of £20 as vicar of Auckland.[25] William Garnett, the Master of Staindrop hospital, drew a pension of £10, and in addition was appointed to the re-endowed vicarage of Staindrop at a stipend of £20. These two emoluments he apparently held concurrently, in contravention of the statute. William Warren, Dean of Chester, was awarded a pension of £18 9s., and appointed to the vicarage of Chester at a stipend of £16. Cuthbert Marshall, already a considerable pluralist, received no pension, but two promotions to the value of £24. The vicarage of Lanchester was given to Richard Cliff, the ex-prebendary of Esh, who, as far as I am aware, held no other preferment.[26] Some of the prebendaries and most of the ministers were turned adrift with pensions corresponding to their previous meagre stipends, and clerical unemployment was consequently a problem for a number of years.

If one can draw any conclusions from so minute a fragment of Reformation history, they are probably these: the dissolution of the four major colleges was justified even without a religious reformation, on account of the pointless state to which the prebends had deteriorated. The needs of the old religion would have been more efficiently met by the diversion of their revenues to the endowment of extra chapels and the better maintenance of the existing ministers. The new religion, with its need for fewer but better-educated clergy, added another justification. Had the major portion of the college revenues been allocated to the maintenance of resident, preaching clerics, then the dissolution would have been a genuine act of religious reform. In the event the new establishments in the parishes were probably no better (and no worse) adapted to the needs of Protestantism than the old were to the needs of Catholicism. While it is not just, on the evidence, to accuse the government of wholesale plunder and hypocrisy, it is clear that religious reform was not the principal motive behind the change. In the cases of Staindrop and Norton, the indictment is clearer. The revenues of both these establishments, which had served some useful purpose for charity and education, were simply appropriated without any provision for the continuance of their functions. Before the dissolution these revenues were inefficiently and inadequately applied – after the dissolution they were not applied at all. Perhaps it should also be added that the greatest single sufferer from these changes was the Bishop of Durham, whose patronage was severely reduced without any real compensation.

Notes

1. John Leland, *De rebus Britannicis Collectanea*, Oxford 1774, II, pp. 332, 388.
2. A. Hamilton Thompson, 'The Collegiate Churches of the Bishopric of Durham', *Durham University Journal*, XXXVI, 1943, 33–42.
3. Ibid., 37.
4. These included men as exalted as Walter Langton, Treasurer of Edward I. Ibid., 38.
5. Sir William Dugdale, *Monasticon Anglicanum*, London 1817, VIII, p. 1335. Provision was made for resident prebendaries, but only a small minority ever took advantage of it.
6. *Taxatio Ecclesiastica*, Record Commission, 1802, pp. 315, 315b.
7. Dugdale, *Monasticon*, pp. 1335, 1337.

8. W.H.D. Longstaffe, *History and Antiquities of the Parish of Darlington*, Darlington 1854, p. 193 ff.

9. *Taxatio*, pp. 315, 315b. The vicar had occasionally been known as dean before the refoundation, as when Robert de Curtenay was presented in 1238, *Calendar of the Patent Rolls, 1232–47*, 223.

10. *Valor Ecclesiasticus*, Record Commission, 1828, V, p. 315 ff. [*Valor*]

11. Barbara Wilson, 'The Reformation in Northumberland and Durham', Ph.D., Durham, 1939. Appendix II (iii).

12. *The Registers of Bishops Tunstall and Pilkington*, Surtees Society, CLXI, 1952, 17.

13. Wilson, 'Northumberland and Durham', 215.

14. *Letters and Papers, Foreign and Domestic, of the Reign of Henry VIII*, ed. Brewer et al., London, 1862–1910, XIII, pt.1, pp. 221–3, 318.

15. E.G. Hamsterley. *Valor*, V, 315.

16. He was bound to provide ministers for the chapels of Tanfield and Lamesley, which he was not, apparently, doing. Robert Surtees, *History of Durham*, London, 1816–40, II, p. 143.

17. This is the value given in 1535 (*Valor*, V, 312). It is practically certain that the entry of its value in the certificate of 1548 – £28 2s.8d. – was the result of an error. *The Ecclesiastical Proceedings of Bishop Barnes*, Surtees Society, 1850, XXII, p. 1xix.

18. Ibid., p. 1xxv.

19. Wilson, 'Northumberland and Durham', 619–20.

20. *Tunstall and Pilkington*, p. 80. Five of the eight portions were leased in 1548.

21. Public Record Office [PRO], Exchequer; Augmentations, continuance warrants, no.9 (E 315/9).

22. This sum does not include the pensions paid to the inmates of Staindrop hospital, which amounted to £51 11s.4d. In 1548 there were five 'poore gents', who each received £6 1s.4d.; six 'poore yemen' who received £3 0s.8d.; and two 'poor gromes' who received £1 10s.4d. *Bishop Barnes*, p. lxxv.

23. BM Harleian MSS, 605, fols. 31a, 77–8. Wilson, 'Northumberland and Durham', 283.

24. There may have been such schools at Auckland (*Valor*, V, 315) and Staindrop (*Bishop Barnes*, p.3), while chantry priests and other clergy frequently gave elementary instruction to children without the formal establishment of a school.

25. Public Record Office [PRO], Exchequer; Augmentations, Miscellaneous Book 247, (E 315/247) nos 10, 11.

26. Continuance warrant no.9.

13 The Dissolution of the Diocese of Durham, 1553–4

For just over a year, from March 1553 to April 1554, the diocese of Durham had no legal existence. This strange interlude is normally dismissed by local historians as being of no significance, since the shortness of its duration and the national political situation at the time enabled the whole administrative machinery to continue without any break which is now discernible in the records. Cuthbert Conyers, Sheriff of Durham and Sadbergh, blithely accounted 'from the feast of St. Michael the Archangle in the twenty-third year of the pontificate of Cuthbert, by the grace of God Bishop of Durham, to the feast of St. Michael in the twenty-fourth year of the pontificate' (1552–3) and again in the same terms for the following year.[1] This not only ignored the brief statutory dissolution of the see, but also the fact that Tunstall had been deprived by royal commission on 14 October 1552, so that the diocese was technically vacant for six months before the statute came into effect.

When the status quo *ante* was restored by Mary, the whole process was explicitly retrospective, Tunstall being granted all issues, profits and jurisdiction from 14 October 1552,[2] so that the continuity preserved by the diocesan officials was formally sanctioned and approved. At the local level the whole episode is indicative not only of legal and administrative conservatism but also of the dilatoriness and reluctance with which the radical interventions of the Edwardian council and legislature was received in the north. However, at the national level it has a much more positive significance and provides some very interesting indications of the ways in which policy was being shaped and implemented during the last two years of Edward's reign.

By the summer of 1550 Cuthbert Tunstall, bishop since 1530, was in deep disfavour with the council in London. In spite of his acceptance of the royal supremacy and his great skill and experience in the administration of the north, he had become a liability to a regime which was concerned to impose a Protestant religious settlement.[3] At the beginning of September he was summoned to London to answer charges of concealing a treasonable plot against the government. The details of this alleged plot never emerged,[4] but the Earl of Warwick took advantage of Tunstall's presence with him at Ely Place to question the bishop about his failure to send certain letters to the council and concluded a brief report to Cecil with the significant words: 'the matter will touch him wonderfully and yield to the King as good a return as the B(ishop) of Winchester is like to do if the cards be true'.[5]

The Bishop of Winchester, Stephen Gardiner, was in the Tower at the time, having refused subscription to the Act of Uniformity. In December he was to be deprived by royal commission and the revenues of his see, the wealthiest in England, taken into the king's hands.[6] When a Protestant bishop, John Ponet, was appointed to Winchester in the following year, the unprecedented step was taken of paying him a stipend of 2000 marks, the king retaining lands and profits amounting to almost twice that sum.[7] The explicit connection between the cases of Gardiner and Tunstall made in Warwick's letter is thus a clear indication of what was in the earl's mind at that time. Durham was the second wealthiest see in England and, although Tunstall's conservatism was much more cautious than that of Gardiner, a pretext of a different kind had arisen to justify a similar course of action. Nevertheless, the process against him was slow and in many respects obscure. For over a year he remained under house arrest at his own residence, Cold Harbour in Thames Street, while attempts were made, first to compel him to testify against Gardiner and then to extract an explicit submission to the Protestant settlement. According to a report which reached the imperial ambassador, Jehan Scheyfve, in January 1551, Tunstall had offered to renounce his see and submit to the council, but that this offer had not been accepted.[8] Warwick seems to have been determined to secure a conviction for treason, but lacked adequate means to accomplish his purpose. An interrogation of Tunstall by the full council in May 1551 having failed to produce a satisfactory result, a formal commission to investigate the case was set up in October, but again no conclusive evidence was found.[9] Only after the second arrest of the Duke of Somerset was this impasse broken; perhaps (as it was claimed) because his papers yielded the vital testimony,[10] or perhaps because the removal of his restraining influence had made the council more amenable to Warwick's wishes.

On 20 December 1551 Tunstall was finally committed to the Tower 'to abide there such ordere as his doings by the course of law shall appear to have deserved'.[11] By that time Warwick had been created Duke of Northumberland and Scheyfve drew the obvious conclusion – that the attainder of the Bishop of Durham was intended to clear the way for the establishment of a new secular palatinate which would give the duke overwhelming power in the north of England.[12] In the event, however, Tunstall was not attainted. No formal charges were brought against him in any court and although a Bill of Attainder for misprision of treason passed the House of Lords at the end of March 1552, it disappeared in the Commons and was not revived.[13] It seems that, despite his ingenuity and possible unscrupulousness, John Dudley could not produce enough evidence against Tunstall to make even a charge of misprision stick. On the other hand he may have come to realise that such draconian methods were not necessary. Gardiner had not been attainted, merely deprived, but the temporalities of Winchester had been effectively sequestered. It may have been felt that the resumption of a palatinate jurisdiction by the Crown needed greater legal certainty, for there was no precedent for the dissolution of an ecclesiastical franchise and with or without an attainder such action could only have been based on the royal supremacy and the overriding authority of statute.[14] After the failure of the Bill of Attainder no further attempt was made to press charges under the common law and the commission which was finally issued to Sir Roger Cholmeley the Chief Justice of King's Bench and six others on 14 September 1552 was almost certainly an *ad hoc* commission to exercise the royal supremacy, similar to those which had already been used against Bonner, Gardiner, Heath and Day.[15]

The commissioners sat twice at the Old Whitefriars, on 4 and 14 October, and after the latter session declared the bishop to be deprived of his see and sent him back to prison during the king's pleasure. Two weeks later Scheyfve reported that he had been found guilty of 'minor treason', but he was presumably describing the substance of the charges and not the legal verdict.[16] The bishopric, its revenues and jurisdiction thus passed into the hands of the Crown, as would have been the case during a normal vacancy; but for the time being no attempt was made to make a new appointment and those who believed that more drastic action was intended were soon justified by events. Nevertheless, the traditional view, expressed by Burnet and Strype (and foreshadowed, as we have seen, by Scheyfve) that the whole process was part of a deep-laid plot 'to add another title to the ambitious Duke of Northumberland, viz. Earl of Durham', will hardly stand up to close examination. There is no evidence prior to the parliamentary session of March 1553 that Dudley sought autonomous power for himself in the north, in spite of a thoroughly misleading entry in the *Calendar of State Papers, Domestic, 1547–1580.* A letter from Northumberland to Cecil, there dated 7 April 1552, is summarised as containing a request that the palatinate jurisdiction of Durham be conferred upon the writer.[17] The original document presents a number of problems: it is slightly damaged and only one part of it consists of a note signed by Northumberland. However, the relevant passage runs

> Che[sic] as now the jurisdiction of the County Palatine of . . . oprike[sic] of Durham is in the King's Majesty's hands . . . it is thought good that the same be used still as . . . Palatine like as Chester is at this day. I . . . therefore in my absence to move Mr. Vice Chamberlain . . . also to the means to the King's Majesty that . . . his Highness Chancellor and Steward of the same . . . to me and my sufficient deputies with such fee . . . office as shall be thought meet to his Majesty to appoint to the . . . whereof I shall be the better able to serve . . . in those parts.[18]

This corresponds very closely to the scheme eventually implemented in two patents which passed the Privy Seal early in May 1553. One of these created 'the King's County Palatine of Durham' in place of the Bishop's County Palatine;[19] the other granted to Northumberland for life 'the Office of Chief Steward of all the King's lands . . . which belonged to the late Bishopric of Durham' with 'the rule and leading of all the King's men and tenants . . . and all profits . . . as amply as Thomas Tempest Kt., Richard Bellasis Esq. and John, Lord Lumley deceased, or any other had them'.[20]

Had time permitted these patents to come into effect, Northumberland's position in the north would certainly have been strengthened. However, the traditional terms in which the stewardship was granted conferred no kind of palatine authority upon the duke himself. Nor was there any intention to dissolve the palatinate and convert Durham into ordinary 'shire ground'. The jurisdictional structure would have remained intact, although the county would have sent members to parliament.[21] The main effect would have been to divorce the county palatine completely from the bishopric and it is in terms of ecclesiastical rather than secular policy that the main purpose of the scheme has to be viewed. Burnet was quite wrong to conclude that only Edward's death prevented Northumberland from establishing himself as 'a Prince in the North'.[22] Recent historians, notably Barrett Beer, have recognised the strict limitations of the grant which was actually made and have tended to conclude that this demonstrated the limited nature of the duke's power – the fact that he could not dominate the council, which had the last word in all such matters.[23] It would, however, be more in accordance with the evidence to conclude that, in this respect, Northumberland obtained almost exactly what he set out to achieve and that he was concerned rather to carry further the policy which had been represented by the Franchise Act of 1536 than to establish a satrapy for himself.

Before the patents expressing this policy could be drawn up, however, the ground had to be more thoroughly cleared. The vacancy created by Tunstall's deprivation could have given an adequate opportunity to make a stipendiary appointment, as at Winchester, but could not, in itself, give the Crown sufficient legal grounds to alter the nature of the palatinate. Nor did it allow the king to divert a significant proportion of the endowment for the creation of a new bishopric. For these purposes the greatest certainty lay in an Act of parliament and on 21 March 1553 a Bill was introduced into the House of Lords, for the dissolution of the see of Durham.[24] This was read a second time on 22 March and committed. After a week's delay, which probably reflects some dissension,[25] it was approved and sent to the Commons on 29 March. There it was rushed through three readings in 24 hours and passed without any recorded debate. Although somewhat misleadingly described in the *Commons Journal* as being for 'the erection of the two bishoprics of Durham and Newcastle', this Act in fact accomplished no such thing. A long preamble declared that

> for as much, as the circuit and compass of the ordinary jurisdiction of the said Bishopric is large and great and extendeth into many shires and counties . . . the charge thereof may not conveniently be supplied and well and sufficiently discharged by one ordinary . . .[26]

and because the area was backward and deficient in godly preaching and ministry, the king 'of his most godly disposition' had decided

> to have two several ordinary sees of bishops to be erected and established within the limits bounds and jurisdictions of the said Bishopric of Durham. Whereof the one shall be called the see of the Bishopric of Durham and the other the see of the Bishopric of Newcastle-upon-Tyne . . .

Each of these sees was to be endowed with 'manors, lands, tenements and other hereditaments', Durham to the value of 2000 marks and Newcastle to the value of 1000 marks.[27] At the same time Newcastle was to be elevated to the status of a city and provided with a dean and chapter, similarly endowed but to an unspecified level. However, none of these intentions were implemented by the Act, which merely authorised the king to carry out his godly purposes by Letters Patent.[28] The operative clause of the statute ran:

> Be it therefore enacted by the authority of this Parliament that the said Bishopric of Durham together with all the ordinary jurisdictions thereunto belonging and appurtaining shall be adjudged from henceforth clearly dissolved, extinguished and determined. And that the King our sovereign Lord shall from henceforth have, hold possessed and enjoy . . . all and singular honours, castles, manors . . . etc.

Only the establishment and endowments of the dean and chapter of Durham Cathedral were specifically exempted and preserved.

Had the plan outlined in this preamble been put into effect, there would have been very little direct financial benefit to the Crown, as Burnet noticed.[29] The total value of the see was not much in excess of £2800 in peacetime and a good deal less during intermittent warfare with the Scots. If £2000 of that was to be allocated to the new bishops and a further endowment provided for the new cathedral at Newcastle, a profit of no more than £300 or £400 a year would be left in Augmentations. This did not at all correspond with the expectations that Northumberland had expressed to Cecil at the end of October 1552, when he was calculating the benefits of Tunstall's deprivation: 'His Majesty. . . . (may) resume to his Crown £2,000 a year of the best lands within the North parts of his realm, yea I doubt not it will be 4,000 marks a year of as good revenue as any within the realm . . .'[30], he had written optimistically. This great profit could be realised, he claimed, and still leave 'all places better and more godly furnished than ever it was from the beginning until this day . . .'. His 'plan', if it can be called such, was to promote Robert Horne, the Dean of Durham, to be bishop and shuffle round the other senior diocesan officers.[31] In doing this he blandly ignored the fact that the bishopric and chapter were separate institutions, apparently regarding their funds as interchangeable. This may indicate a tacit hope that the chapter would be sequestered as well, but too much should not be read into a single hasty letter. What does seem clear is that Northumberland's priorities had not changed since he had written to Cecil in September 1550; and although he envisaged the creation of a bishopric of Newcastle, there was no mention of endowment, or of a second chapter. A few days after writing this letter he was urging Cecil to keep a vigilant eye upon the bishopric accounts and to summon the bishop's auditor to London 'otherwise it is impossible to have any profit or true knowledge . . .'.[32] The council took the same view and instructed Lord Wharton to seek for the same accounts and to send them up as a matter of urgency.[33] In fact proprieties seem to have been very correctly observed and Robert Hindemer, Tunstall's Chancellor, continued to administer the temporalities of the see until after the Act of Dissolution, at which point the responsibility was taken over by the Court of Augmentations[34] – although this fact does not seem to have been noticed in Durham!

In the light of this evidence it seems very unlikely that Northumberland was responsible for drawing up the generous scheme described in the Act. Nor is it surprising that Horne refused promotion on the disadvantageous and legally uncertain terms upon which it was actually offered to him.[35] Although it is possible that the concern and indignation which Northumberland expressed about the Durham situation in January 1553 was the result of genuine anxiety about the pastoral neglect of the diocese, that would not be consistent with his earlier attitude.[36] His criticism of Horne, as a man unwilling to serve and too much concerned with 'great possessions', suggests rather that he was indignant because the dean's uncooperative attitude seemed likely to frustrate a financial 'killing' on behalf of the Crown – as indeed turned out to be the case. However, the battle over the see of Durham was never fought to a conclusion and we do not know how it might have ended. The Act of Dissolution may have been a direct consequence of Northumberland's failure to persuade Horne, or it may have been simply the result of more informed thinking. The preamble may have been no more than a device to disarm opposition and facilitate the passage of the Act or it may have represented the serious intention of someone other than Northumberland – perhaps the king himself, whose religious priorities were perfectly genuine. The one positive achievement of the Act was to lift the threat to the Durham chapter which had certainly been implied in Northumberland's letters. Ridley was named for the reconstituted see of Durham and William Bill for the new see of Newcastle,[37] but neither was appointed because the Letters Patent creating and endowing the sees were never issued. This may have been because of the king's death early in July, but as we saw, the corresponding patents relating to the palatinate were issued in early May. It was certainly not the case that, as Burnet declared, the lands, revenues and jurisdictions were granted to Northumberland instead, but the conflict between religious and fiscal priorities may well have remained unresolved to the end.

The ancient bishopric of Durham, although legally dissolved, was not, therefore, plundered in the same way that the great abbeys had been. Its endowment suffered no more than a few chips around the edges. One of these was the loss of the bishop's London residence. Henry VIII had retained Durham Place in the Strand after Wolsey's fall and in July 1537 Tunstall (in a weak position after his performance during the Pilgrimage of Grace) formally conveyed it to the king, together with certain lands and tenements in Westminster. In return he had received the reversion of Cold Harbour and eight messuages in London, a transaction which was confirmed by the statute of 28 Henry VIII c.33.[38] On 30 June 1553 the Cold Harbour and its attendant messuages were granted to the Earl of Shrewsbury and valued at £66 16s.1½d.[39] Only one other formal grant of bishopric property was made, but that was the substantial one of all lands in Howdenshire to Sir Francis Jobson. These lands had a clear annual value of £284 19s.8½d., but since Jobson was required to pay a rent of £200 a year into augmentations his own profit was relatively modest.[40] Other grants were of a less straightforward nature. One, as we have seen, conferred on Northumberland the office of chief steward, a position which carried with it formal fees of about £40 a year, together with many perquisites and opportunities for influence. Another assigned the profits of the bishopric lands in Norhamshire (£163 6s.8d.) to the captain and garrison of Norham Castle.[41] A third conferred the mastership of Sherburn Hospital, worth £135 7s., upon Sir Richard Rede.[42] Sherburn was not a parcel of the bishopric, but the mastership was in the bishop's gift. The most serious depredation, however, was contained not in a grant, but in another statute. At the same time as the Bill of Dissolution was going through parliament a second Bill, sponsored by the burgesses of Newcastle upon Tyne, sought to detach the town of Gateshead from the bishopric and annex it to their own jurisdiction. This expressed a long-standing ambition on the part of the larger town, which regarded its southern neighbour as a nuisance and a refuge for delinquents.[43] Officially, Gateshead was only worth about £35 a year to the bishop, but in practice its revenues were probably a good deal more and well worth the passage of the Act of Dissolution. 'An Act for the uniting and annexing of the Town of Gateshead to the Town of Newcastle-upon-Tyne' (7 Edward VI c.10) was also completed.[44]

At the time of Edward VI's death, therefore, there was no lawfully constituted see of Durham (let alone of Newcastle); but there was a secular palatinate in the hands of the Crown, coextensive with the former ecclesiastical franchise except for Gateshead; and about 75 per cent of the property of the bishopric remained under the control of the Court of Augmentations. In Durham itself, although some leases had been approved in Augmentations, both the diocesan and the palatinate administration continued without interruption, presumably awaiting the attention of the royal commissioners who would sooner or later have appeared to 'take further order' for the whole organisation.

With the accession of Mary after a brief period of uncertainty, any possibility that this might happen rapidly disappeared. The new sovereign had many preoccupations and it was not likely that the settlement of Durham would be given a very high priority, but her initial actions served to make the situation even more anomalous and confused. Cuthbert Tunstall, now 79 years old, but still active, was released from the Tower on 6 August, and was sworn of the Privy Council as Bishop of Durham, on 14 August.[45] He promptly appealed against his deprivation and on 23 August a commission was established under the Earl of Arundel to hear the appeal.[46] In the circumstances the result was a foregone conclusion; the commissioners declared the earlier sentence void on the specious grounds that those pronouncing it had all been laymen.[47] By the beginning of October Tunstall was again functioning officially as Bishop of Durham; on 18 November he instituted the new dean, Thomas Watson,[48] and was summoned to the House of Lords in Mary's first parliament by that title. On 27 November a Bill was introduced into the House of Commons 'for the confirmation of the Bishopric of Durham and Durham Place, to Cuthbert Tunstall, bishop there, and his successors'.[49] The use of the word 'confirmation', and the reference to Durham Place, were both significant of the council's attitude. Legally Tunstall had no standing apart from that conferred by his episcopal orders and the main purpose of the Bill must have been to repeal the Edwardian Act of Dissolution. However, the whole process of repealing her predecessor's ecclesiastical legislation was extremely distasteful to Mary, who preferred to regard it as invalid *ipso facto*, and the word 'confirmation' suggests a formula which tried to avoid recognising the authority of the earlier Act.[50] Similarly, Durham Place had been conveyed to the Crown in 1537 in exchange for the Cold Harbour. In April 1551 it had been granted, along with other properties, to Princess Elizabeth, who was still in possession in 1553.[51] Whether any compensation was offered in the original draft Bill we do not know, but when it came back for a second reading on 1 December, a proviso was inserted 'for the Lady Elizabeth's Grace, for Durham Place'.[52] Even with this amendment the Bill failed on its third reading, on 5 December, without the necessity to count a division.

Mary's first parliament was, in other respects, reasonably co-operative and had repealed the Protestant Act of Uniformity, together with several other measures of the previous regime, without a great deal of acrimony.[53] These measures did not, however, affect particular property rights and it seems likely that the burgesses of Newcastle (striving to retain their newly won control over Gateshead) succeeded in persuading their fellow MPs that the restoration of Durham would create a precedent for reversing the whole process of statutory acquisition, going back to 1536.

Monastic and chantry lands were soon to be an extremely sensitive and important issue and it looks as though the first shots were fired over this abortive Bill.[54] In any case its failure was a serious embarrassment for the government and left Tunstall himself in an even more ambiguous position than he had been at the beginning of the session. If a remedy were not found quickly, local opponents of the bishop or those with grievances against his administration would be bound to challenge the whole legal basis of his authority in the royal courts and the result might well be further and worse embarrassment. Consequently, on 18 January 1554 in response to a further petition from Tunstall, the queen issued Letters Patent erecting a new bishopric in Durham

> with ordinary episcopal jurisdiction to extend throughout the said city and the county and precincts lately called the bishopric and royal liberty of St. Cuthbert of Durham between the waters of Tyne and Tees, throughout the whole county called Norham-shire and Bedlingtonshire . . .[55]

This patent recited the whole story of Tunstall's deprivation, the annulment of that sentence and the passage of the Act of Dissolution. It also 'nominated and elected' Tunstall to this new bishopric: 'he and his successors to be from henceforth a body corporate with perpetual succession by the name of the bishop of Durham . . .'.[56] and proceeded to grant him the temporal and spiritual possessions of the previous see. Contrary to what is sometimes claimed, this patent did not pretend to repeal or annul the Act of Dissolution; rather it took advantage of the empowering clause in that Act to re-erect the ancient see instead of the two new sees that had been envisaged. What it did annul, implicitly rather than explicitly, was the patent of March 1553 establishing a secular royal palatinate. Since the palatinate jurisdiction and the bulk of the possessions of the former see were in the queen's hands, however, the patent was in no sense *ultra vires*.[57]

Nevertheless, it was not a satisfactory solution to the problem. The grants of Cold Harbour and Howdenshire and even more the annexation of Gateshead to Newcastle were bound to create thorny legal problems unless the two relevant Edwardian Acts were repealed. Whether this was clear to the queen's legal advisers all along and the patent never intended to be more than a stop-gap measure, or whether the new creation was challenged almost at once, we do not know. However, on 7 April 1554 a Bill of Repeal was introduced into the House of Lords of Mary's second parliament.[58] This covered both the offending measures, which were roundly (and characteristically) described as having been

> compassed and brought to pass in the tender years and minorities of our said late sovereign Lord the King by the sinister labour, great malice and corrupt means of certain ambitious persons then being in authority, rather for to enrich themselves and their friends with a great part of the possessions of the said bishopric than upon just occasion or godly zeal . . .[59]

The preamble then went on to recite the whole story, up to and including the patent of January, concluding

> Yet the said Reverend Father in God, Cuthbert, now Bishop of Durham, notwith-
> standing the repeal of the said sentence, cannot by virtue thereof, nor by force of the
> said Letters Patent, have, possess and enjoy to him and to his successors all and
> singular honours . . . (etc) . . . for the said two several estatutes remain yet in their
> perfect force and effect . . .

The Lords passed this measure without demur but the Commons, once again, were recalcitrant. This time we know that the burgesses of Newcastle led the fight, calling legal counsel to their aid.[60] As the debate went on, various provisos and amendments were introduced; protecting the interest of the Earl of Shrewsbury in Cold Harbour, that of Sir Francis Jobson in Howdenshire and, more generally, that of all grantees of bishopric property.[61] Eventually only the first of these was incorporated in the Act of Repeal, but the city of Newcastle had to be bought off with leases and grants which were very disadvantageous to the bishopric, and the House made its feelings clear by instructing '. . . that Mr. Speaker in their names, shall require the Bishop of Durham to show favour to Sir Francis Jobson in his suit'.[62] On 19 April, after an intervention by Tunstall himself, the Commons passed this extremely controversial measure by 201 votes to 120 – a measure of the strong feelings it had aroused and a marked contrast to the passage of the original Bills just over twelve months earlier.

Once the Edwardian Acts were repealed, since all the relevant grants had been made retrospective to 14 October 1552 the episode was, as far as Durham was concerned, closed. Its implications were certainly grasped by those most concerned and written large in terms of the struggle to restore papal jurisdiction which occupied the latter part of 1554; but there was hardly a shadow of weapon left to use against the Bishop of Durham, should anyone have wished to do so. Nevertheless it was not forgotten. In 1559 Tunstall was again deprived and in appointing Robert Tempest to be sheriff of Durham during the first year of his episcopate the new bishop, James Pilkington, was careful to recite the rights of the Crown over the bishopric, including his own appointment.[63]

In spite of its brief duration, and somewhat theoretical nature, the dissolution of the see of Durham was an interesting and significant development. Northumberland, the villain of the peace to generations of church historians cannot, I think, be exonerated from the charge of placing secular priorities (particularly financial ones) ahead of religious – although we cannot be entirely sure of his final attitude towards the 'statute scheme'. There is, however, no evidence to support the charges that he intended primarily to enrich himself or to give himself autonomous power in the north of England. It would be fairer to conclude that the duke's true concern was to strengthen the position of the Crown, and that in placing palatinate jurisdiction and extensive ecclesiastical revenues in the king's hand he was acting in the true spirit of the Cromwellian tradition in which he had been trained. Mary, in spite of her profound distaste for what had been done and her willingness to ignore technical impediments in the path of justice as she saw it, was nevertheless forced to recognise the immovable obstacle of an unrepealed statute. In spite of the strict legality of her patent recreating the see, there could have been no peaceful possession for the restored incumbent until that obstacle had been removed. This was in several ways a very useful 'trial run' for the policy of ecclesiastical restoration and clear proof (if that was needed) of the extent to which the capacity of statute had developed during the previous twenty years; a capacity which could in no way be diminished by charges of unworthy motivation, however heartfelt – or justified.

Notes

1. Public Record Office [PRO], Durham Sheriffs' Accounts, Durh. 20/51, 52.
2. *Calendar of the Patent Rolls, Mary*, I, 378, PRO, C 66/877 m.32. [*Cal. Pat.*]
3. C. Sturge, *Cuthbert Tunstall*, London, 1938, pp. 281–96. D.M. Loades, 'The Last Years of Cuthbert Tunstall, 1547–1559', *Durham University Journal*, LXVI, 1973, 10–21. Tunstall had consistently opposed every step in a Protestant direction, short of actually defying the law. The latest issue in 1550 was over the reformed Ordinal.
4. Tunstall was accused by Ninian Menville, a former dependant of the Nevilles, perhaps on a personal grudge. Sturge, *Tunstall*, p. 288.
5. PRO, SP/10/10/31. Warwick to Cecil, 16 Sept. 1550.
6. The troubles of Stephen Gardiner are examined at length in J.A. Muller, *Stephen Gardiner and the Tudor Reaction*, London, 1926, pp. 183–203.
7. *Acts of the Privy Council*, III, 231; 8 Mar. 1551. Ponet was admitted to the office on condition of surrendering the revenues.
8. *Calendar of the State Papers, Spanish*, x, 214. [*Cal. Span.*]
9. APC, III, 449.
10. A letter from Tunstall to Menville was alleged to have been found in a casket, which the bishop confessed to the council that he had written when interrogated on 20 December; Sturge, *Tunstall*, pp. 289–90. APC, III, 449.
11. APC, III, 449.
12. *Cal. Span.*, x, 425; 27 Dec. 1551.
13. *Journals of the House of Lords*, London, 1846, I, 418 *Journals of the House of Commons*, London, 1803–52, I, 21.
14. The main precedent for altering the status of franchises was the Act of 27 Henry VIII c.24, which had not only deprived the Bishops of Durham of the right to issue writs and appoint justices in their own names, but had also affected the Bishop of Ely's liberty in the Isle of Ely and that of the Archbishop of York in Hexhamshire.
15. PRO, SP/10/13/49.
16. *Cal. Span.*, x, 582; 29 Oct. 1552.
17. *Calendar of State Papers. Domestic*, I, p.38, 7 April; Chelsea; Northumberland to Cecil. To remember the Dean of Worcester's licence. Desires a grant to himself of the Palatine Jurisdiction of Durham. Lady Margaret Douglas wishes to return home, being pregnant.
18. PRO, SP/10/14/18. The first paragraph, relating to the licence, is dated 'from Chelsea this vii . . . ell 1552' and signed 'your assured loving friend, Northumberland'. The other two paragraphs follow the signature in the same hand (a clerk's), but it is not clear whether they are intended to be part of the letter, or are memoranda subsequently written on the blank page. The jurisdiction of Durham was not in any sense 'in the King's hands' in early April 1552, since Tunstall was not deprived until October. The reference to Lady Margaret Douglas is not much help, since the birth date of her second son Charles (subsequently Earl of Lennox) is given only as 'about 1556'; *Complete Peerage*, ed. G.E. Cockayne, rev. V. Gibbs, London, 1910–49, VII, p. 600. Since he was admitted to Gray's Inn in 1572, he could have been born in either 1553 or 1554.

19. *Cal. Pat., Edward VI*, VI, 177; 4 May 1553, PRO, C66/858 m.20.
20. *Cal. Pat., Edward VI*, V, 175. PRO, C66/858 m.17.
21. PRO, Chancery, Patent Rolls C66/858 m.20. It may be significant that the office of chancellor was not conferred along with that of chief steward, as Northumberland had suggested. The terms of the creation of the new palatinate made the office of chancellor a very powerful one. The chancellorship was not bestowed before the king's death. According to the terms of the creation, Durham County would have been represented by one knight and each town by one burgess, on the model of the new counties created in Wales by 27 Henry VII c.26. PRO, C66/858 m.20.
22. G. Burnet, *The History of the Reformation of the Church of England*, ed. M. Pocock, Oxford, 1865, II, pp. 194, 216.
23. B.L. Beer, *Northumberland*, Kent, Ohio, 1973, pp. 142–3.
24. *Lords Journals*, I, 436.
25. The Bill was committed to the Bishop of London, the Lord Chief Justice, the Attorney-General and the Solicitor-General, which suggests legal snags rather than objection of principle. Ibid.
26. PRO, Parliament Roll, 7 Edward VI, C65/161 item 12.
27. Ibid. It is quite clear that this plan did not envisage Durham and Newcastle as stipendiary sees on the lines of Winchester.
28. 'And for the better corroboration and perfecting of the erections and establishments of the said two new Bishoprics . . . which the King's Majesty mindeth presently to do and accomplish by his most gracious Letters Patent and to appoint them severally by the said Letters Patent their episcopal and ordinary jurisdictions, circuits and authorities. Be it therefore enacted by authority of this present Parliament that the said Letters Patent . . . shall be good and available in the law to all intents, constructions and purposes . . .' Ibid.
29. Burnet, *Church of England*, II, p.216.
30. PRO, SP/10/15/35. 28 Oct. 1552.
31. '. . . if His Majesty make the Dean of Durham Bishop of that see and appoint him one thousand marks more of that which he hath in his Deanery and the same houses which he now hath as well in the city as in the country will serve him right honourably . . . and the Chancellor's living to be converted to the Deanery and an honest man to be placed in it, the Vice Chancellor to be turned to the Chancellor, the Suffragan who is placed without the King's Majesty's authority and also hath a great living, not worthy of it to be removed . . . and the same living with a little more to the value of a hundred marks will serve for the erection of a Bishop within Newcastle . . .' Ibid.
32. PRO, SP/10/15/57: 15 Nov. 1552.
33. APC, IV, 155: 31 Oct. 1552.
34. On 7 March 1553 the council wrote direct to the Chancellor of Augmentations to grant a lease of bishopric property at Northallerton. Presumably Hindemer would not have been permitted to commit property in this way, since the dissolution of the ancient see had already been decided upon. APC, IV, 232.
35. Horn, an advanced Protestant, had been appointed to the deanery only in November 1551, after the death of Whitehead, and Northumberland presumably thought him to be as amenable as Ponet. His refusal to accept the see becomes easier to explain if he was expected to be party to the plunder of both the bishopric and the Cathedral and was offered a mixed package of revenues without any secure title. There is no reason to suppose that Horn doubted the legal validity of Tunstall's deprivation. J. Strype, *Ecclesiastical Memorials*, Oxford, 1822, II, ii, 22. It is important to realise that Horn was not offered the see on the terms later outlined in the Act.
36. The duke always professed great zeal for 'God's service' and wrote frequently to Cecil

about the situation in Durham, but by the beginning of 1553 sincere Protestants as diverse as John Hooper, John Knox and Thomas Cranmer had ceased to believe his professions. Beer, *Northumberland*, pp. 141–3.

37. PRO, SP/10/19/28. Burnet, *Church of England*, II, p. 216. Nicholas Ridley was Bishop of London and William Bill a royal chaplain.

38. *Statutes of the Realm*, III, 687–8. [SR]

39. *Cal. Pat., Edward VI*, V, 230.

40. Ibid., 133; 22 June 1553.

41. Ibid., 6; grant of the office of Warden of Norham Castle to Richard Bowes.

42. Ibid., 134; 5 Feb. 1553, Rede, described as 'the King's councillor', received this grant for his services with the Duke of Northumberland. He had also been a member of the commission which deprived Tunstall.

43. 'Where the quiet order regiment and governance of the corporation and body politic of the town of Newcastle-upon-Tyne hath been not a little disturbed and hindered . . . by reason that the said town of Gateshead is parcel of the said County Palatine of Durham and without the liberties of the said haven town . . .'; statute 7 Edward VI, c.10.

44. *SR*, IV, i, 173–4.

45. Loades, 'Last Years'; Mary accepted Tunstall as Bishop of Durham without hesitation or enquiry. Sturge, *Tunstall*, p. 297.

46. *Cal. Pat, Mary*, I, 76.

47. Ibid. This was one of the main grounds for Tunstall's appeal, the other being that he had had inadequate time to prepare his defence. In fact there was no established legal procedure for these commissions under the royal supremacy, as they were a new development in Edward's reign. Precedent, in the shape of Thomas Cromwell's Viceregency in Spirituals, suggested that there was no valid objection to laymen exercising the royal supremacy, provided that they were properly commissioned. Mary, of course, objected to the whole exercise of the supremacy, but could not use that as a ground of nullity, since her own commissions had to sit by the same authority.

48. Loades, 'Last Years'; Horn had fled, one step ahead of arrest, C.H. Garrett, *The Marian Exiles*, Cambridge, 1938, p. 188.

49. *Commons Journals*, I, 31.

50. Mary's conscience, prompted by Reginald Pole, urged her to regard all heretical (and schismatic) legislation as invalid, but she quickly became convinced of the necessity for parliamentary repeal: 'it was first necessary to repeal and annul by Acts of Parliament many perverse laws made by those who ruled before her', as she told Henry Penning in August 1553. For a full discussion of Mary's attitude to the royal supremacy and its consequences, see D.M. Loades, *The Oxford Martyrs*, London, 1970, pp. 104–8.

51. *Cal. Pat., Edward VI*, VI, 91.

52. *Commons Journals*, I, 31. Elizabeth's interests were not touched by the successful Bill of the next session.

53. Resistance to the government's religious policy in the House of Commons was determined, but limited in scale – about 80 members out of 350. It was clearly property, not doctrine, that provoked opposition in parliament. Loades, *The Reign of Mary Tudor*, London, 1979, pp. 154–7. [see also J. Loach, *Parliament and the Crown in the Reign of Mary Tudor*, Oxford, 1986.]

54. The issue over these lands was one of legal title. Did the Henrician statutes confer a valid title to confiscated ecclesiastical property upon the Crown? If so, then the Crown could convey that title to the purchasers, and the church's interest ceased. If not, then the purchasers had no secure title in return for an investment almost twenty years old in many cases. The settlement of December 1554 was ambiguous;

English common lawyers interpreted it as a concession of title by the church, but Pole clearly regarded it as a *de facto* concession only, dependent on the will of the Pope for the time being. BL, Add. MS 41577, fol. 1661; J.H. Crehan, 'The Return to Obedience: New Judgement on Cardinal Pole', *The Month*, n.s. XIV, 1955, 221–9; Loades, *Oxford Martyrs*, pp. 144–5. *Reign of Mary*, pp. 327–9. [and Loach, *Parliament and the Crown*.]

55. *Cal. Pat., Mary I*, 377. PRO., C66/87 m.32.
56. Ibid. This wording makes it clear that the new bishopric would have had no legal continuity with its predecessor, and corresponds with the terms of the bishop's petition, as cited '. . . Cuthbert Tunstall nuper Dunelmensis Episcopus nobis humilitate supplicavit ut Episcopatum et sedam Episcopaleum apud Dunelmensis praedictam de novo erigere et stabilire . . .'.
57. As I formerly argued; see 'Last Years'.
58. *Lords Journals*, I, 450.
59. I Mary st.3 c.3. SR, IV, i, 226–8.
60. *Commons Journals*, I. 34. Counsel was called on 16 April and appeared on 17 April.
61. Ibid., 18 April when the Newcastle counsel also appeared again.
62. Ibid. There is no evidence that Tunstall paid any attention to this representation.
63. PRO, Durh. 3/82 m.l.

14 Anabaptism and English Sectarianism in the Mid-Sixteenth Century

From about 1528 onwards radical Protestants of various kinds from the Low Countries began to seek refuge in England from the pressures of persecution in their homelands. Until the advent of Thomas More as chancellor, persecution in England was sporadic and rather lax. The royal authority had not hitherto been invoked, and the Lollards were not commonly of the stuff of martyrs, which induced a certain complacency in the English bishops when faced with the challenges of nascent Protestantism. After More's brief tenure of office was over, persecution under royal auspices continued, but on a very much smaller scale than in the Netherlands, so that the incentive for radicals to come to England, either permanently or temporarily, remained. Hundreds, perhaps thousands, of them lived in London, Norwich and other towns of the south-east over the next twenty years. A few, like Jan Mattijs, were burned in England, others, like Anneke Jans, met the same fate on their return home, but many lived and worked peacefully, attracting remarkably little attention.[1] Considering their numbers, and the radical nature of their views, they seem to have made only a very slight impact upon their adopted country. A few Englishmen, like that 'Henry' who turned up as the sponsor of the Bergholt meeting in 1536, embraced their ideas wholeheartedly, but for the most part the effect seems to have been extremely piecemeal and diffuse, producing a wide variety of individual eccentricities rather than anything in the nature of a coherent movement. However, the presence of these radicals and their English sympathisers has always served to confuse students of the Reformation, not least by appearing to justify contemporary conservative attempts to discredit Protestantism as a Tower of Babel.

> As holy Doctours all write this
> and constantly agree
> To whom Christs church no mother is
> God will no father be . . .[2]

To Catholic polemicists the innumerable disputes and divisions among their opponents represented clear proof of their error and iniquity. Miles Huggarde, one of the most articulate and readable defenders of the Marian reaction, may be taken as a representative voice:

But if these good felowes wyll nedes be of Christes churche, as arrogantly they presume by their own confession; They must have one unitie of doctrine as ye churche hathe, which surely they have not . . . The punishments are not so divers in hell (as Vergill described) as are the sundry opinions of these Protestants . . .[3]

That these disputes existed is not seriously in doubt, and yet the polemical conclusion need not be accepted by the modern scholar. Where Protestant churches became established they set up, and enforced, standards of orthodoxy; the Confessions of Augsburg, *Confessio Belgica*, the Forty-Two Articles, and many others. There were quarrels between the adherents of these various confessions, and there were also disagreements as to how the confessions themselves should be interpreted, but these provided only a small proportion of the targets for Catholic satire. The bulk of the attack rested upon the idiosyncratic opinions of individuals and small groups whom the Catholics insisted on labelling as 'Protestants', but who were just as objectionable to Calvin, Cranmer or John Hooper as they were to the fathers at Trent. They were usually known at the time as Anabaptists, and the name has stuck, but it is not a very helpful label, implying as it does some degree of sectarian coherence.[4] English Anabaptism as it was first known and condemned in the 1530s was a generic term, embracing some views which would earlier have been known as Lollard, and were indigenous, for instance that the validity of a sacrament depended on the spiritual standing of the celebrant; and some derived from the teaching of particular continental leaders such as Melchior Hoffman,[5] which were brought in by the refugees.

A list of eight beliefs ascribed to these Anabaptists was drawn up in 1538,[6] and several of these occur in subsequent denunciations; particularly that Christian men hold all goods in common, that it is not lawful for a Christian man to hold office, that Christ took no flesh of the Virgin Mary, and that baptism should be administered only to believing adults. Writing ten years later, John Hooper reported that some of the London Anabaptists were arguing that 'besides that will of his which he hath revealed to us in the Scriptures, God hath another will by which he altogether acts under some kind of necessity', and that others denied 'that man is endued with a soul different from that of a beast, and subject to decay'.[7] Huggarde naturally cited his own examples: 'there was a tyler dwelling in S. Sepulchres paryshe in London that helde opinion how Christe was only incarnate and suffered deathe for all those that died before his incarnation, and not for those whych dyed since . . .',[8] and again, 'a bricklayer taking upon him the office of preachyng, affirmed that he myght lawfully do it though he were not called thereunto by the church for spiritus ubi vult spirat . . .'.[9] Writing of the late fifteenth-century Lollards, J.A.F. Thomson recently concluded 'that one cannot talk of a single Lollard creed, but must always remember that beliefs varied,· not only from group to group, but even from individual to individual within the same group'.[10] This seems to have been just as true of the later Anabaptists, and although these groups probably owed some of their assorted beliefs to the main stream of Reformation, they seem to have owed more to Lollardy, and to the radical and apocalyptic movements in the Netherlands which all the leading reformers had repudiated. Consequently, although it was inevitable that Huggarde and his fellows would use the proliferation of eccentric beliefs as a stick with which to beat the Edwardian reformers, it would be a mistake to accept their arguments at face value. Only in one respect can the reformers clearly be blamed for this embarrassing development, and that was in making the scriptures available in English. However, in spite of some urging, Mary never withdrew these bibles, and her Catholic propagandists were muted on this point.

The English reformers cannot justly be accused of encouraging Anabaptism, but they can be accused of failing to suppress it. This was a charge to which Cranmer himself pleaded guilty, when he wrote 'O good Lord be merciful unto us; for we have been too remiss in punishing offenders, and many things we have winked at.'[11] The failure to establish an effective reformed discipline in England was not the fault of the church leaders, but it left them in an exposed position when they faced their Catholic critics. But there was more to this diversity of opinion than a mere failure of discipline, as Cardinal Pole was to discover in his turn. Later sects, such as the Brownists, and continental Anabaptist groups like the Hutterites and the Mennonites, were not just vague associations of people who more or less shared the same ideas and objected to being bullied by the ecclesiastical authorities. They were 'gathered churches' sharing a special sense of election and separation from the world. There was a great deal of difference between the sect in this sense and the non-separating nonconformist. To the latter (who included the great majority of the Elizabethan and Jacobean puritans) the issues were specific points of doctrine or usage.[12] To the former the issue was the fundamental nature of the church itself. As Philip Schaff wrote: 'The first and chief aim of the radicals was not (as is usually stated) the opposition to infant baptism . . . but the establishment of a pure church of converts in opposition to the mixed church of the world.'[13] In other words the true sectarian drive was positive rather than negative and went well beyond the mere act of separation. This is an important distinction, because the early history of English sectarianism has been confused by the fact that all resolute Protestants became separatists under Mary. Writing in 1648, William Bradford claimed that the London congregation of John Rough 'professed and practised that cause (separatism) before Mr. Brown wrote for it'.[14] But we have it on contemporary testimony that the same congregation used 'all the English service without any diminishing, wholly as it was in the time of King Edward VI'.[15] They would hardly have done that if they had not accepted Ridley's definition of a true church as 'permixt' – that is, embracing both elect and non-elect. The congregation presided over by Rough, and at other times by Edmund Scrambler and Thomas Bentham (both Elizabethan bishops) was no more sectarian in intention than those groups of Catholic recusants who were later to refuse the communion of the Church of England.

It seems to me that those scholars who have recently explored the early history of religious dissidence in England have made their own task more difficult by not distinguishing with sufficient clarity between nonconformity, separatism and sectarianism. I.B. Horst, who has revealed the beginnings of Anabaptism in this country with great thoroughness and skill, can find no positive evidence of the practice of rebaptism.[16] He also finds only one specific reference to a 'bishop or reader', a Fleming called Bastiane who was almost certainly no more than an occasional visitor.[17] It therefore seems probable that the 'gathered' Anabaptist congregation of the kind which was flourishing in Franconia or Switzerland before 1530[18] was never transplanted to England during this period in spite of the influx from the Netherlands. The plentiful evidence of beliefs of a broadly Anabaptist kind certainly indicates a fair measure of nonconformity, enough to account for numerous prosecutions for heresy, but does not prove the existence of self-consciously separatist congregations, let alone true sects. In fact the evidence for the existence of separatists before 1553 is very meagre. People stayed away from church for all sorts of reasons, and the existence of conventicles or house meetings 'for talke of the scriptures' is no more proof of separatism than the prophesyings of a later generation. When Thomas Cole and others admitted to the Privy Council in 1551 that they had refused communion 'above ii yeres' they were probably confessing to a deliberate schism, although the reasons for their action are less clear than the fact itself.[19] The group to which they belonged, which centred on Bocking and Faversham in Kent, was loosely called 'Anabaptist', but seems to have been principally under the influence of Henry Hart. Hart had had dealings with the continental Anabaptists, but as J.W. Martin has pointed out in a recent article, there is no evidence that he professed any of the characteristic Anabaptist beliefs.[20] He was not much interested in doctrine, but urged a 'common-sense' interpretation of the Bible, and fell out with official Protestantism mainly because he denied predestination. In 1555, when they were all in prison, he and his followers, the 'freewillers', conducted a celebrated skirmish with John Bradford, which amused and encouraged their persecutors, but neither side seems to have regarded itself as irrevocably 'separated' from the other. This may help to explain why Cuthbert Simpson, who was imprisoned for his nonconformity in 1551 and was almost certainly a follower of Hart, appears in 1556 as the deacon of John Rough's London congregation – which followed orthodox Edwardian teaching.[21] Before 1553 Hart's followers, both in Kent and Essex, do seem to have practised a measure of separatism, calling each other 'brother' and 'sister' in the manner of the later sects, but Hart's teaching was not particularly conducive to a 'gathered' church, and they seem to have been at no particular pains to maintain their distinct identity during the persecution. Joan Bocher, who was executed in 1550 for Anabaptist views on the incarnation, is alleged to have claimed at her death that 'a M in London were of her secte',[22] but this seems to have meant no more than the undoubted fact that there were a lot of radical and eccentric theological ideas about in the capital. If her meaning was more precise, there is no surviving evidence to support this claim. The Lollard tradition that had survived from the fifteenth century is perhaps best described as one of 'occasional conformity'; '. . . more concerned with self preservation than with revolution, conforming to the normal practices of the church to avoid detection . . .', as Thomson says.[23] In spite of its radical tenets, its family groups and 'known men' it was not, by the early sixteenth century, a separatist movement, let alone a sect. And it is here, I think, that we must look for the model of the way in which newer radical and nonconformist ideas were received and developed in England before 1553, rather than to the 'gathered' Anabaptist or 'covenanted' Calvinist churches of the continent.

After 1553 the position changed. Protestants and Anabaptists were equally heretics to the Catholic government, and no serious attempt seems to have been made to distinguish between them. One result of this has been a tendency among modern scholars to claim that John Foxe exploited the confusion to represent as Protestant martyrs men and women who were really Anabaptists, and who would have suffered the same death at the hands of the Edwardian regime had Cranmer's reformed canon law ever come into force.[24] There is some truth in this, at least to the extent that Foxe was often unable or unwilling to distinguish between genuine Protestants and those whom the church disciplined for other reasons, whether radical beliefs or mere hooliganism.[25] However, to claim with Smyth or Philip Hughes that the great majority of Foxe's martyrs came from the nonconformist rather than the orthodox tradition of the previous period is to fly in the face of both evidence and probability. Where separatist congregations can be identified, such as that in London, their doctrine and practices were usually Edwardian. Robert Samuel continued to minister to his erstwhile flock at Bergholt in Suffolk until his arrest.[26] A prayer-book congregation continued to exist in Hadleigh, much to the annoyance of Rowland Taylor's Catholic successor, and a group arrested in Brighton was specifically accused of trying 'to have up again the English service and communion in all points as was used in the latter days of King Edward VI'.[27] Four parishes in Essex were still unobtrusively using the 1552 Prayer Book as late as June 1555.[28] In other cases where groups were accused of absenting themselves from church and 'having your conventicles, a sort of you, in corners', the form of their worship is uncertain. The fact that several of these groups operated in the same areas of Essex and Kent, which were notorious for nonconformity between 1549 and 1553, is circumstantial evidence for their radicalism, but their separatism in that period is a matter of some uncertainty, and their attitude towards orthodox Protestantism during the Marian persecution can only be dimly glimpsed in the dispute between Bradford and the 'freewillers'.

There does, however, seem to have been at least one congregation which was self-consciously separatist. In Lent 1555 Miles Huggarde received word that a certain preacher whom he calls 'father Browne, the Broker of Bedlam' was holding conventicles in Islington. Browne, according to Huggarde's satirical account, dressed as a shepherd, affected a prophetic style, and attracted large audiences, even from among the more respectable citizens:

> Could his pevishe prophecies be hadde in suche estimacion amonges the warme brethren without his dissimulate vesture and his staffe like a shepehooke? Would the marchant men of London with Pat Peny Ale, Sympering Sysse, and other fleerying flurtes their wives use their accustomed peregrinacions and pilgrimages to visit the blissed Rode called poore father Browne, that hathe the lordes gyfts, at Islington, Barnet and other places about London, were they not moved with the spirite?[29]

Huggarde, according to his own account, 'resorted thither with two gentlemen of mine acquaintance' and discovered 'by secret meanes' that Browne 'laye in a typling house, nexte the signe of the Mermayd'. They had no difficulty in gaining access to the tavern where Browne could be seen in earnest conference with some of his followers, who had brought him various presents. 'I trowe he was tellyng their fortunes, or suche lyke', Huggarde comments. After a while the preacher withdrew into a private room where another group was waiting. At this point the observers

. . . with divers other stepped to the dore, partely to here what he sayde, partely to marke the countenance of thassemblye. For no man except he was of special acquaintance, could be admitted to go in . . . But for the moste parte we could hear no worde, but the lorde be praysed, and some sundry devotions of their eyes towardes the top of the house, and suche lyke . . .[30]

This meeting was eventually interrupted by the arrival of a woman who was clearly some kind of patron of Browne's, and who was addressed by him as 'mother', in spite of her comparative youth. She was accompanied by a boy bearing a testament, and praised Browne generously for his constancy under affliction:

O good father Browne . . . howe have you been persecuted for the wordes sake . . . But the lorde be prased for your delivery and constancie in quiet suffering thereof. The prophetes, Christ saith, hath bene so handled. Therefore be of good chere man and take no thought, for one daye I truste we shall all be mery in the lorde, and shal have the dewe of the worde once more besprinkeled upon oure faces . . .[31]

Meanwhile another crowd was gathering in the courtyard outside 'one askyng another when the preaching time was', and after an interval, Browne went into the stable, where he preached, 'alledg(ing) certen places of ecclesiastes without booke, one upon another in heapes'.

Then beganne he to talke of thre religions, (Huggarde goes on), The one he termed my lorde chancellors religion; the other Cranmeres Latymers and Ridleys religion; and the third he calied goddes religion. My lorde Chancellors religion, he sayd, was nought. Cranmers and the others religion not good; but Goddes religion was best.[32]

At this point Huggarde and his friends left 'lamenting the great folly of the people which in this sorte dyd dayly spend theyre tyme to heare such lying spirites. And goyng homewardes we met divers companies both of men and women, of purpose going to Islyngton to heare the sermon of this peltyng prophet.'

It is difficult to know how seriously to take all this. Huggarde was quite frank in his intention to discredit not merely Browne and all who resorted to him but all Protestants. On the other hand the circumstantial detail of the episode is convincing, and makes it very unlikely that the author simply invented it. There is no corroborating evidence beyond the fact that anonymous 'prophets' are known to have been operating in the London area. Foxe mentions several Brownes, but none fits this description.[33] John Rough and several of his congregation were arrested at the Saracen's Head in Islington, but that was not until 1557 and there is no reason to associate these arrests with Browne and his followers. Why did Huggarde not alert the authorities, if he knew the whereabouts of such an heretical preacher? Perhaps he did, for he also says '. . . within a while after I hearde saye thys father Browne and his broode, with the congregation were removed from that place and were dispersed into corners . . .', and he added 'this opinion I have of Browne, that he woulde rather lyve a proude confessor than burne a stynking martyr'.[34] If he was indeed so explicitly hostile to 'Cranmeres, Latymers and Ridleys religion', and especially if he escaped burning, it is not surprising that Browne does not feature in the pages of Foxe. On balance the substance of Huggarde's account seems to me convincing.

Although he represents Browne as a crank 'newly crept out of Bedlam', the assembly he describes clearly had some organisation, and an established congregation of a sort; nor was Browne a wise man or necromancer, but a radical preacher familiar with the scriptures. Through this unflattering description it seems to me that we can catch a genuine glimpse of a group which was separated, not merely from the Catholic church, but also from the Protestantism of the Prayer Book.

If this is so, and Browne and his immediate followers were Anabaptists rather than Protestants, then it is clear that Huggarde was following the common Catholic practice of lumping the two together. This would help to explain why he claimed that 'it is thoughte of manye of these protestantes that no man ought to suffer death for his conscience', which was certainly not the position taken by the Edwardian authorities. Other observations may also be accounted for by the same confusion. Huggarde was quick to condemn those who would later be known as 'mechanick preachers' for 'rayling upon the doctours of the church, comparing themselves to the apostles, saying where went Peter or Paul to schole, and why maye not we have the spirite as well as they', also a view which Cranmer or Ridley would have condemned with equal emphasis. Huggarde also seems to have regarded it as typical of Protestantism that it was much influenced by women, a bias that emerges in his description of Browne's congregation, and in his scathing condemnation of 'these London ladies and other the lyke, whose talke is of nothing but of religion, of Peter and Paule and of other places of scripture. Whose scripture mouthes are ready to allure their husbandes to die in the Lordes veritie, because they would faine have new . . . .'.[35] It was not uncommon for women to play a prominent role in persecuted groups, as they did later among the Catholic recusants, but again it seems likely that Huggarde was speaking of those radicals who were without a regular ministry.

By the time that official Protestantism was restored in 1559, nonconformist and radical tendencies had probably been strengthened by the sheer impossibility of maintaining orthodox discipline during the persecution. English Protestantism had been bred as an establishment, and did not readily convert into autonomous congregations. However, the experience of congregational autonomy, both in England and in exile, was exhilirating to some of those who experienced it, and sowed the seeds of a new kind of separatism.[36] John Smith, the leader of a group of nonconformists who appeared before Grindal in 1567 declared: 'there was a congregation of us in this city in Queen May's days; and a congregation at Geneva, which used a book and order of preaching, ministering of the sacraments and discipline, most acceptable to the word of God . . . which book and order we now hold . . . .'.[37] To those who were firmly convinced that the Genevan order was more acceptable to God than the Book of Common Prayer, the memory of recent separation was very tempting, and Smith conveniently ignored the fact that this order was not used in Marian London. In the event, in spite of the experience of exile (when several experiments had been conducted with liturgy and church order) and the equally relevant example of the licensed separatism enjoyed by the foreign congregations in England under Edward VI, the vast majority of 'Genevans' either conformed to the Elizabethan settlement or indulged in a limited and rather precarious nonconformity. This was largely because, like the earlier congregations of John à Lasco and Valerand

Poulain, they accepted the 'permixt' nature of the church. They also accepted that the Elizabethan church was a 'true' (that is reformed) church, and these two facts together made separatism very hard to justify, in spite of all the nostalgia for the 'most perfect school of Christ'. The evidence for genuine separatism in England in the first twenty years of Elizabeth's reign is fragmentary, and seems to relate mainly to that fringe of 'Genevans' who insisted on congregational discipline. The Anabaptists of earlier years seem to have been absorbed into the ill-defined Lollard tradition of nonconformity, and sectarianism in the sense of 'gathered' churches hardly existed, for the Family of Love cannot really be classified in this way.

In view of the obscure and uncertain history of sectarianism throughout the period after 1530, this is perhaps not surprising. It cannot be positively proved that any 'gathered' congregation, rejecting the whole concept of a state church, existed in England at any time between 1530 and 1570. There were individuals who held such ideas, as well as an extraordinary range of idiosyncratic heresies, and nonconformist groups such as the 'free-willers' and John Smith's Plumber's Hall congregation of the late 1560s. There may also have been congregations which deliberately separated from official Protestantism, such as 'father Browne's conventicle' in Islington and Richard Fitz's group of radical puritans, who were denounced to the authorities in 1571. But in spite of Richard Cox's denunciation of the latter for 'establishing a private religion . . . as the donatists of old and the Anabaptists now', they do not seem to have held a sectarian ideal, rather appealing to the queen to 'bryng home the people of God to the purity and truth of the Apostolyke church'.[38] Throughout this most turbulent period in the history of the English church, the notion of public worship and an established faith was virtually unchallenged, despite the bitter quarrels over the form which that faith should take.

Notes

1. Cornelius Krahn, *Dutch Anabaptism 1450–1600*, London, 1968, p. 215. In theory the English authorities remained consistently hostile, and in 1538 a proclamation denounced 'Anabaptists and Sacramentaries who lurk secretly in divers corners and places', but in practice the pressure was neither uniform nor severe. P.L. Hughes and J.F. Larkin, *Tudor Royal Proclamations*, New Haven, Conn. and London, 1964, I, p. 270.
2. Anon., *Holy churches complaynt for her childrens disobedyance*, n.d., Lambeth Palace Library, 1488 (4a).
3. Miles Huggarde, *The Displayinge of the Protestantes*, London 1556, p. 14.
4. Anabaptists proper were characterised by a belief in 'believers' baptism', as it was preached by the Swiss leaders Grebel and Mantz, and this necessitated rebaptism, which was a specific renunciation of any orthodox church.
5. I.B. Horst, *The Radical Brethren*, Nieuwkoop, 1972, p. 27 ff.
6. *Statutes of the Realm*, London, 1810–28, III, 812.
7. John Hooper to Henry Bullinger, 25 June 1549. *Original Letters Relative to the English Reformation*, ed. H. Robinson, Parker Society, 1846, I, 65–6.
8. *Displayinge*, p. 18.
9. Ibid., p. 18V.

10. J.A.F. Thomson, *The Later Lollards*, Oxford, 1965, p. 239.
11. T. Cranmer, *Works*, ed. J.E. Cox, Parker Society, 1844–6, II, p. 191.
12. On the reluctance of puritans to separate, see particularly P. Collinson, *The Elizabethan Puritan Movement*, London 1967.
13. Horst, *Radical Brethren*, p. 97.
14. *A dialogue, or sum of a conference between some young men in New England*, cited by N. Morton, *New England's Memorial*, Boston, 1855, pp. 346–7.
15. The information of Roger Sergeant. John Foxe, *Actes and Monuments*, London, 1580; ed. J. Pratt, London 1853–70, VIII, p. 458.
16. Horst, *Radical Brethren*.
17. Probably Herman Bastian, a printer who was arrested with several other Anabaptists in Hesse in 1536. Ibid., pp. 52–3.
18. C.P. Clasen, *Anabaptism, 1525–1618*, Ithaca, New York, 1972, p. 103 ff.
19. C. Burrage, *The Early English Dissenters*, Cambridge, 1912, II, pp. 5–6. There seem to have been two Thomas Coles involved with this group. Another man of the same name preached before Cranmer in Lent 1553 at Maidstone, denouncing a long list of heretical errors which he ascribed to the local Anabaptists. Horst, *Radical Brethren*, p. 123.
20. J.W. Martin, 'English Protestant Separatism; Henry Hart and the Freewillers', *Sixteenth Century Journal*, VII(ii), London, 1976, 55–75.
21. This congregation moved its meeting place frequently, and varied greatly in size from one period to another, but it seems to have retained its identity throughout. Simpson was eventually burned in 1558. B.R. White, *The English Separatist Tradition*, Oxford, 1971, pp. 12–13.
22. M. Huggarde, *A new treatyse which sheweth the excellency of mannes nature*, London, 1550, sig. M, 3V.
23. Thomson, *Later Lollards*, p. 19.
24. Philip Hughes, *The Reformation in England*, London 1953, II, p. 262.
25. For some discussion of this problem, see D. Loades, 'Subversion and Security 1553–58', Ph.D., Cambridge 1961, 118–58, 188 ff.
26. Foxe, *Actes* (ed. Pratt), VII, pp. 371–4.
27. Ibid., p. 324.
28. *Acts of the Privy Council*, V, 150.
29. *Displayinge*, p. 122.
30. Ibid., p. 124.
31. Ibid., p. 129. Browne's response was to declare 'I am of goode chere . . . for I am cheryshed of suche good women as ye are . . .'.
32. Ibid., p. 130.
33. For instance Thomas Browne 'who dwelled in Fleet Street' and was burned in January 1556. Foxe, *Actes*, VII, p. 746.
34. *Displayinge*, p. 131.
35. Ibid., p. 79. Huggarde seems to have regarded female influence as characteristic of all heresy: 'in all ages at any time when one had devysed some folishe error or other, straight waye women were readye to applye to their fancies . . .'.
36. Although various attempts were made to keep the different English congregations in line, no serious attempt was made to impose episcopal authority. Cox and his followers at Frankfurt used the 1552 Prayer Book to 'maintain the face of a English Church', but essentially each community was left to work out its own worship and discipline, in consultation with Calvin, Peter Martyr or Bullinger. There was, and could be, no 'tarrying for the magistrate'. (See above, p. 50.)
37. White, *Separatist Tradition*, p. 2. Smith and his followers were part of the Plumbers Hall group. There were several such groups of nonconformists and semi-separatists in the aftermath of the Vestiarian controversy.

38. Cox to Gualter, 12 Feb. 1572. H. Robinson, *Zurich Letters*, Parker Society, II, p. 221. Burrage *Dissenters*, p. 93. There has been considerable debate about exactly how sectarian Fitz's congregation was. For a further discussion of this, and related problems of London nonconformity between 1567 and 1572, see H.G. Owen, 'A Nursery of Elizabethan Non-conformity, 1576–1572' (the Minories), *Journal of Ecclesiastical History* XVII (1966), 65–76. [Many specific aspects of the problem of early English sectarianism have now been examined in J. W. Martin, *Religious Radicals in Tudor England*, London, 1989]

15 The Bishops of the Restored Catholic Church under Queen Mary

The enactment of the royal supremacy between 1533 and 1535 had cut off the English episcopate from its canonical roots. Despite the fact that English kings had in practice nominated most of the bishops of the *Ecclesia Anglicana* for many generations, those bishops had nevertheless been appointed by the Pope. The presence of an occasional Italian, such as Sylvester Gigli,[1] on the episcopal bench, and periodic disputes over provisions had served as reminders of this fact. After 1535 the retention of the tortuous fiction of the *congé d'élire* did not conceal the fact that bishops were appointed solely by the king. At the same time, the Convocations had surrendered their jurisdictional autonomy by agreeing to submit their canons for royal approval, and the Act in Restraint of Appeals had reserved the final decision in all ecclesiastical causes to the Archbishop of Canterbury, from whom appeal could only lie to the Supreme Head – the king himself. None of this had anything to do with Protestantism, but by the strictest canonical interpretation it was at this point that the English became lost sheep, not when they abandoned the mass for heresy. To Cardinal Pole, looking back on these developments in 1556, Henry VIII's doctrinal orthodoxy was irrelevant:

> And in lyk maner (he told the citizens of London) all the tyme the arche was in the Kynges hande, as yt was, he takyng that strange tytle upon him to be Hedd of the Churche in his realm; all that tyme, we maye saye, he pretended to keep that was yn yt, those sacraments with reverence (as I understand ye dyd a good whyle) yet you being out of the unyte of the churche, cowlde receyve no more grace or profyt of them than did the Philistiens of the arche, having the same among them, they not being incorporate with the people of God . . .[2]

Pole's view of these developments, both at the time and subsequently, was unusually clear and emphatic, and was shared by few in England apart from John Fisher and Sir Thomas More. To most, and that included the bishops themselves, the spiritual and jurisdictional positions were alike confused. The activities of Thomas Cromwell as Viceregent in Spirituals resolved some of these ambiguities. The king claimed the right not only to supervise ecclesiastical jurisdiction but also to inhibit it, and to carry out visitations and issue injunctions on his own authority.[3] The dissolution of the monasteries between 1536 and 1541, and the erection of six new bishoprics were the most important demonstrations of this authority in action. Nevertheless, much remained obscure. The king never explicitly claimed the *potestas ordinis*, nor the right to define true doctrine, but he came very close to acting as though he possessed the latter power.[4] He never attempted to deprive a bishop who displeased him, although two were forced into resignation, and one beheaded. Nor did he make it clear to what extent he believed a bishop to derive his authority from his appointment and investment with temporalities, and to what extent from his consecration. Thomas Cranmer, the Archbishop of Canterbury, and Stephen Gardiner, Bishop of Winchester (both equally upholders of the royal supremacy), took opposite sides on this issue. To Gardiner a bishop was an ordinary, and his authority stemmed from his spiritual status, not from his appointment to any particular office; while to Cranmer the appointment was all important, consecration being merely a customary, but not strictly necessary, adjunct.[5]

That particular conflict did not come to a head until after Henry VIII's death, and by then the position of the episcopate had been further weakened in several ways. The enforced resignations of Latimer and Shaxton in the wake of the Act of Six Articles had revealed how vulnerable bishops could.be to changes which were partly inspired and mainly carried out by the laity in parliament. They were also vulnerable in another way. The dissolution of the monasteries had revealed that neither king nor parliament was prepared to acknowledge the sacrosanct nature of the church's landed endowments. When the king began to put pressure on his bishops to accept unfavourable exchanges of land they were in no position to resist, and dozens of fine manors were lost. Between 1529 and 1540 lands to the annual value of about £2250 passed to the Crown while the recompense (largely from monastic estates) amounted to £1900.[6] Later in the reign the balance became even more unfavourable. Between 1540 and 1547 losses amounted to £3700 a year and gains to £2850.[7] Thus between 1535 and 1547 both the economic and the jurisdictional strength of the episcopate had declined sharply; a process which also seems to have been accelerated by the anxiety of lay people to find remedies and redress wherever possible through the king's courts rather than through those of the churches.[8] The disappearance of monastic immunities and exemptions, and of the mitred abbots from the House of Lords, did nothing to halt the general decline; in the former case because the immunities were often attached to the place rather than the order, and in the latter because the bishops simply found themselves in a permanent minority *vis-à-vis* the lay peers. Peculiars such as Greyfriars remained thorns in the flesh of their diocesan bishops for generations, and even the most united episcopal stance in the House of Lords would be unavailing without lay support – as was to be demonstrated in 1559.

After the death of Henry VIII the position continued to deteriorate as the government of Protector Somerset endeavoured to clarify relations between the Crown and the episcopate. No sooner had Somerset taken power than Cranmer petitioned for a fresh commission, on the ground that his archepiscopal authority had lapsed with the king's death.[9] In spite of furious protests from the conservatives, led by Gardiner, that they were not simply royal officials, all the bishops received new powers in the name of Edward VI (the only occasion, in fact, upon which this was done). Towards the end of 1547 the statute 1 Edward VI c.2 carried this process a stage further. The *congé d'élire* was abolished on the reasonable grounds that it was fraudulent, and replaced with a system of direct appointments by Letters Patent. It was also decreed that all summonses and citations which had hitherto been made in the name of the bishop were henceforth to be made in the king's name, that the seals of spiritual courts were to bear the king's arms, and that all process and certificate of trial in the spiritual courts were to be in the king's name.[10] One of the purposes of this Act was probably to enhance respect for the church courts by emphasising the fact that they were a part of the royal jurisdiction, but the effect was to reduce the bishops still further to the level of servants and functionaries. A prime reason for this was almost certainly the growing influence of continental, and particularly Swiss, reformers in England. Unlike the Lutherans these men, such as Peter Martyr and Martin Bucer, had no particular use for bishops, although they had not yet got to the point of describing them as unscriptural.[11] The campaign of their English disciples to 'unlord' the bishops in the cause of making them effective preachers and pastors on the reformed model, gave a welcome ideological justification to the efforts of both Somerset and Northumberland to reduce the traditional status of the episcopate yet further.[12]

As the reign of Edward VI advanced, the church became increasingly a department of state. Successive statutes took over the regulation of such canonical matters as liturgy, ordination, clerical marriage and abstinence during Lent. As this happened, the role of the bishops became equated with that of the secular justices. For instance the First Act of Uniformity provided that

> Bishops and Archbishops shall, at their own pleasure and discretion, by virtue of the Act, joint and associate themselves to Justices of Assize or of Oyer and Terminer at any place within their dioceses to hear and determine of offences arising under the Act.[13]

Similarly, another Act passed in the same session in 1549 declared that bishops might, by virtue of the Act, enquire of offenders and present them to such as had power to hear and determine the same – the justices of the peace. In this case the offence was eating meat in Lent.[14] By 1552 even Cranmer had come to the conclusion that the church had too little autonomy, and both English and continental reformers were alarmed by the extent to which the English experiment had fallen into the hands of the 'carnal gospellers'.

Cranmer's determined attempt to remedy this situation by securing the promulgation of a new code of canon law foundered – ironically but inevitably – because the Duke of Northumberland would not allow it through parliament!

As the episcopate lost what was left of its jurisdictional autonomy, its economic fortunes similarly declined. Between 1547 and 1549 six bishoprics alone lost lands worth over £3500 a year, and this time the compensation was no more than nominal.[15] By 1550 the bishopric of Bath and Wells (admittedly an extreme case) was valued at £480 a year, as against £1844 in 1535.[16] The most notorious case of this kind was probably that of the bishopric of Winchester. When the advanced reformer John Ponet was appointed to the see in 1551 he accepted a salary of £1333 in place of the endowed revenues of the see, which were worth about £3000.[17] Although they were conscious of the fact that they had contributed to their own downfall, by 1553 the Protestant bishops were bitterly disillusioned with the treatment they had received from their ostensible allies. In a sense they had sacrificed in vain, because the reduction in their own revenues had not resulted in better preaching or education. There was a little to be said on the other side. However hostile or indifferent Somerset or Northumberland may have been to the episcopate, they did not attempt to discredit it by advancing fools or knaves to the bench. In learning, efficiency and integrity the Edwardian bishops stand up very well by comparison with their predecessors – or successors. It is indeed possible that Northumberland had more genuine concern for the reformed church than he is usually credited with,[18] but there is no doubt that when he fell from power in July 1553, after the death of Edward VI, the English episcopate was weaker and more demoralised than at any time in its thousand years of history.

This was the situation which Mary set out to remedy, and the simplicity of her original approach can be illustrated by the fact that she immediately recognised the imprisoned Gardiner as lawful Bishop of Winchester, and appointed him Lord Chancellor within a few days of her accession.[19] By so doing she strayed into a legal minefield, although the general strength of her political position concealed the fact from all but the most observant. Gardiner, along with several other conservative prelates – Bonner of London, Day of Chichester, Heath of Worcester and Tunstall of Durham – had been deprived by royal commissions sitting between 1550 and 1552 for their resistance to Protestant reform. Mary clearly wished to regard these deprivations as *ipso facto* unlawful and invalid, but could not do so because she was herself the inheritrix of the authority by which they had been carried out – that is, the royal supremacy. Having realised that some legal pretext would have to be found to reverse the sentences, a variety of unconvincing excuses were produced; one had had an appeal ignored, another had been given inadequate time to prepare his defence, a third had been judged only by lay commissioners.[20] Since Edward's commissioners had been operating without precedents it was not difficult to find fault with their procedures, but the result was legal confusion. If the deprivations were invalid, then such well established Edwardian prelates as Ridley and Ponet had been no true bishops. Consequently all their acts were invalid, including the surrender of land to the Crown, and the granting of perfectly ordinary leases. On the strength of this assumption, both Gardiner and Bonner conducted themselves with a high hand, ignoring their predecessors dispositions, until it became clear that such legal tangles could not be resolved by simple first principles.[21] The most revealing case of all was that of the bishopric of Durham, which had actually been abolished by statute in 1553. Blandly ignoring this fact, Mary called Tunstall to her first parliament by the title of the non-existent see, only to witness what she clearly regarded as the formality of the statute's repeal come to grief in the House of Commons.[22]

For the first few months of the reign, the episcopal bench was in total disarray. Several of the Protestants, including Cranmer, were in prison but not deprived, others had been ejected as intruders.[23] Two sees, Rochester and Bangor, were vacant. Tunstall had no legal standing. Nevertheless the initial successes of Gardiner and Bonner in recovering lost temporalities, the powerful conservative reaction in the Convocation of October 1553, and the queen's obvious

intention to restore as much as possible of the traditional church pointed the
way to a strong recovery of episcopal status and jurisdiction. The first parliament
of Mary's reign repealed both the Edwardian Uniformity Acts, the Act
permitting clerical marriage, and the Act for the election of bishops.[24]
Consequently the *congé d'élire* was restored, and process in the episcopal courts
was again issued in the bishops' name. Needless to say, Mary did not issue fresh
commissions to her bishops, but rather accepted their jurisdiction as being
ordinary in the traditional sense. At the same time the queen began to
appreciate the difficulty of the situation in which she found herself. For a variety
of reasons she could not immediately restore the realm to the Roman obedience,
and was consequently constrained to restore obedience to the ancient canon law
by means of an authority which that law did not recognise – the royal
supremacy.[25] Although she stopped using the title at the end of 1553, the first
disciplinary campaign, launched in March and April 1554, would have been
impossible without it. Royal commissions sitting on 13 and 15 March deprived
seven of the imprisoned Protestant bishops for various infringements of canon
law – in four cases marriage.[26] On the fourth of the same month a comprehensive set of royal articles had been sent into every diocese, ordering the
suppression of heresy and unlawful preaching, the deprivation of married clergy,
and – paradoxically – an end to the use of the term *Regia auctoritate fulcitus* in
connection with the exercise of the episcopal office.[27] At the same time, in the
wake of the deprivations, seven new Catholic bishops were appointed, ostensibly
by the Henrician procedure, but in reality secretly nominated by the queen to
Cardinal Pole, and confirmed by him in the name of the Pope.[28] Pole, who had
by this time arrived in the Low Countries, had been appointed legate to England
in August 1553, but the complex and sensitive political situation surrounding
Mary's marriage negotiations had kept him out of the country, an embargo
which Pope Julius III (although not Pole himself) had reluctantly accepted.[29] By
the spring of 1554, therefore, a double standard was being applied to ecclesiastical
jurisdiction, with the queen's conscience and the canon law on one side and the
law of England on the other – and a considerable gulf lay between the two. It
was mainly for that reason that those who were being held upon the most serious
of ecclesiastical charges – heresy – were not to face their judges for another
ten months.

The resolution of this unsatisfactory situation depended (much to Cardinal
Pole's chagrin) upon political negotiation. By the spring of 1554 the lay
aristocracy had revealed with distressing clarity that they had no intention of
surrendering the ecclesiastical property which they had acquired over the
previous twenty years, and had little desire to see the revival of a powerful and
autonomous church.[30] The two issues were connected, but not identical. When
Stephen Gardiner made a somewhat obscure attempt to push a settlement with
the papacy through parliament in April 1554, the main reason for its failure was
alleged to be the reluctance of the lay Lords to see a revival of ecclesiastical
jurisdiction.[31] The stronger the church became, the less guarantee the laity
would have for the security of their gains, whatever theoretical immunity they
might secure. Meanwhile, Mary had done what she could to relieve the poverty
and distress of her bishops. The restored conservatives were allowed to regard all
alienations since their deprivations as void, and although this involved some of

them in protracted legal wrangles, their sees benefited immediately and substantially. Even Tunstall eventually recovered almost the whole of his former patrimony.[32] At her accession the incumbent bishops owed the queen a total of £10,000 for arrears of first fruits and tenths, and since about a third of them were replaced within the first year, that indebtedness should have increased. Instead Mary followed a generous (although not universal) policy of forgiveness. Henry Morgan, appointed to St David's, was exonerated of almost £1000; James Brookes at Gloucester was forgiven £500; and Bonner of London was not only allowed to recover his former estates, but was granted additional lands worth over £500, and an exoneration for £552 of debt.[33] Another *ad hoc* measure of relief was the grant of cathedral patronage hitherto in the hands of the Crown. Heath of Worcester was given control of all the ten prebends there in 1553, and John Chamber of Peterborough of the six there.[34] This soon became a regular policy, and most sees benefited in this way before the end of the reign. There were, however, limits to Mary's ability, or willingness, to re-endow the episcopate. With the exception of London there were very few actual grants of land,[35] only a fraction of what was returned to old noble families such as the Courtenays or the Percies or bestowed upon the new monastic foundations.[36] Later in her reign the queen persuaded parliament to return first fruits and tenths (worth about £25,000 a year) to the church; but this benefited the bishops hardly at all since the money was placed at the disposal of Cardinal Pole and was used almost entirely to pay the monastic pensions which had formerly been paid by the Crown.[37] By 1558 there was a surplus on that account which should have been used to supplement poor livings, but that did nothing to help the bishops, who were then being squeezed hard by clerical subsidies to help pay for the war.[38]

The only other consistent policy of restitution that Mary followed related to advowsons, and we do not know whether the main consideration there was pastoral or economic. In the last few months of her life she granted almost 500 advowsons remaining in the hands of the Crown to seven bishops, York being the main beneficiary, with 195.[39] Such grants were less valuable than land, but must have been very welcome none the less, and substantially increased the control of the bishops concerned over the spiritual life of their dioceses. The economic rehabilitation of the episcopate therefore continued steadily, if somewhat patchily, throughout the reign. The most serious of the ravages which had been wrought since 1540 were repaired, and bishops returned to their traditional roles in high office and public life. First Gardiner and then Heath as Lord Chancellor, Tunstall and Thirlby to the Privy Council, and Pole to a position of personal influence which was unique, and peculiar to himself. Nevertheless, it would be a grave mistake to regard Mary as a puppet of the restored Catholic church. Not only was her material generosity restrained, her attitude towards ecclesiastical jurisdiction had its reservations as well.

In theory the settlement that Pole negotiated with parliament in January 1555 simply restored the situation which had existed before 1530, but in practice a strong odour of the royal supremacy continued to linger. The common lawyers had successfully insisted that all property issues relating to the church should be tried exclusively in the royal courts.[40] And however vehemently Pole and the queen might deny it, the failure of the church to recover the monastic endowments – followed as it was by the bull *Praeclara* which canonically extinguished the English houses – created a legal precedent for the confiscation of ecclesiastical property by statute. Moreover, the use of royal commissions for ecclesiastical purposes had proved far too effective to be readily abandoned. So although the commissions for the trials of particular heretics, which began to be issued in February 1555, came from the cardinal legate, very similar commissions to investigate heresies and seize heretical and seditious books were passed under the Great or Privy Seal. The line between the two jurisdictions was a very fine one. Pole commissioned Bonner, Thirlby and Maurice Griffin of Rochester in February 1557 to enquire into pluralities. The Crown commissioned Bonner and Henry Cole in November of the same year to seek out books denying the Pope's authority.[41] The Privy Council continued to issue its instructions, not only to the bishops but also to the justices of the peace, as though the restoration of ecclesiastical jurisdiction had never taken place. Bonner, in particular, was far more often badgered by the council than he was by Pole over the discharge of his canonical functions.[42] The main reason for this was the priority placed by both the queen and the cardinal upon discipline. On more purely pastoral matters, such as preaching or absolution, the queen might have her opinions but the execution of policy was left entirely to the legate.

We have also to remember that the Acts of provisors and praemunire had not been repealed, and that the English Crown had by no means been subservient to the papacy before 1530. Thus William Glyn was provided by papal bull to the see of Bangor on the queen's nomination, but when the royal mandate was issued in September 1555 to the Exchequer at Caernarfon to deliver the temporalities of the see, it was recorded that the bishop had 'publicly renounced all words contained in the said Bull prejudicial to the Crown, and made his fealty'.[43] Similarly, when Pole convened his legatine synod in November of the same year he took the precaution of obtaining a grant under the Privy Seal of permission to hold the same synod 'without let of any statutes, customs or prerogatives', and for the clergy 'to appear thereat and to consent to such canons as shall be there ordained'.[44] This may read strangely in the Patent Rolls of so papalist a queen, but in spite of her well known enthusiasm for the Holy See, Mary's attitude was by no means one of unqualified submissiveness. This was to become increasingly obvious after the outbreak of hostilities between Philip and Paul IV in September 1556, and the withdrawal of Pole's legatine commission in April 1557. The latter move cut the ground from under the cardinal's feet, put an end to the uncompleted synod, and left him only with the traditional jurisdiction of the archbishopric of Canterbury.[45] Not only did the queen's protest go unheeded, but Pole was soon facing recall to Rome to stand trial on charges of heresy. In these circumstances Mary showed something of her father's spirit, refusing point blank to admit the emissaries bearing Pole's letter of recall, and totally rejecting the Pope's attempt to replace him with the octogenarian friar, William Peto.[46] Any charge against her archbishop, she declared, with a fine disregard for canonical niceties, would have to be tried in England. It is not surprising that rumours were soon circulating in Rome that England would again go into schism.

Mary had no such intention, but her poor relations with the papacy considerably damaged the English church. Paul IV did not deliberately neglect

English business, but he handled it with indifference and dislike. Private suits got bogged down in the curial bureaucracy, and public business became inordinately protracted. Four bishops died between September 1557 and May 1558, and all four sees were still vacant when the queen died in November,[47] making Elizabeth's task slightly, but appreciably, easier. In these discouraging circumstances, the episcopal bench stuck manfully to its task, struggling to the very end of the reign to restore sound discipline, good devotional habits and financial probity. Mary's bishops were not men with the fire of the Counter-Reformation in their bellies, but they were scholars and preachers; men like Owen Oglethorpe with long and worthy academic careers behind them.[48] They were also conscientious visitors and pastors, very similar in many ways to their Edwardian predecessors or their Elizabethan successors. Mary restored old-fashioned lawyer statesmen like Gardiner and Tunstall, but the men of her own appointment were cast in a more spiritual and theological mould. If their behaviour in 1559 was less than heroic, it was certainly not disgraceful, and by the time that they were forced out of office by the Elizabethan settlement, they had done much to put the affairs of their dioceses in order, and to restore a measure of respect for episcopacy.[49] Their time had been short, and there is little sign of any recovery of their jurisdiction in terms of popular demand, but without their efforts, and those of the queen who nominated them, it is difficult to see how the episcopal order could have survived. Elizabeth's record of dealings with her bishops was to be a shabby story of ill-supported jurisdiction and financial coercian. If the Elizabethan bench had been forced to start at the low point which the Edwardian bench left, then the prospects would have been poor indeed. It may be an exaggeration to say that Mary saved episcopacy for the Church of England – but it is a proposition well worthy of discussion.

Notes

1. Bishop of Worcester, 1498–1521. Worcester was in the hands of absentee Italians from 1497 to 1535.
2. John Strype, *Ecclesiastical Memorials* Oxford, 1822, III, 488. Reginald Pole's oration to the citizens of London. [*Eccl. Mem.*]
3. The first set of Royal Injunctions, issued by Cromwell in the king's name, were sent out in August 1536, and were described by a contemporary chronicler as 'the first act of pure supremacy done by the King'. W.H. Frere and W.M. Kennedy, *Visitation Articles and Injunctions*, London, 1910, II, p. 1.
4. *A necessary doctrine and erudition for a Christian man*, commonly known as The King's Book, was published by royal authority in 1543.
5. Thomas Cranmer, *Works*, ed. J.E. Cox, Parker Society, 1844–6, II, p. 117.
6. Felicity Heal, *Of Prelates and Princes*, London, 1980, p. 115.
7. Ibid., p. 123.
8. With the exception of probate cases, the business of the church courts declined steadily in most areas after the break with Rome. R.A. Houlbrooke, *Church Courts and the People during the English Reformation 1520–1570*, London, 1970. For the thesis that in London at least that decline had set in much earlier, see R. Wunderli, *London Church Courts and Society on the Eve of the Reformation*, Cambridge, Mass., 1981.
9. John Strype, *Memorials of . . . Thomas Cranmer*, Oxford, 1694, II, p. 1.

10. *Statutes of the Realm*, London, 1810–28, IV (i) 3.

11. Neither Martyr, who was Italian, nor Bucer (from Strasburg) was Swiss by nationality, but both were friends of Heinrich Bullinger, Zwingli's successor at Zurich, and stood in the tradition of civic and republican reform. For the origins of Zurich influence on the English Reformation see E.F.M. Hildebrandt 'The English Protestant Exiles in Northern Switzerland and Strasbourg, 1539–47', Ph.D., Durham, 1982.

12. John Hooper, within the episcopate, and William Turner outside it, were among the principal advocates of a redistribution of ecclesiastical wealth. Heal, *Prelates and Princes*, p. 168. For a comment by Bucer on the 'covetousness' of the conservative bishops see *Original Letter Relative to the English Reformation*, ed. H. Robinson, Parker Society, 1847, II, 247.

13. Statute 2/3 Edward VI c. 1. *Statutes of the Realm*, IV, 37.

14. Statute 2/3 Edward VI c. 19, ibid., p. 65.

15. Heal, *Prelates and Princes*, pp. 130–1. The principal sufferers were Lincoln and Bath and Wells. Such compensation as was offered took the form of impropriated rectories.

16. Ibid., p. 133.

17. *Literary Remains of King Edward VI*, ed. J.G. Nichols, Roxburgh Club, 1875, III, p. 312. The imperial Ambassador, Jehan Scheyfve, believed that this represented the beginnings of a consistent policy. *Calendar of State Papers, Spanish*, 214.

18. The plan eventually evolved for the bishopric of Durham in 1552 was not nearly as detrimental to the church as is sometimes claimed. D.M. Loades, 'The Last Years of Cuthbert Tunstall', 1547–1559, *Durham University Journal*, LXVI, 1973, (see also above, p. 172) and Heal's comments on his exchange with the Bishop of Worcester in 1548, Heal, *Prelates and Princes*, p. 131.

19. D.M. Loades, *The Reign of Mary Tudor*, London, 1979, p. 87.

20. For discussions of the legal implication of these restorations, see D.M. Loades, *The Oxford Martyrs*, London, 1970, 113–4 and F. Heal, *Prelates and Princes*, pp. 151–3.

21. A test case was fought over the manor of Bushley, leased by Ridley to one Car, and by Bonner to Lethmore. 'The case was learnedly argued by the Common lawyers, and also by the civilians, and the judges inclined to be of opinion for the plaintiff. But the defendant perceiving this preferred his bill in Chancery, and there obtained a decree against Letchmore . . .' (Strype, *Eccl. Mem.*, III, 89). According to the imperial ambassadors, Gardiner was demanding restitution of revenues from the Earl of Pembroke as early as 27 July 1553, *Calendar of State Papers, Spanish*, 120.

22. *Commons Journals*, London, 1803–52, I, 31. [See above, p. 173.]

23. Ponet and Coverdale were ejected from Winchester and Exeter; Holgate (York), Ridley (London), Hooper (Gloucester and Worcester), Scory (Chichester), Bush (Bristol), Harley (Hereford), Taylor (Lincoln), Farrer (St Davids) and Bird of Chester were eventually deprived. Barlow of Bath and Wells resigned. Cranmer, as a canonically appointed archbishop and *legatus natus* presented a special problem, and was not degraded until after a technical trial in the papal Curia in 1556. Loades, *Oxford Martyrs*, pp. 229–31.

24. Statute 1 Mary st. 2.c.2, *Statutes of the Realm*, IV, 202.

25. For a full discussion of the legal complexities of this operation, see Loades, *Oxford Martyrs*, pp. 101–37.

26. *Calendar of the Patent Rolls, Philip and Mary*, I, 175. Holgate, Ferrar, Bird and Bush. [*Cal. Pat.*]

27. W.H. Frere and W.M. Kennedy, *Visitation Articles and Injunctions*, London, 1910, II, pp. 322–9.

28. Pole's Legatine Register (microfilm in Lambeth Palace Library) f.3r. The list is dated XV Kal. apr. (18 March) – a bare three days after the second commission of

deprivation. The candidates were all canonically absolved from the sin of schism by proxy on 19 March.

29. Loades, *Reign of Mary*, pp. 174–77.
30. Heal, *Prelates and Princes*, pp. 150–1. Loades, *Reign of Mary*, pp. 322–9.
31. *Lords Journal*, London, 1846, I, 452. The measure actually rejected was for the revival of the fifteenth-century heresy laws. In the absence of any revival of papal authority, this would have given the bishops an unprecedented degree of autonomy in a very sensitive area.
32. Only Durham Place, the bishop's London residence, was not returned.
33. Public Record Office, SP11/12 'Account of arrears of the tenths and subsidies of the clergy due by divers bishops at and before Christmas Last', 20 July 1553. *Cal. Pat.*, I, 112, 8 May 1554. *Cal. Pat.*, I, 119, 3 Mar. 1554.
34. *Cal. Pat.*, I, 112–13; Heal, *Prelates and Princes*, pp. 156–7 and n.
35. Archbishop Heath received back the lordships of Southwell, Ripon and Scrooby, lost to the see of York in 1543 and 1545. *Cal. Pat.*, III, 18, 264. Reginald Pole also received lands to the annual value of £1250, and an annuity of £290, but these were grants for life, not to the see of Canterbury, *Cal. Pat.*, II, 69–72.
36. Public Record Office, SP12/1/64 (an estimate of grants made to individuals and religious houses during Mary's reign) shows grants of land totalling about £10,000 a year. About £4500 of this went to the restored religious orders.
37. Statute 2/2 Philip and Mary c.4; R.H. Pogson, 'Revival and Reform in Mary Tudor's Church', *Journal of Ecclesiastical History*, XXV, 1974, 240–65. Before the Act was passed, Mary occasionally granted first fruits and tenths to a diocesan bishop, as a dispensation from the statute of 26 Henry VIII. See the grant to Richard Pate of Worcester on 13 March 1535. *Cal. Pat.*, II, 168.
38. Loades, *Reign of Mary*, p. 439.
39. *Cal. Pat.*, IV, 401, 420, 449, 399, 402, 437, 450.
40. Statute 2/3 Philip and Mary, c.7, section XIII.
41. Pole's Legatine Register, f.7. *Cal. Pat.*, IV, 14.
42. G. Alexander, 'Bonner and the Marian Persecutions', *History*, LX, 1975, 374–92.
43. *Cal. Pat.*, II, 158; 25 Sept. 1555.
44. Ibid., 23; 2 Nov. 1555.
45. See Pole's letter of protest to Paul IV, of 25 May 1557. *Calendar of State Papers, Venetian*, VI, 1111. Pole had been provided to Canterbury by the same pope in the previous year.
46. Loades, *Reign of Mary*, pp. 430–1.
47. Salcot of Salisbury (6 Oct. 1557); King of Oxford (4 Dec. 1557) Glynn of Bangor (21 May 1558); Parfew of Hereford (22 Sept. 1557).
48. Four of Mary's nominations were heads of academic colleges, one a professor of theology, and one headmaster of Winchester. Three leading controversial writers were also chosen. Only three were lawyers by training. For a further discussion of Mary's and Pole's policy in the appointment of bishops, see R.H. Pogson, 'The Legacy of the Schism; Confusion, Continuity and Change in the Marian Clergy', in J. Loach, and R. Tittler (eds) *The Mid-Tudor Polity 1540–1560*, London, 1980, pp. 116–36.
49. The schism had created all sorts of confusion over orders, which Pole had tried to resolve through his legatine synod. These conscientious attempts to follow the correct procedures – made necessary by the need to restore the canon law – still further reduced the time and energy available for spiritual revitalisation. They did, however, have the effect of re-establishing the bishops firmly in the canonical chain of command, Pogson, 'Legacy of the Schism'.

16 The Piety of the Catholic Restoration in England, 1553–8

Of the observation of ceremonies begynnythe the very educatyon of the chylderne of God; as the olde lawe doythe shewe, that was full of ceremonyes, whiche St. Paule callythe *Pedagogium in Christum* . . .[1]

There was very little in Reginald Pole's previous record as a scholar, confessor or ecclesiastical statesman, to suggest that he attached great importance to the externals of traditional worship. However, in his task of restoring the church in England to the Catholic fold, he felt constrained to use whatever methods and materials were available to his hands. Ceremonies, as Miles Huggarde rightly observed, were 'curious toyes',[2] not only to the Protestants but also to those semi-evangelical reformers of the 1530s whose exact doctrinal standpoints are so hard to determine. Along with the papal jurisdiction had gone the great pilgrimage shrines, not only St Thomas of Canterbury – that monument to the triumph of the *sacerdotium* over the *regnum* – but also Our Lady of Walsingham and a host of others. Down, too, had gone the religious houses, lesser and greater, with their elaborate liturgical practices, and many familiar saints' days had disappeared from the calendar before the austere simplifications of 1552.[3] Such changes had provoked much opposition and disquiet, but they had left intact the ceremonial core of the old faith, the mass in all its multitude of forms, and the innumerable little sacramental and liturgical pieties which constituted the faith of ordinary people. The recent researches of Professor Scarisbrick, Dr Haigh, Dr Susan Brigden and others have reminded us just how lively these pieties were before – and during – the Reformation, even in places heavily infiltrated by the new learning, such as London.[4] It was at this level that traditional religion seems to have been at its most flourishing; in the small fraternities and guilds attached to parish churches; in the ornamentation and equipment of the churches themselves; and in the provision of gifts and bequests for obits, lights and charitable doles.

Consequently, it was the Chantries Act of 1547 and the Uniformity Act of 1549 which were really felt at the popular level, not the legislation of 1533–40, but popular piety was ill equipped to defend itself. Considering the short time it had at its disposal, the achievement of the Edwardian government in suppressing such piety was remarkable. Despite the disturbances of 1548–9, by the time that the Protestant campaign culminated in the Commission for Church Goods in 1552, a very high outward level of conformity had been reached.[5] Altars and rood screens had disappeared from the great majority of churches, along with the traditional service books and liturgical equipment. It was, as Martin Bucer pointed out at the time, a negative achievement.[6] Much of the banished equipment was quietly secreted, and there was little sign of enthusiasm for attendance at Protestant sermons – even where these could be provided. The stream of gifts and bequests to parish churches virtually ceased, and secular charities did not gain to anything like a proportionate extent. Vocations to the priesthood fell away dramatically.[7] However, before the Commission for Church Goods could even complete its work, King Edward was dead, and within a month of her accession his successor Mary had made it clear that she intended to pursue a very different policy.

By the end of August 1553, sometimes through the initiative of 'Lords and Knights catholic', as Robert Parkyn tells us, and sometimes through the spontaneous actions of clergy or parishioners, the mass was again being widely celebrated.[8] Service books and vestments came out of hiding, and All Saints' Day provided the occasion for the reappearance of many traditional ceremonies and practices. Indeed, considering the brief duration and undoubted unpopularity of the Edwardian Protestant regime, it is the patchy and hesitant nature of the restoration rather than its speed and enthusiasm which is surprising.[9] Both Robert Parkyn and Henry Machyn testify with some indignation to the existence of those who 'would not away' with the new order until they were commanded by public authority.[10] But this may well have been the result of suspicious caution rather than Protestant zeal, and the general picture is one of a happy willingness to go back to the religious practices of the recent past. It was this popular piety, therefore, which formed the raw material out of which the Catholic church in England had to be refashioned, but it was recalcitrant matter and, paradoxically, it probably distorted the Marian church into which it had to be absorbed, more than the Edwardian church, which had rejected it.

At first this problem seems scarcely to have been perceived. Both the queen and Stephen Gardiner, the Bishop of Winchester and Lord Chancellor, acted as though the only procedure necessary to restore the church to its pristine state was a proclamation of the government's intention, and the repeal of heretical laws.[11] Several chronicles bear witness to the conservative euphoria of these early days:

Item, in August was the alter in Pawles set up againe . . .

The 5th of August at seven at night, came home Edmond Bonner, bishop, from the Marshalsea, like a bishop, that all the people by the way bade him welcome home, both man and woman, and as many of the women as might be kissed him . . .

Item, 17th September, the Bishop of London, Bonner, sang masse in Pawles . . .[12]

The xxiii day of August . . . begane the masse at sant Nicolas Colaby, goodly song in Laten, and tapurs, and (set on) the owtter, and a crosse, in old Fysstrett . . .[13]

There were warning signs that some Protestants would fight the new order, but for a variety of reasons the dispossessed hierarchy confined itself to passive resistance, and by the end of the year it seemed that official optimism had been largely vindicated: 'In this newe and miraculous reign of mercifull Marye . . .' wrote the enthusiastic John Procter, 'wherein (we) see so many good olde orders newely restored, and so many new and erronious novelties antiquated and made olde . . .',[14] a few heretics were not going to be allowed to spoil the party.

The council's first big push in the direction of Catholic conformity, which began with the royal Articles of March 1554 revealed increasing anxiety about sacramentaries and 'persons . . . infected or damned with any notable kind of heresy', but in other respects encouraged established opinions and traditional practices to reassert themselves.[15] This was particularly the case in the treatment of the erstwhile married clergy, who seem to have been especially unpopular with the rank-and-file laity, whose sentiments echoed the queen's own. The unremitting pursuit of these men and of their former wives is one of the most curious and revealing features of the Marian church. At the very end of the reign, in Bishop Bonner's *Interrogatories* for churchwardens of 1558, articles 2, 3 and 4 relate to this issue 'heresye and unlawfull doctryne' only making an appearance in number 5.[16] Clerical marriage seems to have been regarded by the conservative of all shades of opinion as symbolic of that moral laxity and disorderly behaviour which they claimed to be the characteristic of all reformers.[17] Ironically, marriage was a poor test of Protestant opinions. Perhaps a substantial proportion of the 243 who were deprived for that reason in the diocese of Norwich did hold the views of Luther or Zwingli, but that was certainly not the case with the 16 'clerici coniugati' detected in the remote rural diocese of Bangor, where Protestantism had barely pierced the skin.[18] Clerical celibacy, like the familiar ritual of the mass, and the liturgical processions which marked out the church's year, was a part of the 'right order' of things – an order at once comforting and propitiatory, which was disrupted only at the peril of the whole social and natural order.

> there was never such unthriftiness in servants, such unnaturalness in children, such unruliness in subjects, such fierceness in enemies, such unfaithfulness in friends, such beastliness of mind

as under a Protestant regime.[19] The remedies were obedience to the godly authority of 'miraculous Marye', and a return of the good old ways: '. . . come home, come home, gentle brethren, to youre lovynge and tender mother's lap . . . .'[20]

Up to a point this was both a straightforward and an appealing message, but as the restoration gathered pace, it began to develop problems of its own, which had nothing to do with the defiance of genuine and committed Protestants. It was easy to call for a return to the 'good old order', but less easy to say exactly what that order had been, or to agree that all aspects of it had been good. The queen herself made it clear at an early date that she intended to restore the papal jurisdiction, but amid all the popular rejoicing, and the numerous displays of Catholic zeal in the autumn of 1553, the general silence on that subject was palpable. I have discussed the problems which attended the actual restoration of the Roman obedience on many occasions, and I do not intend to do so again.[21] It is, however, worth remembering that both Gian Francesco Commendone who came secretly from Julius III, and Henry Penning who was Cardinal Pole's personal envoy, recognised the difficulties, and reported that there was little enthusiasm for the papacy.[22] This was not simply a question of apprehensive 'possessioners' concerned for their monastic lands, it was a reflection of the fact that Rome had never occupied more than a peripheral place in the religious consciousness of Englishmen, and that twenty years of constant anti-papal propaganda had also had its effect. The author of the *Greyfriars Chronicle* considered it worthy of especial note that the Pope was prayed for at the opening of parliament in November 1554[23] – the parliament which was actually to revoke the royal supremacy. John Procter's fulsome *The waie home to Christe*, based on St Vincent of Lerins and published in 1554, despite its praise of Mary and constant emphasis upon the unity of Holy Mother Church, makes no specific mention of either the Pope or his office. Nor was any such mention inserted when the work was reissued in 1556.[24] On the whole after 1555 references to the papacy in official works like Bonner's *A profitable and necessary doctrine*, are careful and correct. In expounding the creed he points out that the unity of the church is preserved by its having one single head and governor, appointed by Christ as the successor of St Peter, and that anyone who rejects the authority of that head cannot be a member of the church universal. Nevertheless, when it came to awakening the laity to an awareness of that authority, the priority accorded was a low one.[25] It was not until the 44th (out of 49) article addressed to the churchwarden of London that they were finally asked to identify any who 'deprave or condemn the authority of the Pope'.[26] No one could have been more dutiful in his deference to the Holy See than Reginald Pole, but the rôle that King Philip played in negotiating the settlement and his subsequent quarrel with Pope Paul IV left the cardinal stranded in a political wilderness, and effectively destroyed any chance there might have been for the papacy to recover real prestige and influence in England.[27]

English Catholics consequently always felt that they owed far more to Mary than they did to the Pope, and with their constant emphasis on 'the Queen's Godly proceedings', reinforced the paradox of a Catholic church by law established. No one could have been less insular than Cardinal Pole, who had spent most of his adult life in Italy, and who had brought with him to England a papal commission to negotiate peace between the King of France and the emperor, yet by 1555 he was completely out of sympathy with current thinking in the Curia. As Dermot Fenlon has pointed out, his experiences over the *Beneficio di Cristo* and the Tridentine decree on justification had exhausted him physically and mentally.[28] His friends and allies had either died, like Contarini, or lost influence, like Morone. The death, in March 1555, of Pope Julius III who had sent him to England was a further heavy blow. Significantly, when Pole was looking abroad for help in revitalising the English church, it was to the reformed congregation of Monte Cassino that his eyes turned, while the assistance offered by Ignatius Loyola was rejected.[29] In the event, the Cassinese did not come, and there was very little direct continental influence on the restored English church. Pole modelled his legatine synod of 1556 on the Council of Florence rather than that of Trent,[30] and the only foreign divines to be active and to hold preferments in England were Philip's Spanish confessors, Pedro de Soto and Juan de Villa Garcia.[31] The Spanish scholar Tellechea Idigoras has recently argued that Pole wsa greatly influenced by Bartolomé Carranza, but those who were subsequently responsible for Carranza's protracted misfortunes clearly believed that the influence had worked the other way.[32] Worst of all, in April 1557 Pole's legatine commission was withdrawn, and from then until his death he controlled the *Ecclesia Anglicana* by virtue of his primatial office and the unwavering confidence of the queen, whose own relations with the Holy See varied from the chilly to the downright hostile.

Pole's lack of theological self-confidence, and his profound distress and disillusionment at the actions of Paul IV go a long way towards explaining his attitude to his mission in England. He had become a reluctant preacher, believing that sermons merely stirred up controversy. When the queen set out her priorities for the church in January 1555, immediately after the question of church property, she wrote, 'touching good preaching, I wish that may supply and overcome the evil preaching in time past . . .'.[33] The cardinal never openly demurred, but he seldom preached himself, and when his synod came to draft its decrees, sermons were accorded a much lower priority, as they were in most of the visitation articles of the reign.[34] For Pole, sound doctrine could only be inculcated by good habits. He was profoundly convinced that ordinary Christians were incapable of comprehending their faith, except in the mot simple visual and ceremonial terms. In the address quoted above, in praise of ceremonies, he went on to declare

> But this I dare saye, whereunto scrypture doth alsoe agree, that the observatyon of ceremonyes for obedyence sake, wyll gyve more light than all the readynge of Scrypture can doe, yf the reader have never so good a wytt to understand what he readythe . . .[35]

Obedience was a key concept. The laity were 'lytle chyldern', and the imagery of the nursery and the schoolroom came readily to his lips. In spite of his earlier humanist record, and his continuing belief in the importance of education – for the clergy – Pole's view of his flock as a whole was both paternalistic and negative. The function of the layman was to perform his sacramental and ceremonial duties, to pay honour (and tithe) to the clergy, and to restore the battered material fabric of his parish church.[36]

Up to a point, this was a sound, common-sense approach. The need for order and stability was desperate, and in supporting ceremonies the cardinal was appealing to the mainstream of popular religious consciousness. It was, however, significant that he should have chosen to urge ceremonies in preference to the reading of scripture. In spite of its Lollard and Protestant associations, there was nothing specifically heretical about reading the English Bible, and it seems to have been a habit which had grown upon Englishmen over the previous fifteen years. Moreover the English primers which had gradually replaced the Latin books of hours after 1529, and which had come to contain substantial portions of scripture as well as prayers and devotional verses, had become generally popular, and some of them had run to many editions.[37] Thirty-nine primers were published in England during Mary's reign. Of these sixteen were in both Latin and English, five in English alone, and eighteen in Latin alone. Although this last group clearly represents a deliberate return to an earlier practice, the official primer, issued in 1555, was in both Latin and English, and reflected the influence not only of the official Henrician Primer of 1545, but also of the Protestant formularies of Edward's reign. As Helen White wrote several years ago, 'the fact remains that there is . . . striking evidence of regard to opposing points of view even in the restoration of the old primer in this book of Philip and Mary'.[38]

More remarkable still, the Great Bible was never withdrawn, nor was its use prohibited, although it was forbidden for any lay person to 'expound or declare any portion or part of Scripture in any church or elsewhere, or put the same to printing or writing . . .'.[39] Orthodox writers repeatedly inveighed against the 'fantasies' of those who interpreted the scriptures 'after their own wit', but the habit of bible reading seems to have spread well beyond the narrow circles of the explicitly Protestant, and to have become too widespread to be easily suppressed, no matter how suspicious to the ecclesiastical authorities.[40] Perhaps, also, Pole's humanist conscience was at odds with his pastoral and disciplinary instincts, and he deliberately confined himself to making discouraging noises. John Standish published two editions (in 1554 and 1555) of *A discourse wherein is debated whether it be expedient that the scripture should be in English for al men to reade that wyll*, but his forceful condemnation was never translated into action.[41]

The reading habits of pious laymen had also changed in other respects since the 1520s. That one-time bestseller the *Legenda Aurea* disappeared from the publishers' catalogues after 1527, and the lives of the saints in general had obviously gone out of fashion by the mid-1520s. Very few were published during Mary's reign, in spite of official insistence on the worthiness of praying to saints, and explicit orders to restore their images and calendar festivals.[42] Richard Brereton of Middlewich, dying in 1558, left a total of fifty-seven books which were inventoried in his will. His collection included many traditional liturgical works, and an English translation of the *Imitatio Christi* published in 1556; but it also contained several English bibles and parts of bibles, and no controversial theology from either side.[43] Sir William More of Losely's collection, inventoried in 1556, although much larger, shows a similar profile. Neither of these can be described as a 'typical layman', but there is no reason to suppose that they were unrepresentative of the literate gentry. Clerical reading, too, had changed since the early days of the Reformation. Myrc's *Festivall* had long since gone out of fashion as a handy *vade mecum*, and when Edmund Bonner decided in 1554 to provide some help for overworked or inadequate clergy, the model he followed was Cranmer's *Homilies* of 1549.[44] In contrast to the laity, the clergy were encouraged to read the Bible, in both Latin and English, not least to avoid the embarrassment of having their ignorance exposed by such Protestants as still ventured to challenge them. Bonner's *profitable and necessary doctrine*, the classic statement of Marian orthodoxy, was not based on any pre-1529 formulation but on the *Necessary Doctrine and Erudition* of 1543.

The reactionary nature of Marian Catholicism can therefore easily be overestimated. The queen herself may have hankered after the pious days of her childhood, but Pole and Bonner, and indeed Gardiner, knew that too much water had passed under the bridge, both in England and in Rome, for such a simple policy to be feasible. No serious attempt was made to revive even the most important of the pre-Reformation shrines. Images of St Thomas of Canterbury reappeared, and were promptly subjected to Protestant vandalism, but the shrine itself was not rebuilt. When Mary wished to give thanks to God for her victories over Northumberland and Wyatt she made grants to the University of Oxford and to Trinity College, Cambridge.[45] Amid all her numerous and substantial benefactions to pious uses, none went to the old cult centres, and Mary never undertook a pilgrimage as queen, a fact which her mother would certainly have found surprising. Nor is there much evidence of spontaneous popular attempts to revive these cults. There were a few small bequests to St Richard of Chichester after 1556,[46] and no doubt a detailed examination of wills would reveal similar examples elsewhere, but without royal or aristocratic patronage they could make no impact on the religious life of the wider community.

A serious attempt was made, as is well known, to re-establish the regular religious life, an endeavour in which both Pole and the queen were very active.[47] These were new foundation, not revivals, as all the erstwhile religious houses had been canonically extinguished in 1555.[48] They were six in number, and their endowment of rather more than £2000 a year came almost entirely from the Crown. Only Westminster, with an income of £1460 and an ultimate strength of over thirty, was on a significant scale. Two of these communities, at Sheen and Syon, were made up mainly of returning exiles, and of the etimated 1500 or so surving ex-religious in England, only about 100 elected to return to the cloister. This is not surprising, given the lapse of time, and we have no means of knowing whether lay generosity would have been rekindled, given a longer opportunity. Small bequests to monasteries do begin to appear in lay wills, although the caution of Margaret Sutton of Stafford in July 1556 was probably typical: 'my fyne kercher (to) be made a corporas and geven to the freres if go up againe, or if not then to some other chirche . . .'.[49] Certainly there was no immediate surge of lay sympathy or support, and at least two of the communities were subjected to hostile demonstrations.[50] We know virtually nothing about the quality of life in these briefly revived houses, beyond an impression of Westminster recorded long after by Fr Augustine Baker, who wrote that monks 'sett up there a disciplin muche like that . . . observed in cathedral churches, as for the Divine Office', and in other respects followed the 'laws and customs of colledges and innes of court'.[51] A sober and dignified life, but not a strenuous or ascetic one. Perhaps that is why Pole wanted to bring in the Cassinese. The number of new vocations attracted was small, but given that the whole experiment lasted only about three years, nothing can be deduced from that.

Collegiate churches, hospitals and perpetual chantries also began to reappear; the first two mainly on the initiative of the Crown, but the latter through the private benefactions of conservative royal servants, such as Sir William Petre and Sir Robert Rochester.[52] Here too the effect of changing times and fashions can be seen, and most of Mary's pious subjects – or those who wished their piety to be noticed – either endowed educational foundations or returned impropriated livings to the church.[53] The pious instincts were not dead – it would have been remarkable indeed if four years of Protestantism had succeeded in killing them off – and they were flowing in channels already dug before the Reformation, but into learning, charity and parish uses rather than large-scale or permanent liturgical foundations. A similar generalisation can, I think, be applied to religious vocations. The regular life had been in the doldrums since the later fifteenth century, and only the Carthusians enjoyed much prestige in the 1520s.[54] Vocations to the secular priesthood, on the other hand, were high and continued so until the Protestant innovations of 1548–9. It is therefore not surprising to find only a handful of regular vocations, but a positive flood of ordinations. Bonner alone ordained 257 priests and 272 deacons in 63 separate ceremonies over the five and a half years of the reign.[55] There could be no more convincing demonstration of the appeal of traditional religion than these figures, which can be paralleled on a smaller scale in other dioceses. But such striking success was not without its hazards, and it was not only Protestants who began to mutter in alarm that 'the priests are coming back to take their revenge', an alarm reflected in both houses of parliament.[56]

Apart from the crucial matters of money and jurisdiction, which I do not intend to discuss here, Pole and his bishops gave the highest priority to the restoration of parochial life, and the sharp rise in ordinations was both a cause and an effect of that priority. This meant not only a revival of processions and other ceremonies, the repair of fabric and the replacement of equipment but also, and above all, the revival of the sacraments, particularly those of the altar and of penance. These were, *par excellence* the sacraments upon which the authority of the priestly order depended, but Marian writers, unlike their Protestant opponents, placed little emphasis on this fact. The sacrament of the altar was the acid test of orthodoxy, but the way in which it was regarded varied considerably from one author to another. In popular works, such as James Cancellor's *The pathe of obedience*, the emphasis was social and collective; presence at the mass, and veneration of the elements, were what mattered, actions seen in a whole context of ritual acts:

> dyd not our late pretensed bishops, as Lucifer before had done, presume to sytte in Goddes seate, proudly speakinge against God . . . and to set up the abhominable desolaccion, whiche was the ceasinge of the veneration of the Body and Blood of Christ in the blessed sacrament of the alter, and the taking away of oure holye fastynges, holye feates and holye prayinge to saints . . .[57]

To the learned Thomas Watson, on the other hand, worthy reception was the critical factor, and mere presence was passed over in silence. In the first of three sermons of the subject in his *Holesome and catholyke doctryne concerninge the seven sacraments*, he wrote

> And because a man doth dayley offende, and so decayethe in his spiritual lyfe, therefore ought he often to receive this spiritual medicine, whiche is called our dayly bread . . .[58]

Continuing this line of thought in the next sermon, he came remarkably close to echoing the phraseology of Cranmer's Prayer Book:

> for he that eatethe and drinketh the body and blood of our Lorde unworthely, eateth and drinketh judgement and dampnation to himselfe.

Preparation, therefore, was of great importance, and preparation consisted not only of prayer and abstinence, but of confession to the parish priest and the performance of due penance.

Both Watson and Bonner were very careful in their discussion of the sacrament of penance. The mere performance of ritual gestures, whether of penance or of alms-giving, was not sufficient; genuine and inward contrition was needed. But contrition could not be assessed by inquisitive archdeacons, and there was always strict insistence upon auricular confession.[59] Nevertheless it was here, in these official manuals of Catholic instruction, that the Marian church came closest to that individual and contemplative piety which was to be fostered by the Counter-Reformation. Watson's sermons 17, 20, 21 and 23 provide step-by-step guidance in self-examination, designed to convince the sinner of the indissoluble bond between faith and works. Salvation, he argues in a specific attack on justification by faith alone, is never impossible to the penitent: 'The successe of the worke bryngeth sweetness, and the encrease of virtue newe repayred bringeth gladness to our myndes . . . .'.[60]

Despite the strong emphasis on the visible and liturgical expression of all the sacraments, here was no crude quantification of the kind which had so angered the early reformers, but thoughtful and sensitive spiritual counselling. Pole's bishops were, for the most part, men of this calibre and turn of mind, and they represented an indigenous strain of intellect and spirituality running back through Richard Whitford and Thomas More to Colet and Linacre. In 1559 the survivors among them rejected the return of Protestantism, and the royal supremacy, and were deprived. Their pupils and heirs, fostered in the universities by the cardinal's careful oversight, formed the first generation of English Catholic exiles, and the basis for the later recusant movement.

At its best, therefore, as represented by these writers and a few others like them, such as John Christopherson and John Feckenham, Marian piety was intelligent and persuasive, recognising the importance of an informed laity, and accepting many of the changes of emphasis and practice that had occurred between 1520 and 1540. What it lacked at this level was the kind of passion and commitment which was to be found at the same time among the Theatines and the early Jesuits. Pole was significantly described by one of his Spanish critics as 'lukewarm' – a Laodicean.[61] It was an unfair criticism of a man who worked so hard, and under such difficult circumstances, to restore the Catholic church in England, but it had a point. The same point that Professor Dickens was to make when he said that Mary 'never discovered the Counter Reformation'. No doubt, had the restoration lasted, English piety would have assimilated more continental features, but this had not even begun to happen by the time that Cardinal Pole died. There were no meditations on the rosary, no modern hagiography, no cult of the sacred heart or the holy name, and none of the recently established orders recruited or established cells in England.[62] There was passion, but much of it was channelled into persecution, and into the unmeasured denunciations of popular polemic: 'what fylthy frute buddeth out of this frantike franternitie and synfull synagogue of Sathan', wrote William Barlow, in a mood not to be outmatched by John Bale himself.[63] There can be no doubt that some middle and lower-ranking clergy, and some laity as well, were outraged by Edwardian Protestantism, but that was not the prevailing sentiment.

Many aspects of the old faith had been greatly weakened and undermined, not so much by heretical doctrine as by the pressures applied by royal policy between

1530 and 1547, and by the changing fashions of piety which were visible before that and which had helped to make some parts of that policy acceptable. The enthusiasm for the mass, and for traditional ceremonies, clearly visible at the beginning of Mary's reign, was certainly a reaction against the Prayer Book and the brief Protestant austerity of 1550–3. It did not signify a general desire to put the clock back to 1529, even if anyone had known exactly what that meant. Pole and Mary almost certainly realised this and, in spite of their determination to restore the Roman jurisdiction, were not excessively reactionary in the conformity they endeavoured to impose. What they were trying to do was to re-establish a distinctively English type of reformed Catholicism, under the papal jurisdiction; a regiment of the kind which would have appealed to Colet, or the young More. Unfortunately for them such a policy required not only time but also freedom from theological controversy. It was an ideal of order, discipline and peace, which Protestant resistance, papal intransigence and Mary's own political entanglement with Spain conspired to make unrealistic. Evidence for the actual achievement is conflicting. Apathy drifts into conformity quickly under pressure, so between those who wanted the old order restored and those who did not much care, a high level of outward conformity was achieved by 1558.[64] Anxious clergy and gentlemen were requesting all sorts of minor dispensations from Pole, even before he returned to England,[65] and bequests for pious purposes were picking up noticeably by the end of the reign. Episcopal authority was strengthened, and a worthy start had been made with the intractable problems of poor livings and ruined churches. Nevertheless, there was little sign that Protestant dissent had been either suppressed or silenced, and for that purpose weapons were needed of a kind which the Marian church did not seem anxious to acquire. Judicial persecution on its own was not enough, and neither the habit-forming ceremonialism upon which Pole was so keen nor the sensible humanist theology of Watson and Bonner could provide adequate support. Paradoxically, it was the insularity of the Marian church not its ultramontanism, or even its association with Spain, which was its fundamental weakness.

Notes

1. Cardinal Pole's speech to the citizens of London, in J. Strype *Ecclesiastical Memorials*, Oxford , 1822, III, pt.ii, 502. [*Eccl. Mem.*]
2. *The Displaying of the Protestantes*, London, 1556 (STC 13557), preface

   Prelacy is popishe pompe
   Vertuous vowes are vaine
   Ceremonies curious toyes
   Priesthood popery plain.

3. The Royal Injuctions and proclamation of 1538 had caused some saints, such as Thomas of Canterbury, to be removed from the Calendar. By the time the official primer was published in 1545, a very substantial reduction had taken place. H.C. White, *Tudor Books of Private Devotion*, Wisconsin, 1951, pp. 108–9; C.H. Butterworth, *The English Primers*, New York, 1971, pp. 168–70.
4. J.J. Scarisbrick, *The Reformation and the English People*, Oxford, 1984; C. Haigh,

'From Monopoly to Minority: Catholicism in Early Modern England', *Transactions of the Royal Historical Society*, 5 series, XXXI, 1981, 129–47; S. Brigden, 'Youth and the Reformation in London', *Past and Present*, XCV, 1982, 37–67.

5. The evidence for this statement is to be found mainly in the activities of Mary's council to secure the return of church goods in the hands of the commissioners, and in the returns of such Marian visitations as those of Cardinal Pole *sede vacante* at Lincoln (1556) (Strype, *Eccl. Mem.*, III, pt.ii, 389–413) and Archdeacon Harpesfield at Canterbury (1557) ed. L.E. Whatmore and W. Sharp (*Catholic Record Society*, XLV–VI, 1950–1).

6. Bucer to Brentius, 15 May 1550. *Original Letters Relative to the English Reformation*, ed. H. Robinson, Parker Society, 1847, II, 542.

7. W.H. Frere, *The Marian Reaction*, London, 1896, pp. 101, 266. C. Haigh, *Reformation and Reaction in Tudor Lancashire*, Cambridge, 1975, pp. 154–5.

8. 'Robert Parkyn's Narrative of the English Reformation', ed. A.G. Dickens, *English Historical Review*, LXII, 1947, 82. D.M. Loades, *The Reign of Mary Tudor*, London, 1979, p. 153.

9. As late as June 1556 the ecclesiastical authorities in London were still trying to make participation in processions compulsory for at least one representative of each household 'on peyne of forfettynge xii d at every time', but as the conservative author of the *Greyfriars Chronicle* noted '. . . it was lyttyll lokyd upon, and the more pytte'. *Chronicle of the Greyfriars of London*, ed. J.G. Nichols, Camden Society, 1852, p. 97.

10. 'Robert Parkyn's Narrative'; *The Diary of Henry Machyn 1550–1563* ed. J.G. Nichols, Camden Society, XLII, 1848.

11. D.M. Loades, *The Oxford Martyrs*, London, 1970, pp. 109–12.

12. Nichols, *Greyfriars Chronicle*, pp. 82, 84.

13. Nichols, *Machyn's Diary*, p. 42.

14. J. Procter, *The waie home to Christ and truth leadinge from Antichrist and errour*, London, 1556, (STC 2455), preface.

15. E.g. item 13 '. . . the laudable and honest ceremonies which were wont to be used, frequented and observed in the church, be also hereafter frequented and observed'. W.H. Frere and W.M. Kennedy, *Visitation Articles and Injunctions*, London, 1910, II, p. 328.

16. *Interrogatories upon which churchwardens shall be charged*, London, 1558 (STC 10117).

17. The bitter comment of the layman Miles Huggarde, is typical of this sentiment; 'A just plague of God upon such dissolute preistes, who cared not what women they married, common or other, so they might get them wyves . . .'; *Displaying*, f.73v.

18. G. Baskerville, 'Married Clergy and Pensioned Religious in Norwich Diocese, 1555', *English Historical Review*, LXVIII, 1933, 43–64. A.I. Pryce, *The Diocese of Bangor in the Sixteenth Century*, Bangor, 1923, pp. 12–14. These deprivations created 30 per cent of the vacancies during the reign.

19. Procter, *The waie home*, preface.

20. Ibid.

21. Loades, *Oxford Martyrs*, pp. 138–49; *Reign of Mary*, pp. 321–30.

22. Giacomo Soranzo to the Doge and Senate, 11 Sept. 1553; *Calendar of State Papers, Venetian*, 410–11. Penning's report is calendared in *Calendar of State Papers, Venetian*, 429–32. The imperial ambassador, Simon Renard, was even more pessimistic. In May 1554 he reported that the name of the Pope was 'odious', even among those who favoured the old religion, and that there was scarcely such a thing as a true Catholic in the country. *Calendar of State Papers, Spanish*, xii, 243. [*Cal. Span.*]

23. Nichols, *Greyfriars Chronicle*, p. 92.

24. STC 24754, 24755. James Cancellar, in *The pathe of obedience*, London, 1556, (STC

4565) makes frequent reference to 'the churche of Rome', but not to the Pope. As far as I can discover, the only work specifically defending the papal authority was John Standish's *The triall of the Supremacy*, London, 1556, (STC 23211).

25. See, for example, Bishop Brooks' Injunctions for Gloucester diocese (1556), where the only mention of the Pope comes in article 16, in which the clergy are instructed to ensure that the Pope's name is restored to the intercessions. The seventeen articles addressed to the laity make no reference to him. Frere and Kennedy, *Visitation Articles*, II, pp. 401–8.

26. *Interrogatories*.

27. For a full example of the effects of this quarrel see Loades, *Reign of Mary*, pp. 428–52.

28. Dermot Fenlon, *Heresy and Obedience in Tridentine Italy*, Cambridge, 1972, pp. 116–136.

29. D. Knowles, *The Religious Orders in England*, Cambridge, 1959, III, pp. 424–5. J.H. Crehan, 'St. Ignatius and Cardinal Pole', *Archivum historicum Societatis Iesu*, XXV, 1956, 72–98.

30. J.P. Marmion, 'The London Synod of Cardinal Pole', M.A. Keele, 1974.

31. Appointed to the chairs of Hebrew and Divinity at Oxford.

32. J.I. Tellechea Idigoras, 'Bartolomé Carranza y la restauración católica inglesa (1553–1558)', *Anthologia Annua*, XII, 1964, 159–282.

33. BL Cotton MS Titus C. VII, fol. 120.

34. *Reformatio Angliae ex decretis Reginaldi Pole* (1565): Bodleian MS film 33 (Vat. Lat. 5968); Frere and Kennedy, *Visitation Articles*, II, pp. 330–414. The shortage of competent preachers was also recognised to be a problem, although much less emphasised than by the Protestants: '. . . there be not in half a shyre scarcely two habel men to showe their faces in the pulpitt'. M. Glasier, *A Notable and very fruictfull sermon made at Paules Crose*, London, 1555, (STC 11916.5).

35. Strype, *Eccl. Mem.*, III, pt.ii, 503.

36. Ibid., 483: '. . . yet there be other churches, that are nowe fryste to be helpen, and these be your parryshe-churches; which albeyt they have not byn cast downe by coulore of authoyte, as the abbayes were, yet have they byn sufferede to fawle downe of themselves . . .'.

37. Books of hours and primers together (the distinction was not always clear-cut) accounted for 40 titles during the 1520s, and 60 during the 1530s, when they began to reflect the struggle between conservative and reforming churchmen. Alison. F. Bartholomew, 'Lay Piety in the Reign of Mary Tudor', M.A., Manchester, 1979, 16–18. H.C. White, *Tudor Books of Private Devotion*.

38. White, *Tudor Books*, p. 122.

39. Bonner's Articles for London Diocese; Frere and Kennedy, *Visitation Articles*, II, p. 324.

40. An authorised Catholic translation of the Bible was promised at the legatine synod, but never produced. *Reformatio Angliae*.

41. STC 23207, 23208.

42. Royal Articles of 1554; articles 12 and 13. Frere and Kennedy, *Visitation Articles*, II, p. 328. [See also Chapter 10, 'Books and the English Reformation prior to 1558']

43. Bartholomew, 'Lay Piety', 40. *Archaeologia*, XXXVI, 1856, 284–93.

44. These homilies were published as an adjunct to the *Profitable and Necessary Doctrine*, and went through ten editions (STC 3285.1–85.10.

45. *Calendar of the Patent Rolls, Mary*, I, 165–6, 203. [*Cal. Pat.*]

46. Bartholomew, 'Lay Piety', 105.

47. For a full account of these restorations, see Knowles, *Religious Orders*, III, pp. 421–33. Pole, like More, had been greatly influenced by the Carthusians in his youth, and this affected his personal piety deeply. Fenlon, *Heresy*, pp. 27–8. W. Schenk,

Reginald Pole, Cardinal of England, London, 1950.

48. By the Bull, *Praeclara,* 20 June 1555. This was a direct result of the terms upon which the English settlement had been negotiated. Knowles, *Religious Orders,* p. 423.

49. Bartholomew, 'Lay Piety', 158.

50. The Franciscans and Greenwich and the Dominicans at Smithfield. *Acts of the Privy Council,* ed. J.R. Dasent, London 1890–1964, V, 169.

51. 'Life of Father Baker', in *Memorials of Father Augustine Baker,* ed. J. MacCann and R.M. Connolly, Catholic Record Society, XXXIII, 1933, 95–6.

52. *Cal. Pat.,* I, 230 (Collegiate church of Wolverhampton); III, 513 (Manchester College): II, 543 (Savoy Hospital); III. 542 (Petre at Ingatestone): III, 363–4 (Rochester at Terling).

53. For example: Sir Thomas White (St John's College, Oxford); *Cal. Pat.,* II, 322; Sir Thomas Pope (Trinity College, Oxford); *Cal Pat.,* II, 90; and numerous schools. Viscount Montague returned a number of impropriated livings, and others followed his example; *Cal. Pat.,* III, 290; IV, 1.91.

54. Knowles, *Religious Orders.* John Colet was also among those deeply influenced by the Carthusians.

55. Bartholomew, 'Lay Piety', 152.

56. Examinations of John Danyell. Public Record Office SP46, 8, 35. Both the Commons and the Lords expressed unease over the return of ecclesiastical jurisdiction. Loades, *Reign of Mary, passim.*

57. Cancellar, *Pathe of Obedience,* Sig. A. iii.

58. Watson, *Holesome and catholyke doctryne concerninge the seven sacraments,* London, 1538, Sermon IX, f.48.

59. Ibid., Sermon XI, f.66. Bonner, *Profitable and Necessary Doctrine,* 'On the sacrament of penance', sig. D vi, wrote 'When I do say a declaration or uttering, I do use the same to exclude mental confession, whiche though it may and at times ought to be made unto God, yet that is not that sacramental confession of which we heare speake.' These Marian guides have nothing of the systematic intensity of the later Catholic manuals on confession.

60. Watson, *Holesome and catholyke doctrine,* Sermon XV, 'Against desperation', f.86.

61. Don Gómez Suárez de Figueroa, Count of Feria, to Fr Ribadeneyra, S.J., 22 Mar. 1558. *Cal. Span.,* xiii, 370–1.

62. There was a beginning of a hagiography of Fisher and More, the latter mainly promoted by the More family, and associated with Rastell's edition of his collected works, published in 1557.

63. *A dialogue describing the originall grounde of these Lutheran faccions,* London, 1553 (STC 1462), preface.

64. The main deficiencies revealed by visitations in the last year of the reign are concerned with the dilapidation of churches. Churchwardens' accounts, where these have been studied, almost invariably record substantial payments for liturgical restorations. Scarisbrick, *Reformation and the English People,* pp. 136–61.

65. These were mostly for eating meat in Lent, or having a consecrated super-altar for a private chapel. Pole's Legatine Register, Douai Municipal Archives, MS 292 (microfilm in Lambeth Palace Library).

Index of Names and Places